Praise for
What Do You Expect?
She's a Teenager!

"If your little girl has suddenly turned into one big eye roll, then Arden Greenspan-Goldberg's What Do You Expect? She's a Teenager! *is for you. It's the ultimate how-to guidebook that will not only teach you how to survive your daughter's teen years, but how to enjoy them along the way, too."*

—Jen Singer, author of *You're a Good Mom*
(and Your Kids Aren't So Bad Either)

"In a straightforward, user friendly, and totally accessible way, What Do You Expect? She's a Teenager! *overflows with the skills and techniques every mother needs for navigating the precarious yet thrilling road of raising a teenage daughter. Arden Greenspan-Goldberg covers every facet of your ride of a lifetime: sex, drugs, bullying, friends, and more... expertly steering you into realistic expectations that both prepare and equip you for your journey."*

Dr. Jane Greer, marriage and family therapist,
author, *What About Me?: Stop Selfishness From Ruining Your Relationship*, radio host,
Huffington Post contributor

"Thank goodness, a liberating, refreshingly helpful and therapeutically credible road map along the free-falling journey of motherhood. We all win with less 'losing it' around conflict. The personal stories definitely made me feel less alone and empowered to stay open!"

—EMME, TV PERSONALITY, SUPERMODEL,
WOMEN'S BODY IMAGE ADVOCATE, AND MOM

What Do You Expect?
She's a
Teenager!

A Hope and Happiness Guide for Moms with Daughters Ages 11–19

ARDEN GREENSPAN-GOLDBERG,
LCSW, BCD

 sourcebooks

Copyright © 2011 by Arden Greenspan-Goldberg
Cover and internal design © 2011 by Sourcebooks, Inc.
Cover design by Laura Duffy
Cover image © Comstock/Getty Images

Sourcebooks and the colophon are registered trademarks of Sourcebooks, Inc.

Published by Sourcebooks, Inc.
P.O. Box 4410, Naperville, Illinois 60567-4410
(630) 961-3900
Fax: (630) 961-2168
www.sourcebooks.com

Library of Congress Cataloging-in-Publication Data

Greenspan-Goldberg, Arden.
  What do you expect? She's a teenager! : a hope and happiness guide for moms with daughters ages 11-19 / by Arden Greenspan-Goldberg.
    p. cm.
  1. Mothers and daughters. 2. Teenage girls. 3. Parenting. I. Title.
  HQ755.85.G725 2011
  306.874'3–dc22

                            2011007314

Printed and bound in the United States of America
VP 10 9 8 7 6 5 4 3 2 1

To my daughter, Samara, whose enthusiasm, smile, and angelic singing voice bring joy to my heart.

My son, Todd, who rocks my soul and stands tall in his being.

My husband, Larry, the love of my life, forty years and counting.

My mom, Ethel, one very smart woman.

Contents

Acknowledgments

I feel deeply blessed and grateful to have some very special people in my life who have given of themselves tirelessly in helping make this book happen.

My heartfelt appreciation goes to my dear daughter, Samara, whose passion, artistry, being, and essence have inspired me to write this book. You have given me real, firsthand experiences of a powerful and enduring mother-daughter connection. Our relationship is built on a strong foundation of love and respect. Thank you for allowing me to share some of the narrative of your life.

To my husband, Larry, who first said to me, "Arden, you must write a book to help parents better understand their children," and started lobbying for me to record my experiences as a mother and therapist twenty-two years ago. Thank you for reminding me to write about my passion and my loves—moms and their tween and teen daughters. You are a sweetheart, the love of my life, and my biggest champion.

Thanks to my son, Todd, who has always been there for me, as I have been for you. You continue to be a source of courage and sunny optimism. We cheer each other on with words of hope and realization: "You Can Do It, Believe It, and Be It!" You were instrumental in introducing me to your pal

Jon Boswell Jr. and his dad, Jon Boswell Sr., an accomplished writer, who then connected me to my agent, Lauren Galit.

To my agent, Lauren Galit, my north star and unwavering compass point of sound direction, I offer a heartfelt thank-you for your faith, smarts, enthusiasm, determination, and confidence in this project and helping it get off the ground. You have guided me from start to finish and galvanized me to be true and strong.

To Tara Moncheck, a very smart, energetic, and talented producer at Parents.tv and Better.tv. You provided me with so many opportunities to work with you and to reach a core audience of savvy, searching moms.

To Juli Auclair, a wonderful anchor and graceful interviewer. It was so much fun working and appearing with you in numerous segments for Parents.tv. Thank you for both your enthusiasm and your encouragement to write this book.

To Christa Bourg, my book proposal collaborator and quick title changer. Thanks for your insights and humor.

To Suelain Moy, my talented collaborator, whose beautiful, poetic, and instinctive way with words breathed life into my vision of advice, vignettes, and stories. Your old-soul spirit and modern, contemporary edge helped me to achieve greater depth, substance, and compassion on the page.

To Shana Drehs, my brilliant and perceptive editor. You provided sharp clarity and focus to our efforts to keep the book content current, relevant, and fresh to generations of moms.

With great appreciation for their invaluable contributions and support of my book, I thank Hope Edelman, Emme, Sondra Kronberg, Dr. Maureen Cooney, Professor Hannah Fox, and Vanessa Van Petten.

A special thanks to Dr. Jane Greer, my dear beloved,

treasured friend and colleague for over twenty-two years. Jane, your advice, guidance, love, and support have been so priceless and invaluable to me. You are a wonderful, talented therapist, author, and my "pal of pals."

To my "sisterhood of the pants" dearest friends: Jean, Vicki, Karen, Dorothy, Robin, Beth, Lisa, Jessica, Jeri-Ann, Viv, Marsha, Jen, Tatiana, and Kathy, and all the rest of my "family of friends," thank you for countless years of sharing your wisdom, insight, inspiration, support, pride, and love. I couldn't have written this book without you.

Thanks to my mom, Ethel, for your faith in me, and especially your warmth, love, wisdom, support, and excitement for my writing of this book.

To my stepfather, George, I thank you for being my hero, a great joke-teller, and a real good guy.

To my Uncle Larry, for watching over me and looking after me from up above; here's to "Blue Skies" and "100 Million Miracles" forever.

To my dad Gerald, "Jerry," your presence has been felt in mystical and magical ways.

To my talented tweenage niece Julie, whose presence warms my heart and soul.

To many of my close relatives, too numerous to name individually, thank you for your love and positive energy.

To my beloved patients: you, you, you know who you are! Thank you for your faith, trust, and confidence in me, for letting me help, advise, and guide you, and for sharing your struggles and triumphs with me. Writing this book has been an amazing life-charging, life-changing journey and learning experience for me.

Author's Note

Some of the names and details in the questions, vignettes, and stories have been sensitively modified to protect the confidentiality of my patients and friends while maintaining the integrity and essence of the message.

CHAPTER 1

Introduction to Aerial Parenting

Hope is the thing with feathers
That perches in the soul

—Emily Dickinson

You thought your husband or partner could push your buttons, but that was before you had *her*. Daughters, particularly teenage daughters, are gifted in the art of the comeback, the shoulder shrug, the eye roll. And what's really amazing is the way it affects you. Think about how your face gets so hot after your daughter says "You ruin everything!" or "You don't know what you're talking about!"

Perhaps your daughter reminds you of yourself when you were her age and all the growing pains you experienced. Maybe you see yourself in her, your good points as well as your not-so-good ones. Or maybe you feel you don't have anything in common with your daughter and can't relate to her. No wonder the relationships between mothers and daughters can be so emotionally charged. Being the mother of a teenage daughter can be downright alarming. Consider these bald facts:

- More than 30 percent of girls—that's nearly one in three—becomes pregnant at least once *before* the age of twenty.
- In the United States, one in every ten births involves a teen mother.
- Seventy percent of teen girls who are sexually active say they wish they had waited.
- Nearly 63 percent of teens try alcohol before their eighteenth birthdays; 41 percent before they even reach the eighth grade (that's just thirteen years old).
- Sixty-two percent of U.S. high school students attend a school where drugs are used, kept, or sold.
- Eighty percent of fifteen- to seventeen-year-olds have been exposed to hardcore porn on the Internet *multiple* times; in fact, the average age a child is *first* exposed to Internet pornography is just *eleven years old.*

It's a minefield out there, and if you're a mother of a tween or teen daughter, it's enough to make you want to scream and hide. Well, screaming might help to release some of the tension, but you can't really hide. Wherever you go, whatever you do, you're still a mom, and a mom to a daughter between the ages of eleven and nineteen at that. Much of the time it's all we can do to simply react to what's going on and try to keep up with everything that's happening around us. So what's a stressed-out, overworked, underappreciated, woefully-unprepared-for-all-this mom supposed to do?

As a nationally known family and marriage psychotherapist specializing in teen and young adult issues, I have helped countless moms step back from the chaos, manage their worries, and cultivate more open and less volatile relationships with their daughters. This book is that help wrapped into a portable package just for you.

HOW THIS BOOK CAN HELP

This book is the ultimate preparation manual and survival guide for mothers with tween or teen girls ages eleven to nineteen. It's a tool of prevention. We'll discuss all manner of scenarios on the most hot-button topics, from bullying to sex to drugs to eating disorders to stress and depression. We'll also cover everyday confrontations, from her wanting to get piercings where the sun doesn't shine, to her posting racy pictures online, to you trying to get her to talk to you about what's going on in her life and listen to what you have to say in return.

You'll read through real questions that moms typically wonder about, followed by ideas on how to handle the situation calmly and effectively, as well as the relevant info moms need to make good parenting decisions. The questions are based on dilemmas I've encountered as a therapist in my practice, and from questions and emails I get through my website, www.askarden.com. In addition, you'll read some exclusive interviews I've conducted especially for this book with noted experts in their respective fields. These incredible women, many of them mothers themselves, all offer their expertise and insights to Mom to further her understanding and strengthen her connection to her daughter. I also share memories and lessons learned from parenting and guiding my own daughter, Samara, although there were definitely days when it seemed

Samara was teaching *me* how to be a better parent. I share the collective wisdom of all of these experiences, thorns and all.

Why are we covering so many situations? The idea is that the more scenarios you've thought through, the better able you'll be to handle things as they arise.

Because we obviously can't anticipate everything that might happen in your daughter's life, the book will also include general strategies for being a responsive parent, which can help moms with things like how to keep from taking your daughter's outbursts too personally, how to talk to her without escalating the argument, how to stay focused on what's important, and how to be a positive and effective influence on her life. The book includes lots of clearly marked boxes and sections highlighting important facts and advice to make it easy for moms to navigate. That means you can dip into this book wherever and whenever you want to in order to find help dealing with the issue of the moment. But I also hope that you will read this book as a guidebook, a manual for surviving and thriving during the oft-dreaded teenage years, *before* you end up facing their fears and frustrations in real life.

The book is divided into fifteen chapters. This chapter will introduce you to the parenting philosophy that I call "aerial parenting" and give you some guidelines for your overall relationship with your daughter. Chapter 2 explores the main issue, which is that tween and teen girls tend to be volatile creatures in their own right. On top of that, the mother-daughter relationship can be full of change and emotion. But a volatile parent is not a good parent, so how does Mom handle all this and turn turbulent situations into positive outcomes? It's not easy, but this first section will set moms on the right track by arming them with the proper perspective and general parenting strategies. I'll explain where girls are developmentally as they age from tweens to teens, so that moms can have a better idea of what to expect from them. I'll also help moms access their own parenting styles so they can better understand the part they play in creating the dynamic between themselves and their daughters.

The rest of the chapters deal with the most common and feared issues mothers of teen daughters face, from sex and drugs to family fallouts and getting into college. The purpose of my advice is to bring Mom closer to her daughter, to make their relationship more open, more trusting, and even more fun. There will be plenty of sidebars and statistics throughout the chapters to emphasize both the practical and inspirational aspects of this book, along with scripts and conversation starters in case you're not sure what to say. (You'll find **conversation starters** and **scripts** bolded throughout.)

The last chapter of this book will let moms know when to seek out additional help, information, or support they might need, how to find that help, and the right questions to ask. The book ends with a resource section for moms looking for more information and direction.

This book aims to help you learn how to be even more responsive, compassionate, educated, aware, and savvier moms than you already are. I believe as parents we are on a learning curve. Home is not built in a day, and raising daughters is a day-by-day process. For my daughter, Samara, and for your daughters, there are some complicated emotional and physical developmental building blocks that need to be put in place.

As a parent and therapist I have put in great effort to see the bigger picture, what I call the "aerial view." Some of my training as a therapist has helped me to be more objective, to take steps back, to be more curious about where a person is coming from personally and within the framework of her family and culture. I've learned how to listen and not take things so personally. This approach has helped me immensely in finding solutions and inspired my clients to find their own solutions with guidance from me.

I call this approach "aerial parenting."

AERIAL PARENTING

Aerial parenting is all about seeing the bigger picture and getting some much needed perspective, specifically when it comes to parenting your daughter. Aerial parenting involves developing the capacity to gain some objectivity, to learn how to respond rather than react, and to immerse yourself in the present while taking into account your and your daughter's pasts and projected futures. It's seeing yourself and your daughter in a timeline and developing a deep appreciation, gratitude, and joy for her existence and for how much she has enhanced and challenged your life. I have developed a capacity to parent aerially through my work as a psychotherapist, and I practiced this philosophy at home with my two children, Samara and her older brother Todd, with great success.

Let me show you a bit about how this philosophy works using two mini-visualizations. Imagine, for just a moment, that you're a bird flying high in the sky. (I love the image of eagles soaring and gliding through the air because they are able to reach altitudes as high as a jet.) You look down, and laid out on the ground below you is your daughter's life. The details are a bit sketchy from that height, but you can basically see who she is, what obstacles are in her way, and in which direction she might travel. What's more, from that vantage point, the chaos doesn't seem quite so overwhelming. You look around you and realize that this experience can be almost peaceful, even fun sometimes. That's the feeling we're aiming for when we engage as aerial parents.

Or pretend that you are sitting in the audience of a grand theatre, high above the stage in the balcony. From your perch, you can look down on the stage. Playing out before you is the unfolding drama of your and your daughter's life stories, your relationship, and whatever you're struggling to face at the moment.

With the aerial approach, whether you are high in the sky or in the balcony of the theatre of your life, you are watching, anticipating, and preparing. Remember, you are moving in the direction of objectivity, guiding and helping your daughter think through her problems. To me, viewing life from the biggest picture will usually serve both your and your daughter's best interests and deepen and strengthen your connection to each other.

Here's a look at several of the guidelines that make up the aerial parenting philosophy, things that it might be helpful to keep in mind overall with any scenario you encounter.

Anticipate and Prepare
One of the things I like to tell moms who are in a high state of anxiety over what might happen to their daughter is that *prevention is all about anticipation and preparation*. If you prepare

in advance, when things come up—and they will come up; there's no use burying your head in the sand and pretending they won't—you will be able to respond from your heart. It will allow you to be a *responsive* parent rather than a *reactive* one.

What's the difference? Suppose your daughter came to you today and said, matter-of-factly, "Mom, I want to start taking birth control. Can you take me to the gynecologist?" If you've prepared for this moment, for this very question even, you can respond with concern and advice, have an open conversation with her, and perhaps even influence her decision. If you aren't prepared for this moment, well, then you're likely to freak the heck out.

Educate and Inform

As mothers, we need to keep our fingers on the pulse of what's happening in our children's lives and the world at large. We need to be on the lookout and stay informed about current developments in teen culture. If pharm parties are all the rage (see Chapter 12), then we need to check our medicine cabinets and count all the prescription pills. We cannot stick our heads in the sand and pretend our kids are never going to experiment with drugs, alcohol, or sex. Educating ourselves is a big part of being proactive and protective, as kids can be very savvy these days.

No Punishment

Part of my parenting philosophy is an emphasis on *no punishment* when it comes to tweens and teens. This is not because I'm a lightweight pushover. It's for a much more practical reason that comes from years of experience as both a therapist and a mother: punishment simply doesn't work with teens the way you want it to.

Let's say your daughter is at a party and realizes she's about to miss her curfew. As she's standing on the sidewalk wondering what to do, that new kid who's had a little too much to drink offers her a ride home. He's a little unsteady but says he can drive just fine. Will she get into the car, or will she call you for a ride? Well, if she's afraid you're going to yell at her and punish her for missing her curfew, she might be tempted to get into Mr. Tipsy's car and put her life at risk. Check out this alarming statistic: in all drunk driving fatalities, 45% of the passengers are under the age of 21 while a drunk driver is in control of the wheel. Or if he's not as nice as he seems, she could become one of the 44 percent of rape victims who are under the age of eighteen.

But if she remembers you telling her that her safety and well-being come first, then she won't get in the car with a drunk stranger, no matter how cute he is. She won't become a statistic because she'll know that she can call you at any time and count on the fact that your love and concern for her trumps any anger or annoyance you might feel.

Expect Her to Make Mistakes

Although you warned your thirteen-year-old not to go on the "My Life Is Average" website, don't be surprised when your nine-year-old daughter snitches on her older sister: "She's back on there again saying she's seventeen—and chatting with some stranger who says he's seventeen!" You might feel very mad, Mom, but before you walk down to the basement where your older daughter is using the family computer, say to yourself,

"Collect yourself, take a breath. I knew it would take more than once to make an impression on her that it's dangerous to pretend she is seventeen. She really has no idea who she is chatting with on the other end. I need to understand better what compels and lures her to go on that site and behind my back again. I thought she felt comfortable enough to talk with me and have a discussion."

If you *expect her to make mistakes* from the get-go, and prepare yourself for the fact that your teenager *will* mess up, then you'll be better able to help her and guide her when it really counts. This will be an ongoing dialogue between Mom and daughter that transcends the Internet and moves into real life. For instance, you could ask her: "Would you just randomly walk up and talk to a seventeen-year-old?" See what she has to say. She may say, "No way!" "Okay, then, why would you do that on this site?" You need to make her part of the solution, and walk her and steer her to think through what she is doing.

Make Your Daughter Part of the Solution

Making your daughter part of the solution means asking her to help create the guidelines and routines that will affect her life, whether it's coming up with a new curfew or deciding which chore she will handle on a weekly basis. Your daughter is much more likely to abide by these parameters when she has had a hand in making them. Ask her what she thinks would be fair in a situation, and then tell her what you had in mind and be open to negotiation. Let's say you want her home by nine thirty on a school night and she's pushing for ten thirty. Try ten o'clock and see how it goes. You want to show her that you can be flexible and receptive and she can be capable and smart.

She'll be more receptive to any limits and boundaries if she is able to negotiate a more favorable outcome. Negotiating is an important and useful life skill that will come in handy with friends, roommates, teachers, classmates, colleagues, bosses, and romantic partners. And if she breaks curfew, then you can remind her, "But sweetie, you agreed to this," which will help keep the conversation focused on her and her behavior.

Set Up Reasonable Parameters and Guidelines

I prefer to set limits and boundaries and parameters that speak to the possibilities in life. Rules, punishments, and prescribed formulas are way too restrictive and negative in their focus to work effectively for me. I have done my best to eliminate any hard and fast rules from my parenting and practice. The guidelines you set should come from a place of love, not fear or control, and be fluid enough to respond to most situations you and your daughter may encounter.

Talk in Unconventional Places and Spaces

It can happen in the car while you're driving (and not looking directly at each other), while you're making dinner, or while you're walking together at the mall. Suddenly she blurts out something that's been bothering her, maybe that her pal is going through a really bad breakup with her boyfriend and acting crazy jealous. And you are presented with a casual opportunity to discuss a more controversial or serious topic. You have the chance to filter through some of what she's seeing and hearing. By giving her your perspective and your take on these situations, you can help to reframe her perception of it. You can ask her, "How could she have handled it differently?" and share experiences from your own adolescence. Just think, if you were sitting across the table from each other at dinner, face-to-face, this conversation might not have happened at all.

Pick the Right Time to Talk

Your daughter will be much more receptive to what you're saying if she's not tired, sleepy, hungover, upset, frustrated, or mad. If you ask about her homework and rattle off a list of to-dos as soon as she comes through the door, she will likely feel irritated. Translation: enough already, leave me alone, can't I have a minute or sixty to text, Facebook, and IM all of my friends? Avoid the times she'll feel hassled and rushed. And obviously it's not good to have a serious talk with your daughter in front of her friends, her coworkers, or her teachers. If you're not sure, ask her, "Is this a good time to talk?" If your daughter is coming home stoned and drunk at four in the morning making lots of noise, it's not a good time for a talk when your blood is boiling. Table the discussion and wait till tomorrow.

Table It and Try Again Later

Take a few deep breaths before speaking, or wait a few hours (or a few days) until you're able to talk to her calmly. If your daughter is not in immediate danger, you can give yourself enough time to pull yourself together so you can organize your thoughts. You'll be much more likely to get through to her if you can speak with composure, logic, and a clear sense of what you want her to understand. You simply can't do that if you're feeling frazzled or provoked. Here's the question you need to ask yourself, Mom: how often are you really facing an emergency situation that must be dealt with this very minute? Generally, not that often.

REPRINT REPRINT REPRINT REPRINT

Schuler Books
2820 Towne Center Blvd
Lansing MI, 48912

QTY	SKU	PRICE
1 T	What Do You Expect? S	14.99
1 T	WHATS HAPPENING TO ME	6.99

Total Sale	$21.98
Sales Tax	$1.32
Net Sale	$23.30

Master Card $23.30
Card # ************9788
JENNIFER NAUTA
Authorization # 094820 CAPTUREI

X_____

Sale Date: 9/22/2011
 Register: 1
    Store: 3
  Cashier: RW

Refunds - 30 days with receipt.
CD's & DVD's must be unopened.
Used, seasonal, dated, and markdown
items are non-returnable.

www.schulerbooks.com

0000468181

REPRINT REPRINT REPRINT REPRINT

Pay Attention to Her Nonverbal Cues

When she starts rolling her eyes, turning her back, or walking away, respect her limits and let her process what has just been said. Don't push your agenda on a hostile or resistant teen who is unwilling or unable to absorb any more. On the other hand, if she leans in closer to talk or seems like she wants to ask you a question, you can draw her out and continue the conversation. She will signal you when she is ready to receive the information and when she is not, without having to say a word.

Be Aware of Your Own Signals

Check for any negative attitudes, eye-rolling, sarcasm, angry gestures, and bristling impatience on your part. She can sense when you're tense or angry with her and read your nonverbal cues and reactions. Pay attention to your tone of voice, your facial expressions, and your body language. How are you coming across in the moment? Negative or angry signals will only derail and undermine whatever message you are trying to get across.

Be the Role Model

As moms, we need to be clear about our purpose and consistent in our comportment. If you ask your daughter not to text while driving, then you need to stop texting when you're driving. The same goes for smoking and drinking. You need to be the prototype of self-respect, a moral and ethical compass for your daughter. Walking your talk is essential. Demonstrate the behaviors and attitudes you wish to see in her. Your daughter is learning from you. She watches you like a hawk and copies you and picks up your blind spots along with your gifts.

Lend Your Brain

There also will be times when she will be lacking in judgment. That's when you *lend her your brain*. Because the teenage brain is not fully developed yet, your daughter will need to "borrow" yours from time to time. As an adult, you have the ability to think through problems and come up with potential solutions. You have a marvelous capacity to peer into the future and see what's waiting around the bend. Let your daughter know that you and your brain are there to help her sort things out, no matter what the subject. (Even "My boyfriend and I are thinking of having sex." Gulp.) When things come up, you can walk her through your logic and thought process and talk to her about any relevant experiences you may have had. In doing this, you're demonstrating to her how to be creative and resourceful. This is coming from a place of love, calm, and respect for our daughters. We educate and inform our daughters that their brain, specifically their prefrontal cortex, is not fully developed until their early twenties. This is not a put-down; if anything it's all about age-appropriate expectations, what they are really capable of processing and figuring out on their own.

Trust Your Gut (TUG)

Too often we have this gut instinct or inner sense that something is wrong. Some folks call it instinct; others call it intuition or a sixth sense. It's a small, extremely intelligent voice within us that's full of wisdom. We need to pay the closest attention to this kind of inner stirrings. I often hear moms say things like "Why didn't I trust myself? Turns out I knew better." Red flags go up if there is danger or apprehension. At other times, we can sense what the best course of action for our daughters is and summon up a wise strategy. For me, it's like a safety valve, something that has not ever let me down. When I have not listened to my small inner voice, that's when I have gone off course and lost my way. So our work as parents is in developing, building, and strengthening our TUG—and teaching our daughters to listen and trust their guts too.

Let me give you an example of how one resourceful mom trusted her gut. Andrea has two teenage daughters. When she was laying down the law one day, they looked at her and simply said, "Mom, you don't know what you're talking about. You're crazy. We both know it, and all our friends know it too. Every one of our friends who has met you says you're crazy." As a single mom with no one to back her up, that really hit her where it hurt and even caused her to question herself.

Thankfully, rather than just let it go, Andrea decided to investigate the situation further. She sensed something was fishy. It just didn't sound like something her daughters would say. Acting on instinct, she called up the mothers of some of her daughters' friends to get their perspective and discovered something amazing: their daughters had been saying the exact same thing to them. Apparently the tactic of undermining Mom by calling her crazy had worked for one teen and word had spread. This group of moms decided they would launch a coordinated response by confronting their daughters that same evening. Andrea's girls nearly melted in shame when she told them what she had learned and how disappointed she was in their behavior. Our daughters can be masters of manipulation when they want something, but how this mom handled the situation is a lesson in how to be both composed and clever.

Create Age-Appropriate Expectations

Be realistic when it comes to your teen. Don't impose limits and restrictions she can't handle or expect her to be an adult. When I refer to age-appropriate expectations, it's trying to keep within the frame of what your child is both emotionally and intellectually able to understand. When we talk to our tweens and teens like we would talk to our peers or our girlfriends, we are expecting too much. When we expect our teenagers to be compassionate to our exhaustion after we have spouted out a litany of complaints about everything that she is doing wrong, we are expecting too much. Let's take a simple example: if she has always been messy, don't demand that she start keeping her room as neat as a pin during finals week.

Let Her Talk

Give her enough time to finish her sentences, her ideas, and her thoughts. Don't interrupt her. Respect her pauses in the conversation as she is gathering her words. Do not rush in with solutions or answers. It's best not to comment until she gives you the green light that it's okay to do so. Practice active listening. Give her your full attention. This can be the hardest strategy for moms because it requires us to *stop talking and doing* for a moment and get out of our daughter's way. You are giving her the chance to share, vent, and problem-solve creatively, and all you have to do is listen. And when it's your turn to talk and answer her questions, keep it short. As plus-size model and National Eating Disorders Association (NEDA) spokeswoman Emme says, "Remember to *listen* more than to lecture."

Keep It Short and Simple

If you do talk, make your point quickly and clearly. Ask one or two open-ended questions. Don't take so long to illustrate your statement that she forgets what you were trying to say in the first place. Stay focused on the message. Don't go off on tangents. When it comes to talking to a teenager, less is more and don't be a snore. Dawdling, nagging, or lingering on an issue doesn't bolster the effectiveness of your message—such elaboration only dilutes it. No lecturing allowed: your teenager will be turned off if you talk down to her and constantly criticize and find fault with her. She will tune you out and wish she was elsewhere, and your message will be lost in outer space.

Lighten Up with Humor

Humor is a powerful healer. It lightens up the heaviest of conversations with laughter, the capacity to smile, and the gift of not taking ourselves too seriously. As Orison Swett Marden once said, "A good laugh makes us better friends with ourselves and everybody around us." Humor makes us more approachable to our daughters. Kids love it.

Answer the Why

Whys are good because they mean your daughter is talking to you and listening. They present opportunities for you to explain a mystery to her, something she doesn't fully comprehend or understand. "Because I said so" or a flat-out "no" are just about the worst answers you can give a teen when she asks why she needs to do something or why she can't do something. It's important for her to understand that you don't set limits and guidelines to punish her. You set them to protect her.

Be Calm and Come from a Place of Love

Your message to your daughter has a much better chance of being heard if it is stated calmly and comes from a place of love and concern. She will hear and respond to any anger and sarcasm and sharpness in your voice. Don't let your emotions cloud your communication. Staying calm also sets an important example for her to follow—for her to communicate her needs and wants and emotions calmly.

When my daughter, Samara, was young and used to get frustrated and upset, I used her tantrums as an opportunity for me to help her tame, understand, and express herself. When she would get angry, Samara would stomp her feet, start to cry very hard, and say "I hate this family!" and go upstairs to her room. Mind you, I did not ever give her a time-out or put her in her room. She just did that on her own. Usually she slammed the door to her room for emphasis.

I did not get upset. I could see that she was really steamed, and her pattern was that she would soon come downstairs, walk up to me, and we'd talk it out. She would get so frustrated when she did not get her way. During those times, she felt she was not being heard or understood. When I calmly and lovingly said I was sorry that she felt so upset and that she hated us all for not getting her way, she would calm down. I did not ever say to her, as I have heard many parents say, "Hate is a strong word; how could you hate?" Instead I tried to help her process the intensity of what she felt. I validated her feelings and validated her as a person. The turbulence passed like a tidal wave, but it only passed until the next time I could help her process it again.

Lots of moms feel that if they do something once and say it once, their daughters should learn and understand the concept on the spot. It does not work that way. Our daughters need lots of reinforcement and repetition, especially when it comes to expressing the strong emotions that are flooding their brains. Once the storm passed, Samara returned to herself. She even said she was sorry and all was right with her and me. Moms need to understand that if you weather her storm, this too shall pass. Our daughters depend on us to be their anchors, their constants, their rocks. I did not say this was easy to do. It takes lots of practice, patience, perseverance, persistence, determination, prayer, and self-talk.

Focus on Her Health, Safety, and Happiness

I tell my moms that when they talk to their daughters about any subject, they need to *focus on their health, safety, and happiness.* If you think she stays up too late, for example, you can share with her all sorts of facts she may not know, from how the lack of sleep can compromise the immune system to how people who don't get enough sleep often gain weight and get depressed. Could staying up late talking and IMing her friends be affecting her health and well-being? What kind of effect does a lack of sleep have on her studies and test scores?

Look for the Transformative Teaching Moment

You can't stop your kid from making mistakes. In fact, screwing up is a big part of how they learn. But I will show you how to turn a "disaster" into a transformative teaching moment. You can turn any communication "breakdown" into a "breakout" opportunity to connect, protect, and nurture. Drop your expectations and be alert for chances to connect with your daughter. Be invitational instead of confrontational. Make the most of the moment. Surprise your daughter by being open, spontaneous, and relaxed. Face challenges with flexibility and let solutions and insights float to you. As one mom said, "The messages just flow if you take the time to listen."

* * *

I'm in your corner. I know you can do this. I support you because I know moms can do this and do it well; I see it every day in my practice, in the moms who write to me for advice, in those I connect with through various media appearances. I see moms handle the uncomfortable and the unthinkable with grace, calm, and, yes, even humor. They get through it and make their daughters' lives better as a result. They are their daughters' secret weapons and their very best defense.

You can do it too.

CHAPTER 2

Why Is She Like That?

"I can't go back to yesterday because I was a different person then."

—Lewis Carroll, *Through the Looking Glass*

Don't you wish sometimes you could slip your daughter into your pocket? Your tiny Thumbelina would dance on the palm of your hand! Being that tiny, of course, would make her extremely vulnerable to all sorts of creatures, large and small.

Thankfully, *your* Thumbelina will not stay small for long, although you may yearn for the days when she was smaller and sunnier of disposition. She is growing and expanding, upward and outward. Her limbs may be sprinting ahead; suddenly clumsy, she seemingly trips over her feet. She is also struggling internally, trying to fit in with her peers, stand up for herself, and stand out in the crowd. She wants you to see her this way— no, *that* way. As she pulls on you and pushes you and provokes you, you may feel quite pummeled. Or she may go silent and shrink, feeling tiny, not expansive, and wishing she could fit back into your pocket.

A FORCE OF NATURE

Inside your daughter, turmoil is brewing. You wish there was a weather channel that could predict her moods, or a remote control that would allow you to at least change the channel. Part of the frustration is that it's so hard to predict! One minute she wants to cuddle; the next she just wants you to leave her alone. Your child's happy face can move into an unexpected nor'easter with a wind velocity that could uproot your living room from its foundations. Her emotions spill over. Her tempests rattle the entire house and provoke more than a few squalls of your own, leaving you exhausted and unglued. As one mother describes it, "Here comes my little tornado." Inside your daughter is still that sunny nature, only now it's reserved for her friends.

Here's what's happening inside that tiny tornado. In your daughter's brain, the almond-shaped amygdala is a swirl of feelings, instincts, and impulses in charge of processing memories and emotions. That's right, that thing that sounds like a queen from *Star Wars* has control of your daughter's emotional life, and it's running you ragged as well. It accounts for her thin-skinned reactions to routine interactions and her suddenly stronger opinions, feelings, ideas, and tastes.

"Is this the area that's responsible for rational thought processes, logic, and impulse control?" you gasp. "How do I turn it on?" No, that would be the prefrontal cortex, and it's still developing; it won't be completely hardwired and fully functioning until she's a young adult. She's on her own to sort through these things. Give her time. Be her back-up plan. Lend her your brain.

She can't tolerate much frustration now. She needs your help to quell the volcano. Hang in there, Mom. Be determined, patient, and reassuring.

One of the biggest mistakes a mom can make is to tell her child not to feel, to push it down, to say, "Don't talk to me like that, I'm your mother!" Dealing with your daughter's outbursts and temper tantrums by screaming back, slapping, hitting, punishing, talking down to her, calling her names, belittling her, and sending her to her room is a surefire way to alienate her from you. Your daughter is not able to understand what she is feeling on her own, nor is she able to calm herself down. If your daughter's emotions become pent up, where does it all go? You can get away with that to some degree when she is little, frightened, and very dependent on your approval, but all of that accumulated emotion is eventually going to burst forth. Trust me, the older your daughter is, the louder and angrier your mother/daughter power struggles will be.

Here's what you can try instead. Think back to your own experiences while growing up—when you got your first period and how your mom explained (or didn't explain) menstruation to you. What kind of guidance did she give you? Did she patiently explain to you how your body changes during puberty, or were you left on your own to learn the facts of life? Maybe you watched a film in fifth- or sixth-grade health class to learn how your body changes. Now imagine your daughter going through those very same changes and having many of the same questions and concerns that you did. It never ceases to amaze me how many mothers don't talk to their daughters about getting their periods. I recall a particular segment I did for Parents.tv about helping moms prepare their daughters for their periods.

I was amazed by how many moms were still embarrassed and uncomfortable about talking about something so natural and basic with their daughters. When the segment was posted on YouTube, it eventually got over fifty-five thousand hits, and I was swamped with emails through my website from ten- to fifteen-year-old girls who felt too uncomfortable to speak to their mothers and had very basic questions to ask.

Here's a refresher course on what happens, Mom, in case you're having trouble remembering. That little pituitary gland starts to work big time and releases powerful hormones, estrogen and progesterone, setting off an amazing, life-altering process in your little girl. Body hair starts to appear in the underarm, leg, and pubic area. Her breasts start to bud and develop. Depending on her genetic makeup, body type, and diet, she can grow in height, weight, strength, and shape.

These days a girl can get her period as young as seven or as old as sixteen. Every little girl, tween, and teen is unique. Family history can give an indication of when her period might start. When this happens, it would be so helpful for you to explain what's happening to her, and teach her how to be aware of her body. You will both need to be mindful of all the coming physical, emotional, and behavioral changes that can hit the two of you over the head like a ton of bricks.

Not every girl has PMS, but those who do may feel more bloated than usual and more sensitive to touch. She may get cramps, feel uncomfortable in her skin, and lash out at—guess who?!—that's right, her mother.

But along with the major adjustment in her body and her being, there needs to be a shift and adjustment in the way you are around her too.

REMEMBER YOUR OWN TEEN YEARS

It's so important to be mindful of your own adolescence and your relationship with your mom. Remembering your tween and teen years helps you be more attuned with your daughter's struggles, especially her need to be patiently heard, understood, and comforted. I remember when my own mother encouraged me by giving me a subscription to *Psychology Today* for my seventeenth birthday. It was a validation of the person I was growing to become.

We soften our attitude and approach toward our daughters when we remember our moms perhaps being a bit too harsh with us and expecting too much. I want you to consider what was missing for you as a teen. What did you want from your mom? I can show you how to tap into your inner teenager to be a better and more empathetic parent by remembering what did—and didn't—work with you.

TEACH BY EXAMPLE

Our daughters learn from watching us and how we cope with stress, anxiety, anger, sadness, happiness, good news, and other emotions and events. By sharing our own stories—and photos—from our youth, we develop a closer bond with our daughters. We invite them to learn from our mistakes and our successes. But there is another way we can instruct our daughters too—by setting a good example for them on a daily basis. For instance, if our daughters consistently see us taking care of ourselves and respecting ourselves, they will too. In this way, our daughters learn from what we live.

This kind of learning is not absorbed from a book, a TV show, or a movie. It's witnessed and observed. Growing up, I heard my mother say, "I also am a mother's child," whenever she felt that her needs were not being met. I remember how powerfully her words rang in my ears. To me, the words mean "I matter. I deserve to be loved and nurtured and heard." If you encourage your daughter to see herself as a person who matters, as a unique and original individual who is deserving of love, patience, and acceptance, doesn't it make sense to see yourself that way too?

BE CAREFUL WITH THE WORDS YOU USE

We have so much impact as moms with our words. You may think your daughter is not listening, but she is. She hears everything that you are saying, even though she may not let you know it. Don't ever stop saying that you love her, especially after a major fight or rupture. Moms and daughters can be angry with each other. They can physically separate from each other and might not talk to each other for hours or even days. However, moms and daughters really do not emotionally separate. Your daughter still looks for your approval, even when she pulls away. She still wants your blessing. In my practice and during my lifetime, I have seen many mothers connect and reconnect with their daughters time and again. Your relationship can become stronger, with the right effort and intent.

Think of your daughter's separation and connection to you as happening in stages. An eleven- to fourteen-year-old is still very physically and emotionally dependent on her mom. Then, as she turns fifteen and sixteen, your daughter becomes less dependent on you and moves toward interdependence, both physically and emotionally.

A wonderful thing, interdependence is somewhere between dependence and independence. In that growth process, your daughter is more able and capable of caring for herself, mind, body, spirit, while still very emotionally connected to her mom as her guide. She's not quite ready to be fully on her own. Moving from dependence to interdependence gives a higher level of mother/daughter connectedness, more of a back and forth. Your daughter is more open to feedback, running her thoughts, issues, concerns, opinions, and feelings by Mom.

As she gets older, say seventeen to nineteen, she can further refine and develop the capacity to become that much more of an independent thinker, but she can be interdependent as well. At any given time, your daughter may behave on a continuum from dependence to interdependence to independence, based on how capable, needy, or stressed out she may be feeling. (See Chapter 4, "Independence.") Our daughters pull away from us, but they circle back, time and time again, looking for our approval, validation, love, praise, and blessings.

When you tell her how much she matters to you, you build her up. Your praise for her intelligence, her heart, and her soul does wonders. Your words as her mom can have tremendous impact on her self-esteem and self-worth, and I can help you use your words to rebuild and strengthen your connection.

Over the years, I have helped many moms develop deeper and more loving connections with their daughters. I help them see that no matter how challenging or difficult the circumstances they face, nothing and no one can get in the way of how much they care about each other.

STOMPING GROUND

Dear Arden,

When I try to talk to my daughters, Liza, age twelve, and Lacey, age fourteen, about anything, why do they always assume I'm criticizing them and the choices they make? Why? Oh yeah, and when I ask them to do anything, they shoot back, "Why?"

Twelve- and fourteen-year-old daughters can be so hypersensitive, as they are starting to feel some of their oats and stretch their wings. They are uncertain and therefore a bit more stubborn; they see things in terms of black and white, and they hear your questioning as attempts to undermine them. You may have quite innocent intentions, but remember that they need to feel certain in their uncertainty at times.

Start with one question. If you need to ask more, take an open-ended approach. This takes a lot of practice. I've been where you're standing right now, personally and professionally. Instead of saying, "Sweetie, why are you wearing the blue sweater? The gray one goes so much better with your outfit!" try this **script**: "I love the blue sweater and your sense of style. I like the gray one as well. Hmmm...which one do you think enhances your outfit?"

It's about Liza and Lacey needing to make choices to feel a sense of independence. Tempering your questioning, even if it's difficult, can really ease the situation.

If you're asking them to perform a chore or task, however, then it's another ball game altogether. Trust me, you will see them doing more on their own in the future, especially if you are not moaning and groaning and making them feel guilty. With each request, when they question you and ask "Why?" come up with a well-thought-out response, not a lecture, and no raised voice. Be calm and come from a place of love. That's my mantra, and I need to repeat it and reinforce for you how important it is to put this concept into practice. It has saved my neck so many times with my daughter and will work with yours as well.

TOO TOUCHY

Dear Arden,
How do I handle my daughter's outbursts? Sandy's so touchy about every little thing! I feel like I'm constantly walking in a minefield. Honestly, sometimes you'd think we were having two completely separate conversations.

I recall working with a mom and her eleven-year-old daughter over a period of two years. Her daughter was dramatic, high-strung, and verbal. She was a very angry kid with too much power. She'd break into loud outbursts and tantrums, and complain and compare incessantly. Mom would give her daughter reasonable explanations, but that only made her angrier. She just wanted her way and that was that. I remember telling Mom that when her daughter said jump, she needn't reply "how high," and to keep in mind that she wouldn't be like this forever.

The work here is to rise above Sandy's provocations. Do not give in to the tantrum. Do not bribe it away with offers of clothes and money, as one mother I know did. Sandy is watching your reactions like a hawk. She needs to see that having a meltdown will get her nowhere. Right now she is struggling in her skin. She needs space to breathe. Please be patient with her. She needs your calm, warmth, and strength to see her through. Help her to be resilient and teach her coping skills, like listening to music, so she can self-soothe and calm herself down.

MOM TIP: Oh, Baby!

During your daughter's next meltdown, take out her baby picture. Not only will seeing her sweet face make you smile, but it will also make the horrible moments more bearable. Many moms I know keep baby pictures of their teenagers in their wallets for moments just like this. Back then, when she got upset, you thought she was adorable. You can also create a pictorial narrative of your daughter's life, whether it's through scrapbooking, picture albums, or what you may have displayed of family history on the walls of your home. It's amazing how excited we get seeing ourselves and our children. It's that wonderful sense of connectedness flowing over. I see the narrative as a mirror, a reflection of how much we value our family and our daughters. This underscores and reinforces our and our daughters' rootedness and sense of belonging.

SWITCHING GEARS

Dear Arden,
I am menopausal and my teenaged daughter is hormonal. Any advice on how we can keep our balance?

A dear friend of mine had her daughter when she was in her late thirties. By the time her daughter was thirteen, mom was in menopause. As she put it, "She was on the way up and I was on the way down."

One day her children asked, "When are we having dinner?"

Mom exclaimed, "I'm in the midst of a hot flash; I feel like I'm possessed. Leave me alone! Take care of yourselves; I'm suffocating."

"Where is my mommy?" the dumbfounded daughter asked.

"This could be you one day," menopausal mom responded, "so get used to it and take notes!"

This clever mother used gear shifts to describe where she was in a particular moment—first, second, third, fourth, fifth, overdrive, reverse, and so on. The daughter got so used to her mother not being herself that she'd ask, "Where are you today, Mom?" Mom would say something like, "I am just in idle." It got so that her daughter started using the concept of the gear shifts to describe her emotional and physical states as well.

Your situation sounds similar. Your daughter has gone from neutral to first, second, and third with the upsurge of estrogen and progesterone. She may feel moody, bloated, cranky, or tired before her period. Other times, she has an upsurge in energy. You, on the other hand, feel like you are going into reverse or idle. Symptoms like hot flashes, insomnia, and losing your temper over the littlest of things become commonplace. You may even start to get a bit forgetful. Don't worry; it takes a good long while to adjust to these changes in your mood and body.

So how do you prevent a mutual meltdown? By simply letting each other know where you are. Your daughter can alert you with sentences like "I have my period" or "I am expecting it." You can let your daughter know all about your menopausal symptoms. And both of you need to be particularly gentle with each other and let lots of small stuff slide. Know that, in time, as you work on creating balance, you both will become more comfortable with each other and it will be okay.

ARDEN'S MEDITATIONS FOR MOMS

"To keep a lamp burning, we have to keep putting oil in it."

—Mother Theresa

As moms, we need to take care of ourselves and chill out. We can be so stressed out at times. I know you don't have much time, but take two minutes and try my guided visualizations. I guarantee you will feel refreshed, refueled, and more able to come from a place of calm and love when you are interacting with your daughter.

Deep Breathing Meditation

As you breath in and out, oh so slowly, imagine being in a very relaxing spot, like a beach. Visualize sitting by the shore and seeing the ocean, the ebb and flow. It's so mesmerizing. Feel the warmth of the sun and the sand all over you, from your head down to your toes. It's so calming. Hear the seagulls and the sound of the ocean breaking on the shore. Ahh, the beach. My favorite spot to be.

You are feeling refreshed, refueled, and are able to come from a place of patience, calm, and love. Face your challenges with a renewed spirit of hope and faith.

Untying the Knot

Oftentimes I receive my patients in a state of urgency and crisis. Something is troubling them, maybe they're feeling blue and out of sorts, or they feel the pressure from a major exam, starting a new school, or coping with an illness in the family. I am sure that you and your daughter have felt knots in your stomachs at times. It's feeling as if you're falling into a dark abyss. Your anxiety and panic are preventing you from feeling grounded, centered, and focused. (This exercise also works well when you feel a lump in your throat or if you have a racing heart, sweaty hands, or any kind of headache.)

Imagine your knot; what does it look like? Is it a single knot on your favorite pair of sneakers? Is it a double knot with a bow? Imagine both of your hands slowly untying the knot, a double becomes a single, breathe into the knot and out as you untie. Sigh and say, "Ahh, that's a bit better." As you continue to untie, the single knot becomes loose sneaker laces, long and floppy. The laces are hanging. Sigh and say, "Ahh, that's much better." Breathe into your stomach, in and out, feel it go in with the inhalation breath and out with the exhalation breath. Breathe like this a few times. Breathe into the looseness. Feel a calming energy, calming thoughts, soothing words, "I'm okay, my tummy is okay. Ahh, that's much, much better." Breathe deeply, until you can feel grounded and centered again.

Imagining Ourselves Whole

I want you to breathe through your nose and exhale through your mouth very slowly throughout this entire relaxation period. If at any time you feel dizzy or winded, just stop and feel the sensation. By the end of the session, you should feel calm, alert, relaxed, and more accepting of the body you have. Let's start. Remember to breathe.

Imagine a warm and healing light running through your entire body, from your head all the way down to your toes. The warm light is bathing your entire body. Imagine hugging yourself. Start with your head, down to your neck and shoulder area. Roll your shoulders back and forward. We carry so much tension in this area. Breathe into these areas. Move down to your chest area. Imagine your lungs filling up with pure oxygen and then exhaling all worries, tension, and anxiety. This feels so nice. Now continue to move down to your hips, belly, legs, ankles (roll your feet), and don't forget to breathe.

Imagine embracing your entire body. It's the only one you have. Your body is sacred. Respect and revere it and yourself. Your body houses your heart, soul, creativity, potential, mind, and spirituality. Love it, nourish it, soothe it. Be kind to yourself and your body. Take tender loving care of yourself. Treat yourself with kindness and gentleness.

Take a walk with your body into the cool breeze, on the beach, anywhere you love to be. Be with yourself. You are worth it! Value, affirm, and cherish your body and being. Others will mirror this love back to you. Be your authentic self. Your being is so special. Reclaim your body.

Societies that revere the female human body appreciate our curves, fleshiness, and roundness. Let's focus for a few moments on our bellies. Breathe into your stomach. Fill it with self-love. If you contract your belly area, you limit not only your physical self, but your emotional power as well. Imagine looking at a toddler who is playful and emotionally free—they joyfully let their bellies hang loose. We are taught in the Western world to hold our bellies in a tight and unnatural pose. We aspire to tight abs and a flat, washboard stomach. Just breathe into and out of your belly. Fill it with self-love. When negative body thoughts start to crop up, challenge them. When we do that, we reclaim our bodies and take back our power.

Take a moment to digest, assimilate, and integrate your power and wholeness. I will count from one to ten. As I do, you will begin to feel more alert and pleased with yourself. You are basking in the power of your being in the world.

Feeling more and more empowered. Feeling more and more connected to yourself and nature. Feeling more and more pro-active to resist the cultural message that you can't be too thin.

Love your body; it's the only one you have. Love yourself, your mind, body, and spirit…and it will help you love your daughter.

Chapter 3

Technology

"Dear Teachers,
Thank you for teaching us how to text without
looking.
Love,
Ur Students"

—www.dearblankpleaseblank.com

It's hard to remember how we survived, once upon a time, in the ancient age before the technological revolution. Still, many of us parents managed to grow up just fine without cell phones, computers, video games, MP3 players, handheld computing devices, and what-have-you. We actually had to use that part of our brains that allows us to engage in forward-thinking, making plans ahead of time if we wanted to meet up with friends, instead of simply texting them our whereabouts every two minutes until we found each other. We even had to deal with delayed gratification and save big news for school the next day, instead of immediately telling our friends about anything of even remote importance that ever happened to us via email, cell phone, Facebook, Twitter, or all of the above, all at once. You and I grew up in a world that your teen daughter can hardly imagine.

And it may be equally hard for you to understand her world, one in which technological gadgets are a lot more than just cool toys. To her, they are facts of life, even necessities. Technology is here to stay, so if it's new terrain for you, it's time to learn something about it—enough, at least, so you have an idea of what your daughter could be doing!

THE REALITY

- Gadgets, including cell phones, computers, MP3 players, and video game consoles, are an integral part of your daughter's life.
- Because you didn't grow up using technology like she has, you will have very different views on the subject and its level of importance in your lives.
- She likely knows more (potentially *a lot* more) about how these things work than you do.
- Technology is a wonderful source of education and entertainment, but it enables access to images and information to which you would never knowingly expose your daughter. It also makes it easier to keep secrets.
- All this is having an effect on your daughter in terms of what she sees, how she interacts with others, how she thinks about the world, and how she thinks about herself.

Face The Facts

- Eighty-four percent of teens go online each week, spending an average of eight hours per week on the Internet.
- Nearly 70 percent of teens have cell phones.
- Fifty-two percent of teens listen to MP3s, spending an average of four hours of listening time per week.
- As much as Internet use is on the rise, TV is still the teen's favored medium. The average American teen spends more time in front of the television set than she spends in school.
- Thirty percent of parents say they don't think the Internet has had an effect on their children.
- Seventy-five percent of teens say their parents "almost never" monitor the time they spend online, and 29 percent say their parents would disapprove if they knew what they were really doing on the Internet.

SMOKING HOT HANDLE

Dear Arden,
I just found out my fourteen-year-old, Skylar, uses the screen name "hottiegrrlXXX" and her best friends are "sweetsmokinlips17" and "kissyface18"! There are other names on her chat buddy list like "turbocommando124" and "lethalthrust." I told my fourteen-year-old NOT to use her real name, but don't you think this is too much?

Most fourteen-year-old teen females are in such a hurry to grow up and buy too much into our oversexualized culture and scene.

As freshmen, they want to appear cool and appeal to the older guys. They may come on too strong, sending flirty IMs and sexy texts. Most of them are not sexually experienced and do not realize they are getting in over their heads. They can be clueless about the signals they're sending to boys. Guys, who are already very hormonally driven, are very quick to notice these messages, and take them seriously.

Talk to Skylar about the meaning of her name. Does she realize what she is putting out there for all to see? Does she mean to be so disrespectful of herself? Let her know that what she puts out could come back to bite her. "XXX" might sound cool because it could stand for kisses, but it also sounds like a rating for a porn film.

She will surely minimize having such a controversial screen name, but let her know that having others respect her, especially boys, will serve her now and for the rest of her life. Tell her to pick a more age-appropriate screen name, like "14cutiepatootie" or something like that. Now is the time to make an impact, so let Skylar roll her eyes—it's worth it!

SEXTING

Dear Arden,
Last Saturday I walked into my fifteen-year-old daughter Olivia's room while she was taking a shower and accidentally saw something on her laptop. It was an IM between her and her boyfriend in which they were both saying unbelievable things. Her: "I want you to suck my tits." Him: "While I do that, I want you to grab my cock." I was shocked! Do I speak up or just pretend it never happened? If I do say something, she's going to be furious with me for snooping. Help!

It didn't take long for texting to become sexting. For those who don't know, sexting is when someone sends sexually explicit messages or photos electronically. This is typically done via a cell phone (hence the play off the word *texting*) but can also be accomplished via email, IM, or other form of cybercommunication.

Things we never would have dreamed of saying to each other as kids are regularly typed and texted by teens today—graphically sexual things that would make most anyone over the age of thirty blush. And here's the crazy thing: many teens would never say such things out loud either, but sexting is a different matter. Technology offers a sort of veil they can hide behind. They say things in print that they don't have to take full ownership of in the moment. It's a false sense of security, really, and one your daughter may not fully understand.

The quick answer is yes, you do need to face your daughter. What you found is too important to just sweep under the rug. But first thing first. You can begin by apologizing for reading her private IM.

I know it can be hard to find the right words in sticky situations like these, so here's a **conversation starter** you can use to kick things off on the right foot: "Sweetheart, I have something to confess to you. On Saturday, I came into your room to talk to you and I saw an IM between you and your boyfriend on the computer. I'm sorry for looking at something that was private."

If she gets upset, and she likely will, respond from a place of calm. The point here is to diffuse her anger and get past it so you can talk about the subject you really want to address: what's going on between Olivia and her boyfriend? Continue with: "I can understand why you're angry, and I truly am sorry. I'm also concerned and I want to help. I really want to know, is this how boyfriends and girlfriends talk to each other these days?"

Even if she's still angry, it's important to listen to what your daughter has to say and offer some advice. If Olivia responds by saying that this is how everyone at school talks and that it's just talk, believe her. But tell her you worry about whether her boy-friend respects her when he says things like that. Tell her that you hope he isn't pressuring her into doing anything she doesn't want to do, virtually or otherwise. And point out that when you put such things in print, people can show it to whomever they want.

Ask her: "If you and your boyfriend end up breaking up some-day, are you sure he wouldn't show your private communications to his friends? If he did, how would you feel about that?" That's something she may not have thought about.

If she responds by telling you that she and her boyfriend are sexually active, then you have another conversation ahead of you. See Chapter 10 on sex for more on how to handle this tricky subject.

The important thing is to do what you can to diffuse your daugh-ter's anger and open up the channels of communication. You may not get all the answers you want, but you will learn more about what Olivia is thinking. You can end the conversation by making it clear that you are open to talking about these kinds of things in the future.

DIGITAL PHOTOGRAPHY

Dear Arden,
My sixteen-year-old, Jade, left her cell phone in the kitchen, and when I picked it up, I found something very disturbing—nude pic-tures of a girl her age. You can't see the girl's face, and I don't think it's my daughter, but I'm just not sure. Even if it's not her, why would she have such things? I just don't know what to do.

I can certainly understand the fear that this type of discovery can cause. Most moms have heard about the case of the Ohio teen who sent nude pictures of herself to her boyfriend. After the couple broke up, the boyfriend forwarded the pictures to several girls in schools who then mocked and harassed the teen, calling her a slut and a whore. The teen got very depressed and hung herself in her bedroom at the age of eighteen.

These are the kinds of stories that send chills up a mother's spine. And rightly so. Our daughters have access to very powerful technologies, but many of them don't fully understand how damaging they can be.

As a mom, one of the things you need to understand about digital photography is how easy it is to use. Your daughter doesn't need to have a digital camera in order to take pictures. Her phone or her computer might have a built-in camera. Even iPods can come equipped with cameras. What all this means is that she can take a picture and send it off via text or email before she has even had time to think about what she's doing.

Regardless of why Jade has these pictures, take this as an opportunity to "lend her your brain." The teenage mind tends to focus on the present, not the future, so she needs you to help her think through the potential consequences of sending someone a nude photo of herself or even of forwarding on a picture of someone else. Point out that once something is sent, she can't control what happens to it. Anyone can take that photo and post it, forward it, even manipulate it however they want. Talk to Jade about stories in the media, or maybe email her an article so she can better understand how real people have been affected by this. It may take all of thirty seconds to snap a picture and send it, but that picture can end up haunting her for years.

> ## The Controversy Over Nude Photos
>
> There are a lot of reasons why sending a nude photo is a really bad idea. Among those reasons is one that many people don't even realize: the potential legal consequences. Creation, distribution, or even simple possession of a sexually explicit image of a minor can be considered child pornography and thus prosecuted under state or federal law as a felony. The perpetrator, no matter the age, could even be made to register as a sex offender. If your daughter tells you that nude pictures are "no big deal," pointing out this fact may help change her mind. You can remind her of all the young actresses whose wholesome images and careers got derailed by just one moment of poor judgment and lots of "leaked photos."

CELL PHONE OVERUSE

Dear Arden,

We knew our fourteen-year-old daughter, Jasmine, would use the cell phone we got her for her birthday to talk and text with her friends, but it wasn't until we got our bill that we realized just how much. She'd run up a pretty big charge! I wish we had put some restrictions on usage right from the start. How can we do that now, after the fact, and what kinds of guidelines make sense?

A cell phone can be useful, not just for teens, but for parents as well. It allows you to connect with your daughter no matter where she is. If you forget to tell her something or you're going to be late picking her up, a quick call can relieve your anxiety. And you can feel more secure knowing that she has it in case of an emergency.

Many kids these days have cell phones by the time they're in the fifth grade (around the age of eleven or twelve). But kids that young and even Jasmine's age need help understanding that having a cell doesn't mean they get to use it anytime, anywhere, and in any manner they choose.

Clearly defined limits from the beginning would have been a good idea, but it's never too late to implement them. Jasmine is going to come on strong and say something like: "But Mom, *all* my friends have unlimited texting! It will cost less if you get an unlimited plan." She may be right, but what her friends do and what a plan costs are not the most important issues here.

If you get her an unlimited texting plan, she'll likely be texting her BFFs the moment she wakes up in the morning, while she's on her way to school, every lunch period, every evening, and even at night when she needs her sleep. It can easily distract her from things that matter more, like schoolwork, family, and a good night's rest.

This is a good time to employ the "Make Her Part of the Solution" strategy (see Chapter 1). Approach the conversation from the perspective that there must be times when the phone is off but that she can help you decide when those times will be. Then ask her some leading questions. If your daughter has trouble getting herself ready for school, ask if she thinks it would a good idea to have a "no cell phone" policy until she's dressed and ready to go. She may very well see the logic in that and agree. If she doesn't, then the next time she's late, you can bring up the notion again.

Consider using the honor system at first, putting your daughter in charge of sticking to the agreed-upon limits. You want her to feel like you trust her to shoulder this big responsibility. Remember that most cell phone companies make it easy for you to monitor her usage (just check your bill or account online) without having to look over her shoulder all the time.

If she messes up by using her phone when she promised she wouldn't, you can make it harder for her by keeping it with you or in your bedroom during off periods. But resist the urge to take the phone away from her entirely. This is just the sort of punishment that will only inflame her. One of the things we try to teach our daughters is to think about the consequences of their actions. Moms need to do the same. If you take away something Jasmine considers vital to her existence, it's not likely to encourage her to act more responsibly. Instead, she'll end up sneaking around—using her friends' phones or even buying a disposable one that you won't know about. It's best to promote responsible and *open* behavior rather than forcing her into a position where she could end up doing things behind your back.

CELL PHONE GUIDELINES FOR EVERY MOM TO CONSIDER

- Have a designated space in a common area, like the living room or kitchen, where everyone in the family leaves their phones during downtimes and overnight. The practice will mean more if you do it too.
- If you have a strange feeling that something is up with your daughter, it's okay to check her saved texts and pictures

while her phone is in its charger. Don't undertake this lightly, but some careful and respectful monitoring can provide you with vital insight into your daughter's life.

- Designate times during the week when everyone in the family turns off their phones and various devices. Whether it's dinnertime or a family outing, it's a good idea to have periods that you spend together without interruptions.

- Acknowledge to your eleven- to thirteen-year-old daughter that you may periodically look at her cell texts. She may balk, but I suggest you have these parameters set up before or as soon as she starts using her cell. You can then reinforce and remind her of your original agreement as needed. She may also go along because there is nothing to hide.

- What if you haven't set up parameters, and she's upset by the idea? Here's a **conversation starter**: "Honey, I am sorry that you are so upset. I am sorry I made a mistake. This is a big responsibility that you need help with. I was expecting too much of you."

- When it comes to your fourteen- to sixteen-year-old, your snooping may get her feeling resentful and angry, like it's an invasion of her privacy. She may delete any and all potentially incriminating evidence. Try this: ask your daughter before looking and discuss your concerns.

- For your seventeen- to nineteen-year-old, if you are picking something up that causes you strong concern, then talk directly to your daughter. Your position is that of respect and being solidly there for her if something is amiss. Apologize if there is no cause for upset and say that you still can be lovingly protective of her at times, no matter how old she is.

> ## *Mom Alert!*
>
> Included in teen texting lingo are warnings that signify when a parent is afoot, hence the need to censor what they're typing. If you see any of the following abbreviations, she may be trying to hide something from you:
>
> - POS = Parent Over Shoulder
> - PIR = Parent In Room
> - P911 or PA = Parent Alert
> - PAW = Parents Are Watching
> - PAL = Parents Are Listening
> - PBB = Parent Behind Back

COMPUTER ACCESS

Dear Arden,
My fifteen-year-old, Lea, has been bugging us to get her a computer. We have a shared one in the house, but she insists she needs one in her room. I worry about what she'll do with a computer of her own and that she'll never come out of her room. Am I overreacting?

First of all, it is definitely not overreacting to worry about this subject. I managed to keep Samara from having a laptop of her own until six months before she started college. Instead, she had full access to a family computer in a shared space. She would sometimes close the door to the computer room or be on the computer late at night, but even if I didn't always know what she was doing, I knew when she was using it. And since it was a shared room, my husband or I could walk in at any time. Plus, we used the computer ourselves, which made her think twice about what she stored on it. Overall, it was a good strategy for our family.

Lea is not going to like my answer, but I believe that you are asking for BIG trouble if you give in. It will be so hard to monitor how long she is on the computer, how late she is on it, and what sites she's visiting. She may end up wanting to spend all her time in her room, even having meals in there. It's bound to cause tension between the two of you, and you will have your hands full.

Instead, offer a compromise. Suggest that you get a second desktop or laptop that will be kept in an open space. That way she won't have to wait to use the computer if someone else is on it—a particularly useful solution if you have multiple people in the house vying for time.

The main consideration here is to find a solution that allows Lea appropriate access to a computer while avoiding any sort of set-up that makes it easy for her to check out, get lost in cyberspace, and leave her family behind. The research on this is very clear: a child who is not feeling connected to her family, particularly her mom, is more likely to get into trouble, participate in risky behavior, and become self-destructive.

ABOMINATIONS ON THE INTERNET

Dear Arden,

I'm a single, working mother of two girls, Shannon, age fifteen, and Alexis, age twelve. Since it's just the three of us, I put a lot of faith in them, maybe too much. My oldest really wanted a laptop of her own, and she promised she would use it only for homework and IMing friends. I believed her, so I gave in, but then something I never anticipated happened. I came home from work early one day because I was sick and caught Alexis using Shannon's laptop. She was on a porn site! Well, I just blew up at my youngest, and now she won't talk to me. How do I handle this?

This sounds like the right time for the "Table It and Try Again Later" technique (see Chapter 1). You weren't feeling well and you were just getting off work, which means you probably weren't at your best. What you saw was shocking, and you could have used some time to recover before facing the situation head on. The best solution probably would have been to get Alexis off the computer and then walk away.

I know it's not easy to manage your anger in situations like these, but you have to make an attempt. Try breathing exercises to help calm your nerves. Your anger is understandable, but it's also what turned your daughter off. The only way to find out more about what's going on is to *gently* question her.

The reality is that porn is everywhere on the Internet, and the average age that kids are first exposed to it is just eleven years old. That means, as icky and uncomfortable as it is, we all need to talk to our kids about the subject and do it early.

In Alexis's case, she may have just stumbled upon it, or she may be curious. Either way, you need to find out her intentions. When you bring up the subject again, start by telling her she's not in trouble. That will take some of the pressure off her and help her open up. Then follow up by saying you need to understand what happened. Did she just fall on this site or was she looking to push the boundaries of what was allowed? Once on the site, did she feel overwhelmed but couldn't resist looking? Is this something she does on a regular basis, or is this a new thing?

Take an educative approach and make this a transformative teaching moment. Here's a **conversation starter**: "Honey, every tween wants to grow up so fast and it's quite normal to be curious, even if you may be feeling this is not the best visual for me to see. You may be feeling a bit uncomfortable, maybe a little guilty, but can't help feeling that you want to see more. That's how porn works—it pulls you in, overstimulates you, and you just want more. It's a seven-billion-dollar industry that adults are hooked on, and these days it's so easy to access on the Internet."

You may be surprised; she may admit to being pulled in and feeling a bit sneaky. You have set the stage for discussion that can come up spontaneously now when you see or make other opportunities. Your daughter sees that you are not angry and are coming from a place of patience and trying to create a conversation.

It's never too early to start educating our kids about the overstimulating, inappropriate, and racy material on the Internet. For children, tweens, and even younger teens, you need to install safety software that blocks inappropriate sites on any computer she has unsupervised access to. But don't punish Shannon for something her little sister did by taking away her computer. Instead ask for her help. Perhaps she can take the laptop with her or put it in a safe place when she's not home. That way, temptation can be avoided for your youngest.

AGE-APPROPRIATE GUIDELINES
FOR COMPUTER SAFETY

All Ages
Keep computers out of kids' rooms. You'll thank me for this. A computer of her own is a privilege earned after years

of responsible, supervised usage, so put it off until she enters college and her brain can handle the complexity. Instead, have one or more in a common area where everyone in the family can access it. This will foster a more open atmosphere and make teens think twice about what they're doing on the Internet.

Everyone needs to limit their computer time, even adults. The hours can pass quicker than you think when you're absorbed in the Internet, which has the potential to distract from more important pursuits and foster a sedentary and isolated lifestyle. Determine clear time limits and stick to them.

Eleven- to Fourteen-year-olds

You need to install software that blocks inappropriate sites. This age group doesn't need to be overstimulated, nor do you need to be looking over her shoulder all the time. Explain to your daughter why you are doing this, and talk to her about predators and bullies on the Internet.

Fifteen- to Nineteen-year-olds

This group may have ample experience on the Internet, but they need consistent reminders about the hazards, particularly about being mindful of what they post, both in pictures and text. Emphasize that words in print can have a powerful impact. If you wouldn't say it to someone's face, don't post it.

At eighteen, she'll likely be leaving for college, where she'll have twenty-four/seven access to a computer. If you've helped

Social networking sites such as Facebook and MySpace consistently rank among the most visited websites for teens.

her establish good habits and explained the reasons behind them, this transition is bound to be much easier for her.

SOCIAL NETWORKING

Dear Arden,
I was recently inspired to set up my own Facebook account, and now I'm wondering if it's okay to "friend" my eighteen-year-old daughter, Katherine. What happens to my role as Mom if I do this? Will she see me as a peer? I don't know how comfortable I am being tagged as my daughter's "friend."

I know exactly how you feel. I was put in a similar situation when Samara was twenty. After two female pals sent me friend requests, I asked my daughter to help me set up a Facebook account. She did a great job of teaching me how to navigate my page, but when we were done, I didn't know whether it was appropriate to ask, "Do you want to be my 'friend'?"

Beyond what it means for your relationship, moms wonder if they're invading their daughters' privacy. If your teen is younger, you may want to friend her in order to keep track of what she's doing. But for older children like yours and mine, moms have to wonder if there are things we just don't want to see. I know my daughter has a boyfriend, for example, but if she posted a picture of the two of them making out, do I want it staring me in the face?

The funny thing about these questions is they reveal how differently we think from our daughters. I cautiously asked Samara about friending her and she was very agreeable, as if it were nothing. And that's the thing, it *is* nothing to them. Many teens regularly friend so many random people that they don't even think about questions like, *what will this do to our relationship*? To them there are no hidden meanings or complicated implications involved. It's simply NBD (no big deal).

In contrast, what can be a very big deal is unfriending someone. I once noticed that my daughter had someone in her network that she hadn't talked to in a while. "Why don't you delete her?" I asked.

It seemed simple enough to me but my daughter recoiled. "Oh no, Mom, you don't just *do* that. It could create a backlash."

To get back to your question, if Katherine is okay with it, I would recommend becoming her "friend." The title won't change your relationship. Just be aware that you may end up seeing things that make you uncomfortable, like dicey pictures of her drinking, partying, or posing sexily. You'll also see some very harmless, adorable, and silly stuff. My view is that it's always better to know more about your daughter than less, even when it makes you squeamish.

And if you see something that troubles you, please talk to her about it. Don't worry; it's highly unlikely that Katherine will unfriend you as a result.

Have You Considered...

Nearly half of teens on social networking sites say they use them to make new friends. Additionally, on average, teens have seventy-five people they have designated as "friends" (and many even have more than that). Consider how many of your daughter's friends you know well. Is it anywhere close to seventy-five people? Yet online friends can still be having a strong influence on her.

PRIVACY AND THE INTERNET

Dear Arden,

My thirteen-year-old, Avery, posted some really embarrassing stuff on her MySpace page about my recent divorce. She also talked about her latest crush in quite a lot of detail. She doesn't seem to realize this is too much information to be putting out there for anyone to read. How do I make her understand?

Very few teens seem to have any natural instincts about protecting their privacy online. As much as they understand about how to use technology, they just don't connect the dots when it comes to the effect using it can have in the long run. Privacy to them is about closing the door to their room, hiding what's on their computer screen, or whispering to their friends. It's about what happens in the here and now, not about all the things they've posted that strange or unwanted people can read or see anytime, day or night.

This can be more than just embarrassing; it can be a real safety concern. We've all heard stories of young girls connecting with someone in a chat room or through a social networking site, which led to an in-person meeting with disastrous consequences. People who target young girls look for ones who are vulnerable, such as someone who is struggling with her parent's recent divorce and has displayed a strong interest in boys.

This is an area where it's absolutely essential to educate and inform (see Chapter 1). You can't just tell Avery not to go into chat rooms; you need to make her understand the dangers so that she can protect herself. She needs to know what to do if she has a weird feeling about someone online. We teach our kids not to talk to strangers or get in a car with someone they don't know. The same parameters and guidelines apply to the Internet.

Here's a **conversation starter** you can use when talking to your daughter: "Let me know if anyone approaches you in the real or cyber worlds. I will not get mad. I love you and I just want to protect you from people who can take advantage of you. There are unstable people in the world, and you need to keep that in mind when you're away from home *and* when you're on the computer. You're a smart girl, so trust your gut, and if you ever feel uncomfortable when chatting with someone on the Internet, stop the conversation immediately and talk to me about it. Never go alone to meet someone you only know from the Internet, no matter how nice that person sounds. You just don't know who will show up."

(This last point is an important one to reiterate to older teens who may be on dating sites. Encourage them to use their own form of transportation to get to and from a date and meet the person in a heavily trafficked area, preferably with a friend nearby.)

This is an area where you may need to be nosy to ensure your daughter's safety, especially one as young as thirteen. Many moms have access to their daughter's passwords and personal accounts and check them periodically to make sure there is no improper contact going on.

Here's a **conversation starter** for telling your kids why it's so important for you to have their passwords and access: "It's essential for me to have your password and access to your account so that I can make sure that no verbal or pictorial harm or overexposure is directed at you or any of your 'friends,' cyber or otherwise. This is a safety measure coming out of my love for you along with some age-appropriate expectations. I won't punish you if you make some mistakes. I expect that you may. I'm going to be reasonable, patient, and protective." Add some reassurance: "I respect your privacy, but I am helping to teach you how to navigate the Internet, Facebook, etc. Right now having this information is your and my insurance policy that you are safe and secure."

INTERNET TRUTHS TO IMPART TO YOUR KIDS

We tend to think of our kids as the technology experts, but there are still so many things we can teach them about cyberspace. Here are a few crucial lessons:

- **People lie.** Just because someone tells you she's fourteen in a chat room doesn't mean that's the truth. She could really be a he and forty years old. This sort of thing happens routinely.
- **People can be tricky.** Someone may say he met you at summer camp when really that's not the case at all. So how does he know where you went to camp? There could be a picture of you on your Facebook page in a camp T-shirt, or maybe your name is listed on the camp's website. If you don't remember the person, don't believe him.
- **You never know who is looking.** Predators and bullies are not the only people to worry about. There have been stories of young women just out of college who were turned down for jobs because of unflattering pictures on the Internet, usually of them drinking and partying. These young women never thought about potential employers looking at their pictures until it was too late.

- **Once it's out there, it's out there.** Once someone has seen a picture of you or read something about you, they don't just unsee or unread it. You can't control what happens to your personal info or images on the Internet. Even if you delete something from the page where you posted it, people can copy that info and keep it forever.

Even though teens love their social networking sites, it's important to remember that they're not the only ones using them. Only 9 percent of Facebook users and 14 percent of MySpace users are teens. Point that out to your daughter the next time she gets a friend request from a stranger she assumes is her age.

WHEN PAST POSTS HAUNT YOU

Dear Arden,

My daughter, Ro, really dug herself into a hole. She posted pictures from her high school senior spring break on Facebook. Ro commented how gross and disgusting and fat everybody looked, including herself. Her friend, Tia, started a Facebook dialogue with her and the friends about how insulted she was and what a nasty girl Ro is. Initially Ro thought she was joking, their usual typical teen talk, but Tia wasn't! She got a posse of online "friends" to confront Ro.

My daughter was so upset. She deleted the pictures and comments, then turned to me and asked, "What do I do now? Everyone is mad at me. I didn't mean it in the way she and the girls are taking it."

Empathize and say to Ro, "You must be feeling so confused, embarrassed, and ashamed. It's so out there for all of your friends.

Sweetheart, I hope this is an eye-opener for you and will make you think twice the next time you post pictures and make comments that can be taken in a hurtful way."

As for what she can do, she can try a couple of things. She can say online, "I had no idea. I did not intend to hurt you or anyone else." If that still provokes a backlash, she can say, "Let's meet face to face and I can explain myself and apologize for hurting you."

INTERNET ADDICTION

Dear Arden,

My eighteen-year-old, Mackenzie, graduated high school in June and decided to take the summer off before college. Her dad and I wanted her to get a job, but she insisted that after a hectic senior year, she had earned some time off. So we gave in. The problem is that now all she does is spend hours and hours in her room at her computer. She hardly talks to us, never goes out with friends, and sometimes doesn't even bother to shower. If she didn't have to visit the kitchen once in a while to eat, I think I'd never see her. Is this just how kids blow off steam these days? I'm worried...

What you describe is cause for concern. It sounds like Mackenzie is using the computer to withdraw from the real world and may be suffering from an Internet addiction.

Overuse of the computer is often associated with feelings of anxiety, insecurity, and depression. In fact, a recent study suggests that the more time a person spends surfing the Web, the more unhappy that person is likely to be. It's possible that Mackenzie is having trouble adjusting to a new stage in life and is frightened about starting college in the fall. The computer may be her coping mechanism.

Simply threatening to take away her computer would not be a positive solution. If your daughter is addicted, that would be like taking the bottle away from an alcoholic. An addict is an incredible rationalizer and avoider, always looking for a way around you.

It sounds like your daughter needs help dealing with her underlying anxiety. Tell her that you're worried about her and that you miss her. Ask her why she thinks she spends so much time online. If you speak to your daughter out of love and concern and she answers you with a lot of anger and defensiveness, she may have a real problem for which you'll need to seek help. If she isn't willing to try or doesn't think she can cut back, encourage her to see a therapist.

WARNING SIGNS OF INTERNET ADDICTION

Mental health professionals refer to something called the ACE model when talking about Internet addiction. ACE stands for anonymity, convenience, and escape, three basic characteristics of the Internet that reinforce addictive behaviors. Here are some things to watch out for:

☐ She spends more time on the Internet than she realizes.
☐ She uses the Internet with increasing frequency.
☐ She tries to conceal how much time she's spending on the computer.
☐ She regularly passes up chances to do things she used to enjoy so she can be on the computer.

☐ She's on the computer first thing in the morning and last thing at night.

☐ She uses the computer as an escape from negative feelings or stressful situations; conversely, she feels anxious or depressed when she's not able to use the computer for a time.

☐ She gets angry and defensive at the idea of limiting her time on the computer.

ALL THINGS HEADPHONE-RELATED

Dear Arden,
Do I have to worry that my daughter, Daria, never seems to hear me because she constantly has her headphones on? I'm losing my patience!

It can certainly be tough to take when Daria tunes you out, but keep in mind that there are good things about these technologies too. Remember the struggles that used to take place in the car over who got to choose the radio station? Would it be Dad's ball game, Mom's easy listening station, or daughter's rock 'n' roll? Such moments could quickly turn into an argument that ended with no one happy.

When you talk to Daria about the downside of technology, it's a good idea to stick to points related to her own health, safety, and happiness. Simply telling her that the behavior annoys you will only annoy her back and get you nowhere. And there are some real health issues involved that are worth mentioning. For example, those headphones don't only make it difficult for her to hear you, they may make it difficult for her to hear in general. Noise-induced hearing loss is a growing problem that can happen to a person of any age and is often completely preventable. In fact, a recent study suggests that the tiny "ear bud" headphones that come with many popular models of MP3 players are even more likely to cause hearing loss than larger headsets. A good rule of thumb is this: if a person standing next to you can hear the music through your headphones, it's too loud.

Even if your daughter keeps to an acceptable volume, she still may not be able to hear you when you ask her a question. Try not to take it personally. Teens go on autopilot when they tune into their various devices and generally don't mean to be rude. Eventually, she will have to take those things off her head, so if you can, wait until then to talk to her. She'll be more receptive to what you're saying if you don't interrupt what she's doing. If it can't wait, simply take a deep breath, let your annoyance go, then tap her on the shoulder and ask her nicely to take the headphones off for a bit so the two of you can talk.

THE BOOB TUBE

Dear Arden,
I read in the newspaper about this show, Gossip Girl, *that has racy plotlines yet is aimed at teen girls. It made me realize that I didn't know very much about what my daughter, Lizzie, who's fourteen and a half, watches. Is it too late for me to begin monitoring her viewing choices now?*

These days we're all so concerned about the influence of new technologies that we forget about the old ones. The good old television set is still the most used form of technology in a teenager's life. And it comes with its own set of considerations and complications.

The good thing about television is that we know how to use it and we know how to monitor it. We can search the TV listings ahead of time and read reviews of shows to get a sense of what our kids are watching.

Not long ago I happened to stumble on a repeat of the infamous threesome episode on *Gossip Girl*. I was surprised to find that it wasn't as graphic as I'd expected after all the hype. The threesome scene began with kissing among two girls and a guy and then cut to another scene happening elsewhere with other characters. When it cut back to this trio, they were asleep in bed together, so the actual sex was left to the imagination.

Still, is this what we want our daughters to be watching? Probably not. But if it's what they want to watch, is there any real harm? That depends on their age and level of maturity. Our daughters are often a lot savvier than we realize. They know when something is over the top and they know what a play for attention and ratings is all about.

First off, give Lizzie some credit, and if you're not sure what she thinks about something that has happened in one of her shows, ask her. We can use these overstimulating or inappropriate televised situations as transformative teaching moments (see Chapter 1)" and springboards for discussion. Just remember to ask her about it like you're interested, not like, "What could you possibly see in that awful show?!" And if she'll let you, watch an episode or two with her so you can really talk about what's happening.

The American Academy of Pediatrics recommends limiting viewing of all forms of entertainment media (TV, movies, online videos, etc.) to just one to two hours of *quality* programming per day.

TECHNOPHOBIA

Dear Arden,

My fifteen-year-old daughter, Addy, is light years ahead of me when it comes to computers and other technology. The older she gets, the more I worry that I have no idea what she's doing with all this stuff or what it's doing to her. Sometimes I feel like I'm losing her to it. What can I do?

I know it can be intimidating, but we moms have to remember that this stuff is here to stay. So it's time to embrace it, for your own and your daughter's sakes.

Take a computer class, read up on the subject, and ask your daughter for some lessons on how to text, surf the Internet, or play a video game. She may enjoy being the one with the knowledge to impart to you.

You might even like some of these things, and you might also be able to improve communication between you and your daughter. She's used to speaking in IMs, posts, and texts, and might just understand you better if you try speaking her language. (In fact, statistically speaking, texts are the teenager's favorite form of digital communication, followed by instant messages. Interestingly, they're not as into email.) So what are you waiting for? Go ahead and get plugged in!

DON'T FORGET TO UNPLUG

A recent report from the Kaiser Family Foundation confirmed something that many of us had already suspected: children are less active than they used to be, spending an average of seven hours and thirty-eight minutes *a day* utilizing all this technology, from cell phones and iPods to computers, television sets, video games, and more. The same report also noted that in households where parents set limits on usage, kids spent an average of three hours *less* per day plugged in. To me, that speaks volumes about the importance of a parent's role here.

The limits need to start as soon as your daughter starts using technology. It can all seem very harmless at first, even cute, like when young kids play games online that let them care for their own virtual pets or decorate a virtual room. Still, take the opportunity to start creating good habits as early as possible.

If you haven't set limits before, start now. Something in the range of three hours a day on whatever forms of technology she chooses is a good place to start.

In determining what limits make sense, however, try to understand how your daughter is using technology. As members of an older generation, many of us tend to lump together all things technological. But when your daughter is on the computer, she could be socializing, watching videos, doing her homework, reading celebrity gossip, listening to music, or any number of things. Some of these activities you may actually want to encourage, so take the time to talk to her about her habits and try to sort out the good from the bad from the simple waste of time. For example, if she's using the computer to research a paper, learn about colleges, or do some sort of creative project, those are good things. Be careful that your limits don't discourage her from such pursuits.

Regardless of what time limits you decide on, it's key to encourage activities that don't rely on technology. Depending on your daughter's interests, this could mean playing sports, taking art classes, spending time with a church group, or any number of things. Family dinners are to be encouraged in a big way. It can be a wonderful time for everyone to unplug and talk to each other…the old-fashioned way.

SMART STRATEGIES FOR USAGE

- **Set limits and guidelines.** She needs some structure when using any kind of technology. How else will she know that this is an important issue or that you care?
- **Educate, educate, educate.** She needs to fully understand how dangerous these technologies can be. That way, she can make better decisions for herself when you're not there.
- **Take part and take heart.** She does hear you, even if it doesn't seem like it. Make an effort to relate to her through her technology of choice, and she may hear you even better.

CHAPTER 4

Independence

"I remember adolescence, the years of having the impulse control of a mousetrap, of being as private as a safe-deposit box."

Anna Quindlen, *Thinking Out Loud*

Everyone knows the story of Rapunzel, the beautiful girl who was kept locked up in a lofty tower. Sheltered and protected from the outside world, she was isolated and lonely. Her only company was her captor—an old crone who was determined to keep Rapunzel safe from the outside world and away from prying eyes. The poor girl's single freedom was to grow her hair long. Did Rapunzel feel grateful to her protector? No, she felt trapped. And that beautiful, long, flowing hair? That became the means of her liberation and release when an enterprising prince begged her to "let down her hair" so he could use her tresses as a rope to pull himself up.

As mothers in unprecedentedly challenging times, who hasn't wanted to lock up their daughters in order to keep them safe? And yet, our daughters yearn to think and act freely for themselves. They long to dream and explore and imagine the possibilities. They don't see the pitfalls that we do, at least not yet. As parents, we realize that a daughter needs space to breathe and fly and a strong connection at home to anchor her flights. It is simply not possible or responsible to keep our daughters little and dependent on us forever. We encourage them to return home often because hopefully they—and we—miss all the good stuff that a strong, loving connection brings.

As parents, it can be hard to watch a daughter's transformation from a little, protected girl to a curious, secretive, edgy, and experimental teenager, but the alternative—a girl who isn't allowed to grow up—is even worse. What happens to girls on the brink of adulthood who don't get the information they need? In the old days, before the Internet and the hurricane of data that is now available, girls who didn't get "the talk" from their mothers or caretakers didn't learn about their periods or understand how they could get pregnant. They often turned to their peers or older sisters for advice, which was not always reliable or accurate.

This has led to some very sheltered princesses who could be naïve and gullible and, dare we say, vulnerable to the next prince who climbed up the tower. Once out of the castle and on the ground, our poor Rapunzel is looking quite lost and confused. Imagine her sitting with a laptop, talking to strangers in chat rooms, and devouring hours of reality TV, movies, and cable. In an instant, she is suddenly connected to the world. How overstimulating, how overwhelming, how daunting for her to wander through that wilderness alone.

My advice? Give your Rapunzel the information she is seeking from you, right from the get-go, no matter how embarrassed you feel. The conversation does not have to be perfect or proper, just honest and reciprocal. No matter what she says or how much she protests, your daughter depends on you to help her navigate through all the confusing and chaotic elements and influences in her life, internal and external. Be her rock, her wings, her shelter, and her lighthouse in a storm. Remember, your daughter needs you.

APPROPRIATE LIMITS AND EXPECTATIONS

Dear Arden,

I have three daughters: Jessica, sixteen; Jana, thirteen; and Janie, nine. I am a divorced, single mom who has been working full-time since my youngest started kindergarten. I have a college-age girl shuttling my girls to their activities. She also makes sure that they do their homework and stays until I come home. I admit it, I am exhausted and there are times that I come down too hard on the girls. I feel too much falls on me, especially when it comes to the housework. I have spoken to all of them about pulling their weight. My sixteen- and thirteen-year-olds just look at me like I am from another time zone. My nine-year-old looks like a deer in the head-lights. Jessica finally said, "But Mom, I work after school. I have no time as it is, even for my friends."

I have asked Jana to mind and play with her little sister after school and I have stepped that up to her babysitting as well. She gripes a lot, sounds resentful, and says, "Why do I have to do this? It's not fair!" She is taking it out on her little sister, who feels hurt and rejected. I expect more from her. After all, she is thirteen. I was watching my sibling when I was much younger than her.

With my oldest, I am guilty of having done too much for her and babying her sometimes. When I was a full-time mom, it was my pleasure. I was so torn about going back to work. She is still very dependent on me to make some of the simplest decisions. Sometimes she just does not want to think for herself. There are positives—she is driving and she has agreed to work with me on creating and coordinating a schedule to shuttle her sisters when it does not conflict with work and her other commitments.

They are great kids overall. One other thing—I am a stickler for neatness. I am working on them to tidy up after themselves, load the dishwasher, and clean their rooms. None of them do so willingly. Will this ever change? Am I expecting too much because they are girls? What are some good, positive ways that I can encourage my daughters to become more independent and less dependent on me?

I think one of the hardest challenges for you is to know how much is realistic to expect from your daughters and what their age-appropriate responses and reactions are going to be. For instance, a mature thirteen-year-old can be asked to watch her younger sister for a few hours while you run some errands, but it wouldn't be fair to expect her to babysit at night and on most weekends. I think Jana is feeling some of the brunt of your expectations that are based on your minding your sibling at a much younger age. Unfortunately, she is feeling obligated and is losing sight of how much she probably loves Janie.

I would make the effort to talk to Jana on her level and really hear what she has to say to get a sense of what she is able to accomplish independently and handle on her own. I'd also encourage her to share her feelings about her new caretaking role. I would **script** it like this, "Honey, I see that you have been unhappy and not yourself since I asked you to be more involved in babysitting for your sister. Your little sister is hurting too. Can we start all over again? Would you like to sit for your sister sometimes, or is this something that makes you feel anxious, stressed out, angry, and resentful?" You may be surprised at her response. Once you enlist her in the process and "make her part of the solution" (see Chapter 1), she may actually offer some of her time. I think your being flexible, and saying, "Sweetheart, so far this has not been working out too well; maybe we need some adjustments?" may make her feel so relieved. Her input here is invaluable, and I want her to reconnect to her sister in a more loving, fun exchange.

I chuckled to myself as I read about Jessica's dependence on you; it reminded me so much of an exchange I had with my daughter. Samara could be so independent, like your daughter, working and responsible at sixteen. But then there would be some leaks in the dam, and partially it was my doing.

For example, I used to make all of Samara's doctor's appointments, and there came a point where I told her that she could do that for herself. Samara would say, "Mommy, I need an eye exam and a refill of my contacts. Would you call up and make me an appointment?"

Instead of saying, "I'll do it," I responded, "Honey, you know your schedule better than I do. Here's the number. Why don't you call now or tomorrow and make an appointment?"

She looked at me askance the first time, but once she got into the habit of doing it for herself, it became second nature to her and she was less dependent on me and more capable of taking care of herself. Samara and I moved from dependence to interdependence. We need to be flexible about our daughters' growth because most of this is not about when we are ready for them to grow up, but when they are. It's about having our fingers on the pulse and our gut-sensing feeling, that tug, that she is more able.

In some areas, our more grown daughters are very capable of pulling their weight, so to speak, and in others not. So we look to make suggestions, plant seeds, add the water and sunlight, and help them see that they are much more capable than they realize.

With the housework, their resistance and griping (which is very typical of tweens and teens) scream that they want to be doing something else. My advice is to do it with them at first, as I did with Samara. We would make a game of cleaning up her room. It became more playful, less of a chore. For now, be involved in any additional house-cleaning and dishwasher-unloading as well.

Please take heart, take a breath, try some aerial parenting like an eagle, get a sitter for a Saturday night, meet your girlfriends and go out dancing, and kick up your heels. You deserve it!

BE A LITTLE BAD

A friend of mine, Debbie, used to tell her eleven-year-old daughter Lily to "be a little bad." Lily would look at her, horrified, and say, "Mommy, why do you say that?" Debbie would say, "Lily, if you misbehave now, you are more likely not to act out as much when you are a teenager, when you could get into big trouble." Lily would shake her head at her mother, and say, "Oh, Mommy, you are such a kidder." Debbie responded, "No, no, Lily, I really mean it." Lily would just shrug her shoulders and go back to what she was doing. Debbie explained it to me this way, "Lily is a bit too well-behaved. I am not encouraging her to act out in a self-destructive way. It's just that Lily is more on the quiet side. She's a sweet girl of few words. She does her homework as soon as she gets home, has a neat and organized room, has all her ducks lined up, is a high achiever, and is very respectful of her older brother and parents."

You may ask, too good to be true? Luckily for Lily, Debbie was a former social worker and student assistance counselor at a high school, who from her personal and professional experience and wisdom understood that her daughter was a bit too much of a perfectionist for her own good. She saw how important it was for Lily to loosen up and test the boundaries, at least a little. Now at fifteen Lily has a strong moral compass but has loosened up on herself. She has many friends, an adorable sense of humor, and now has both a serious and lighter side to her.

Remember your daughter is a hatchling in an aerie, especially as she moves from her fourteenth to her fifteenth and sixteenth years. You, as her mom, will remain alert and watchful, mindfully observing as your daughter stretches her wings. She may dip and falter, but she is learning how to fly. Yes, she is a bit different from you, and she keeps to her own flight pattern, but applaud her and praise her for trying and persevering. She is going to make lots of mistakes. She may go on the high wire. Promise to be there for her always and to be her safety net. I would let her know in no uncertain terms, "I am here for you, I'm not going anywhere. It's you who needs to keep flying, no matter what challenges lie ahead."

A LITTLE FAITH GOES A LONG WAY

On the other end of the spectrum, if you clip your child's wings and keep her too close to the nest, you inadvertently send her a message of your adequacy and her inadequacy, that you have little or no faith or confidence in her. Vicki, a former patient, was a high-powered corporate executive who ran her daughter and family like a business. Vicki micromanaged her daughter Natalie's life and infantilized her to such a degree that Natalie would scream, "Stop babying me! I can't stand you! Get out of my face." Natalie would deliberately stay out later and later at night and would be icy cold to her mother.

Vicki was clueless as to why her "baby" was behaving so out of control. "I try to be a good mother; I do everything for her." In discussing this with Vicki, it was hard for her to see that that was just the problem. During many sessions, I shared, "Vicki, you don't let anyone help you, you overdo, overkill, and that has been tied up to your identity of being a competent and capable woman." Vicki would insist, "But she's my only child, my little girl."

In her sessions with me, Natalie insisted that she did not want to be in the same room with her mother and say, "My mom is driving me away and driving me to do things that I really don't want to do." Natalie was feeling very guilty about her outbursts and was getting weary of staying angry with her parents. It took a lot out of her.

Meanwhile, with Vicki I was helping her work on mourning the loss of her little girl, who was growing up at rocket speed. "She's sixteen, Vicki. You've got to cut her loose; you have her on such a tight leash. This is what her acts of resistance and rebellion are all about." It took lots of convincing, but I finally had the family in my office to hash out all sides. Vicki started to cry, saying, "Where has my baby gone?"

Natalie rolled her eyes but realized with my prompting that her mom was really having severe separation anxiety. "I don't need to be strangled and suffocated," Natalie said. "You make me feel so stupid, like a baby. I'm sixteen, I have my permit, I can drive, I am not an invalid. I have been sticking it to you, like Arden says, by staying out late and being a bitch because you are controlling me and not listening to me."

"I will try to be what you need me to be," Vicki said. "It's not natural for me. I feel useless without doing for others, especially you."

I loved what Natalie said to her: "Mom, you are a great lady; I am so proud of you. Sit back and give me some more breathing space. I am not perfect. Like Arden says, I will make mistakes, but let me, okay?" There was not a dry eye in the house.

TOO STRICT OR TOO NICE: IT'S A BALANCING ACT

Some of the best-intentioned and most well-meaning moms are unaware of how controlling, strict, and overprotective they come across to their daughters. Listen to one mom's exclamation and you will be clued in big time: "You think I'm strict? You should have seen my mother. Yes, I had to toe the line or else I'd be punished. I learned to be sneaky if I had to. I am much less strict than my mother. Why does my daughter ignore me and tune me out?"

Then again, when mom is a pushover, overly pleasing, needing to be liked and loved twenty-four/seven, she puts her relationship with her daughter at a disadvantage as well. Another mom asks me, "Why does my daughter boss me around? I just want us to be best friends."

It's such a challenge and takes so much effort to find the

balance, but it's so worth it for your and your daughter's sake. Here are three examples that show the two extremes and three committed families that worked hard and figured it out.

Too Strict

I had been seeing my patient Tracy for well over a year when she came in to deal with her frustration over her relationship with her thirteen-year-old daughter, Lucy.

Tracy shared that she was brought up by two strict, old-world parents. There was no talking back; she could get hit and did at times for even a raised eyebrow. Tracy found Lucy's newly executed eye rolls and attitude intolerable and would smack her. Tracy knew how I felt about any kind of physical contact like that. She would even say, "I know this is not the right thing to do, but she is being so disrespectful to me and she just doesn't want to talk about how she is behaving."

Over the course of treatment, she began to see that her own parents were frustrated and did not take or make the time to talk, to share, or to hear what she was thinking and feeling. Tracy saw that their hitting and punishing her pushed her to go underground, within herself, and that she was doing the same with Lucy, with the result that her daughter was as afraid and intimidated of her as she was of her parents.

Tracy was feeling more and more guilty and hungry to learn how she could be less rigid, less of a stickler for the rules, and more tolerant and accepting. She wanted to encourage Lucy to have some attitude and to explore a new testing ground of voicing her thoughts, feelings, and opinions.

I helped Tracy to see that she could be a different kind of mom, one who was more approachable, with the result that

Lucy and Tracy began to experiment with texting each other and having conversations that way. Texting her mom was a great first step for Lucy, who was so scared at times that any mistake she made could be met with anger from her mother. Tracy was willing, with me in her corner, to give Lucy some breathing space for error, but not so much room as to ask for trouble. Lucy was still held accountable for the faces she made and her whereabouts, but not with any ensuing punishment. It was more for accountability, caring about her, and letting Lucy see that she had an impact on her mom.

Too Nice

Another patient in my practice, Linda, came to see me to deal with her confusion and frustration with her daughter Kari, age fourteen, who was able to push her around and treat her like a doormat.

Linda was overly permissive and just too nice. She had a very hard time understanding why she and Kari couldn't be best friends, and my advice to her that such behavior was not in their best interests; in fact, it was an obstacle getting in the way of a closer and more authentic relationship. She questioned, "How can Kari be so respectful to her teachers at school, but walk all over me?"

During our sessions, Linda shared that she had grown up with a very demanding and difficult mother who was hard to please. Whatever Linda did wasn't good enough or right. She would say, "There was the wrong way and Mamma's way!" Linda felt constantly criticized, demeaned, scapegoated, and bullied by her mother. She said to herself, "When I grow up, I am going to be easygoing and a super-nice parent." So, "why," she asked, "is my own flesh and blood daughter behaving at times like a mean, nasty, demeaning bully?" It was déjà vu for Linda. She would say, "Kari is turning into my mother! Where did I go wrong?" Linda was so needy and hungry to be loved that she couldn't see what was wrong with being more like a sister to her daughter than a mother.

However, after being repeatedly clobbered over the head by Kari's verbal insults, feeling that she did not deserve to be treated like a second-class citizen, and feeling her anger for the first time in a long time, Linda realized that she did not have to be either the overly nice, caring mother or the Mamma she grew up with. She saw that Kari would respect her more if she didn't turn herself inside out like a pliable pretzel.

We rehearsed in session how she could approach Kari with clarity and directness. I gave a **script** for what Linda could say to Kari: "I think it's time that we treat each other as equals. No one is better than the other. No one bosses, bullies, or puts down anyone anymore in this family. We all need to work on being kinder to one another. Kari, my voice deserves to be heard, and I hope to be a more empowering role model to you now and for the rest of your life."

Kari initially was baffled and blown away. It took a while for her to adjust to Linda's newfound assertiveness and confidence. Linda continued to have many talks about respect and self-respect. Kari was cut down, in the best sense, to a life-size fourteen-year-old who in time felt far less anxious and arrogant and who grew closer to Linda in a more loving way, which is what Linda wanted to begin with. Linda just needed some help with her approach and clarity about where she was coming from.

The Balancing Act

Finding the balance and working through frustration and anger takes lots of work on all sides, but it's so worth it. It's about reaching the other side of the mountain in a journey toward peace and harmony. My goal with Todd and Samara was always trying to be a benevolent, kind, reasonable, dependable, approachable parent, but not a pushover. They could test me and press my buttons, but I would try my best not to react. My attitude was and still is how I can facilitate their becoming their best selves. My focus has been unwavering in teaching them to think for themselves and to take care of their beings and bodies. I was very aware about walking my talk as well.

Sam and I had some additional accountability and caretaking discussions throughout her adolescence, especially when it came to her driving at night when she was in high school. Even though she would question, "Why do I have to text you when I get to my friend's house?" she would do it the majority of the time, because she knew how important it was for my peace of mind that she was safe, and that she mattered big time to her dad and me.

At times she'd come home extra late on the weekends, well after three in the morning, (she didn't have a curfew). I did not get upset, because teens sometimes lose track of the time. I'd just call out and ask if she was okay, and she'd apologize for waking me up.

Maybe twenty minutes later, I would notice the light in the computer room was still on. I'd check on her, remind her gently that she often got sick without enough sleep, and subtly talk about how she could do things the next day.

Teens just love to stay up all night, and most love sleeping in the next day. Some parents get very flustered and angry. I try to see the bigger picture, and to teach her from the day she could talk about self-care and to not push her own envelope when it came to her health and safety.

As parents, we do the best we can to imbue loving, healthy values. Our teens especially need to hear our voices and to "borrow our brains." We help our daughters remember to use their brakes in the car, and their emotional brakes in life, to not put themselves in risky or dangerous situations.

A IS FOR ANGER

Dear Arden,

I overheard my sixteen-year-old daughter, Sophie, talking on her cell with her girlfriend, saying, "Sometimes I just want to scream!" And then she screamed so loudly I got startled. Later that day I let her know it was impossible not to hear her scream. I asked her what was bothering her. I asked, "Can I help? Do you want to talk?" She was silent. When I said, "Did I do something to disturb you?" she nearly bit off my head and said, "It has nothing to do with you, Mom. Leave me alone." I hope she is going to continue to run this by her friend. It makes me nervous when she gets so worked up and angry. I get angry quick, don't hold a grudge, and then get over it. She gets hurt so easily, stews, and has a hard time letting go. She is generally a light-hearted, adorable, and funny girl. It just takes her a while to come back to herself. Does it serve any purpose for her to get this angry and scream? Is this normal for a teenager?

Something is up with Sophie, and she is not ready to talk about it with you just yet. She is stuck and stewing in hurt and anger for now. Maybe she's frustrated. She is clearly not holding you responsible. She needs to work it out, and I hope her pal can continue to give her an ear.

Squelching, stuffing down, or denying her anger and strong feelings won't make her feel any better. In fact, with some of my tween and teen patients, it has led to increased anxiety, frustration, despair, and the possibility of risky, self-destructive behaviors such as drug abuse and eating disorders. We don't want your daughter or any daughter to withdraw, become overly dependent, and not reach her full potential.

Self-expression is crucial to resiliency and mental health and wellness. Channeled anger can be used constructively to launch our daughters, give them some spark, and fuel their ambitious strivings.

For now, take a few steps back and see the bigger picture. Keep a loving, watchful eye on her, keep your finger on the pulse, and try not to crowd her in. We don't have to do everything for our daughters; that's what friends are for. Let's see if her friend can help her out by being her sounding board. Many times I have heard my daughter Samara vent to a pal and then spring back. I have watched her develop a resiliency that has served her well throughout her life.

Just today, a sixteen-year-old patient texted me a few times with questions revolving around the warning signs of anorexia nervosa, describing her friend's weight loss, wondering if her best friend was developing an eating disorder, and her concern as far as what she could do. There is nothing like a friend who cares.

KEEP OUT!

Dear Arden,
My fourteen-year-old daughter, Cameron, is growing increasingly private. Lately she has started closing her bedroom door when she has friends over—and some of them are boys! What kind of rules can her father and I set up? Are we allowed to make her room a "no-boy zone"?

Ah, one of the hallmarks of a tween and teen girl's push for independence is the push for privacy. This leaves many moms feeling alienated and left out. Mom, I can give you parameters, not rules. Rules are so rigid and inflexible. Parameters can be more fluid and subject to change. I know I can be a stickler for semantics, but I think this will work better for your growing daughter and her changing needs. Try these:

1. Have a discussion about the open and closed door. She is getting older, and the three of you need to figure out how to handle visits from her pals.
2. Rather than making her bedroom a "no-boys zone," ask her to leave the door open. This is reasonable for ages eleven to fourteen, especially with mixed groups of males and females.
3. Every so often, just stick your head in to see how she is doing. I would put away a tiny bit of laundry in a drawer. My daughter, Sam, didn't mind it at all.
4. If she gives you a hard time about the door being open, or she mistakenly closes the door, let her know that you and Dad have been considering a no-boy-zone room. Her eyes will bug out,

but she will understand that it's much better to keep the door open than to not be allowed to have any boys in her room at all. She will feel appreciative, grateful, and relieved. For ages fifteen to sixteen, if you are uncomfortable with a closed door, it's understandable. These are tricky ages, so it's open for debate, but it doesn't have to become an occasion for her to have a nuclear meltdown.

5. So with that in mind, no drugs, smoking cigarettes, smoking pot, pill popping, and drinking are acceptable at any age or any time in her room. Just be around and be a bit of a sleuth.

6. Eventually she will sometimes close her door, from ages sixteen to nineteen, and older. She is entitled to her privacy after all.

7. Once she is in college, it's common to have coed parties and gatherings and sleepovers in dorms and apartments. Some dorms are coed. She will be used to a closed door at school, and that probably won't change when she comes home for breaks.

8. Keep in mind that if you kick and scream, she will do it behind your back when you are not at home.

9. Be open to her growing interdependent and independent developmental needs, along with her taking into some consideration what's in your personal comfort zone.

LICENSE TO DRIVE

Dear Arden,
My daughter Ella, sixteen, just got her driver's license and is a pretty decent driver. I admit I'm an anxious backseat driver. Ella says I drive her nuts with all of my "be careful" comments and my

hitting phantom brakes on the passenger side when she drives. Ella kids around and says I leave fingerprints on the door handle from gripping it so hard. Ha! Everything was fine until yesterday. It was Friday night, about one in the morning, and I heard a kaboom! I ran downstairs to find my daughter in the family car, having backed up into the garage door. I said, "Who gave you permission to take the car out at one in the morning? Where are you going? See what happens when you are a sneak! Look at the car, the garage door! Give me the keys and go upstairs to you room now. I mean it. What's next, Ella?" I was livid. What a ballsy thing to do! My parents would have taken the keys and told me I couldn't drive for a month!

Ella was hysterical and begged me not to be mad. She says she made a mistake, and she begged, "I'm only sixteen, please don't take the keys away from me forever. How am I going to get to school Monday?" I was so upset and told her to take the school bus. So she cried harder. Now what?

The issue is why Ella couldn't let you know that she was taking the car out at one in the morning. Yes, I get that it's an ungodly hour, but your enraged reaction closed her off to your getting to the core of her urgency. The punishment only serves to close her down further.

I love how you and Ella kid around with each other and that you recognize your own limitations when it comes to Ella's driving. And Ella admitted that she made a mistake; she owned it and that's a good thing. But there is a wall that prevents Ella from being more open and honest with you.

The punishment has got to go, and maybe that has something to do with why she snuck around. She expected you to say no, perhaps. Teens make mistakes all the time, and hopefully, if we help them learn from them, they will use their heads next time.

I would start from scratch and **script** a discussion with Ella as follows: "Honey, you know how I get so enraged when you are not direct with me with what you want or think and then go about doing your own thing impulsively and get into hot water. From now on I will try to take a breath, regain my composure, and have a more open attitude and approach with you. No more talk about how my parents were with me and threatening an over-the-top punishment. It's just you and me setting up some new time parameters for the usage of the car, and my trying to be calmer when you drive. Hopefully, this will help you be more open and truthful with me."

I am sure that this arrangement will work much better for you and Ella. Your mutual humor and lightness will help you see the bigger picture, and that's what's missing here. Now you can approach your daughter and ask her about where and to whom she was going at one o'clock on Friday night.

Ella will feel more comfortable in the future running her urgent plans by you. Teach her about accountability and give her time frames of expectancy and responsibility. Emphasize that you are not looking to control her, and that you're first and foremost concerned about her health, welfare, and safety. Make the most of this opportunity to create the type of dialogue that gives Ella the freedom and confidence to talk with you about these kinds of situations. Let's make this a transformative teaching moment (see Chapter 1) for both you and Ella.

ROCKING OUT

Dear Arden,
I found out that instead of sleeping overnight at her friend's house,
my thirteen-year-old daughter, Lauren, went to a rock concert in the
city. Now what? Do I punish her or ground her? She does not seem to
understand how serious this is. She said the fact that she came home
safely only proves how safe it is and that next time I can let her go!

Rather than punish her, you need to understand what she was
thinking and what would compel her to push the envelope like
this. Be an objective detective and a benevolent authority figure. I
would offer the following **script**: "Lauren, you needed to run your
plans by me. You're thirteen, I love you, and I'm concerned about
your safety. I don't want you to put yourself in a position where
someone could hurt you and take advantage of you. It's important
for me to know way ahead of time where you are going, who you
are going with, whether an adult will be present, the time and loca-
tion of the concert, how you are getting there, and how you are
getting home. I don't think you thought this through; it's almost
as if you think you're all grown up and can make decisions on
your own. Honey, you need to be accountable for your actions and
your whereabouts. You are acting like you are packing your bags,
moving out, and getting a job. Are you?"

I am trying to add a little lightness to the seriousness of what
she did. She is fearless, cocky, and acting pseudo-mature, and it
concerns me that she may be hanging with much older teens. If
you are thinking of punishing her, however, keep in mind that she
can easily do something like this again and sneak around you. I
want Lauren to begin to feel that she doesn't have to anticipate an

automatic no from you and that you are open for a back and forth conversation with her. Lurking beneath the surface is a little girl, your little girl, still looking for her mommy's approval.

I hope this was a Justin Bieber or Jonas Brothers concert and that she and a few slightly older youngsters lost their heads and got carried away in the moment. I would suggest you contact the mother whose home she was supposed to be staying in and do some preventive and protective brainstorming to ensure the safety of your daughter in the near future.

BROKEN CURFEW

Dear Arden,

Our seventeen-year-old, Lori, constantly breaks her curfew and comes home hours later than she's supposed to. When we confront her about it, she says that we don't trust her and she's sick of it. We've told her it's the other people out there we don't trust. What's an acceptable curfew time for school nights and for Fridays and Saturdays? She's a senior, and she drives her own car.

Been there, seen that, except for one tiny difference—please don't yell—our daughter did not have a curfew. Why? Because her dad and I thought she'd rebel and test us, just like your daughter is doing now. Instead, Sam, her dad, and I tried to come up with reasonable guidelines and parameters. For school nights, Sunday through Thursday, Sam chose to be home between eleven and eleven-thirty. This took into account that school classes began at 7:40 a.m. and that she would get up and get dressed in fifteen minutes. No fooling, she is the fastest girl I have known to date! On Friday and

Saturday nights she opted for a range between midnight and two in the morning that took into account social commitments, musical theatre, dance rehearsals, and dance competitions.

The point is, try to help Lori set up some reasonable parameters and guidelines based on your daughter's unique life, interests, social obligations, and extracurricular activities—and not on arbitrary, hard-and-fast rules.

Bottom line: you just want her to get sufficient rest. When you look at the bigger picture, it's not so much about her obeying you, but more about her developing an internal awareness, a gut sense of what works for her and what's best for her spirit, mind, and body. It's all about her health and well-being. Soon enough, Lori will be making her own decisions about how to schedule her time and continue to strengthen and develop self-care skills. We can only hope that she has learned some of these life lessons during her senior year and will carry them over to her years in college, when she's more on her own.

TEXTING ON THE ROAD

Dear Arden,

My sixteen-year-old daughter, Brooke, was in a car accident. I'm embarrassed to say I was sitting next to her. I know an accident can happen to anybody. The problem is she was texting her boyfriend. I knew better, but I didn't stop her. She looked down for a moment, a woman was making a left, my daughter slammed on the brakes, our car lightly tapped the rear fender of the car in front of us, but we were slammed from behind really hard by a woman who must have been tailgating or distracted herself.

Brooke begged me not to tell her father or the insurance company that she was texting while driving, and I didn't. Her father is a real stickler for details and very strict. I feel bad for lying to him and covering up the truth.

Mom, you sound so anxious. You didn't rob a bank; your "crime" is not unique. Think about this: before cell phones, sometimes we would be changing the radio station, or sneezing and blowing our noses, or picking up something off the floor, and we would lose our focus and in a moment, BOOM! A car accident. It doesn't take much.

However, there has been such an escalation of accidents because we have become a very impatient culture. We live in a very now-oriented, immediate world. Our teens know no different. We set the precedent. Modern technology is great, and driving is a privilege for all, but we all need to realize that safety comes first. We adults need to realize this, and then we can teach our teens and young adults.

According to the National Highway Transportation Safety Administration, "distracted driving claimed 5,474 lives and led to 448,000 injuries in the United States in 2009, accounting for 16 percent of fatalities. Of all the driving distractions, texting poses the greatest risks, because it distracts drivers visually, manually, and cognitively, creating a trifecta of deadly distraction." Have your daughter check out AAA's new teen driver website, Keys2Drive (teendriving.AAA.com).

So let the dust settle, collect yourself, and then, when you're ready, approach your husband. Talk to him alone first. Let him know what happened. If the daggers are there, let him know that you know that this was a major mistake. Don't explain yourself, justify, or argue the point. Then enlist him in having a conversation, not a lecture, with your daughter. Let him be and let her see his disappointment. That will have quite an impact. Let him share his concern for you and Brooke's safety and how much he values your lives. Let him talk about the internal anxiety and urgency that gets stirred up with the ingrained expectation that texts and smart phone emails have to be responded to immediately. Offer alternatives and options, like "Pull over to the side and stop in a safe place," or "Let the person who is texting you know that you are driving and this needs to wait."

Consider a no-texting while driving contract—and make it apply to the adults too. Thirty states have laws against texting while driving. It can't be said enough: please remember that our lives and our children's health, safety, and welfare are very precious.

CHAPTER 5

Family Dynamics

---

*"Govern a family as you would cook a small fish—
very gently."*

—Chinese Proverb

Our children breathe our air. If our air is joyous, happy, healthy, loving, compassionate, supportive, sensitive, respectful, and harmonious, we bring a lovely awareness of joy and enlightenment to our children.

When our air is heavy, polluted, toxic, dark, hostile, angry, stressed, or full of hate, we bring ignorance and pain to our children. It's too easy at times to slip into a fog, a routine, and not pay attention to our impact as parents. Our lives can seem overscheduled and frenetic in pace. We may feel unfocused, disconnected, as if we're losing our direction. The conditions of family life can be demanding. Clutter—emotional and physical—surrounds us and threatens to choke our living space. We need to do our best as parents to eradicate deep-rooted destructive patterns of behavior that can negatively impact our daughters without our knowledge.

All of us hunger for the safety, refuge, and security of home. It has the potential to be both grounding and peaceful. A loving family is a connected family. Love is a powerful force and healer that helps us to be courageous in the face of hard times, adversity, illness, and loss. Life may be full of ruptures, but the family seals and binds and connects us to each other. The home, the family's center, needs to be a place of peace, a sanctuary from the external stress and storms of our lives. We get great satisfaction and purpose from our families. They give us a very real and rooted sense of who we are and who we wish to be.

A family has a structure, a conscience, a moral compass. My mother was the embodiment of all that and more. As the center of the family, she provided shelter, direction, and heart. Maintaining a family in this way is no easy business. It requires huge investments of our emotional and physical energy.

But who I am today, my love for good people, delicious food, fun times, nature, the ocean, lively conversation, music, and laughter can be directly linked to my family and all the mothers before me. And who my daughter is can be linked to her family. And I have the power to influence that immensely.

Although families can be complicated, they remain unique. No one family or person is alike. I am remembering a childhood with summers spent at Brighton Beach, riding the waves, and having picnics with sandy salami sandwiches, surrounded by sandcastles. What kind of memories and associations come to mind when you think of yours?

Imagine living with more purpose and a more powerful ownership and awareness of your impact on your daughter. This is about getting in touch with your inner teenager and connecting with yourself and remembering what you bring to the plate from your past experiences, hopes, wishes, and dreams.

The family fill-in-the-blanks you'll encounter next are

preventative, a helpful and useful teaching tool and strategy that will bring to light what you may have forgotten and pushed aside, perhaps because the memory might stir up too much pain. Your awareness is the key to prevent replaying, reenacting, and repeating these old scenarios and emotional patterns from your past through your daughter. This exercise will help you become a better and more empathetic parent by remembering what did and didn't work for you.

My family is _____.

I love my family but _____.

I wish my family could be more _____.

I never thought that my family would experience _____.

Growing up, I longed for_____in my family.

I knew that when I had a family of my own one day, I wanted to _____.

My role in the family is_____.

My daughter's role in the family is_____.

BATTLING CANCER

Dear Arden,

I am in the midst of battling a recurrence of my breast cancer. My first bout was five years ago, and I had nine months of chemotherapy. This time I had surgery to remove a tumor. I get all worked up right before a test to see if the cancer has returned. So far I'm okay physically. I am grateful for every day and pray that I remain cancer-free. If my results change, then I would probably need chemo. I was in a survivor support group five years ago, but I just don't want to go back at this point. I talk to my husband and friends for emotional support. I know I am not myself. My patience wears thin and I am more anxious overall.

My concern is for my fourteen-year-old daughter, Abby. Abby has been so supportive; she came to the hospital and stayed with me for many hours at a time and was really there for me in my recovery. It did not all fall on her. My husband took off two weeks from work, and my amazing girlfriends sent food every day, checked in on my daughter, and were my life support. I have discussed Abby seeing a therapist for herself and she insists that she is fine, busy at school, and active with her friends. My husband recently shared with me that Abby thinks about me dying and worries about what would happen to her. I have had long conversations with her, reassuring her that so far so good, but that could change. I assure her I'm a fighter. I am writing to you because I need help to take another step in some direction.

I am sorry for your recurrence of breast cancer. Even though you are currently not going through chemotherapy, you are probably still healing physically, emotionally, and spiritually. The anticipation from month to month, hoping and praying that the cancer does not return, is not foreign to me. My mom has had two bouts of cancer and is so relieved once she gets good test results. My mom, like you, is more than a survivor—she's a thriver! I am grateful that your husband and friends are solidly there for you. That's key to your recovery and healing.

You are picking up your daughter's concern about your current and long-term health and where she fits in all this upheaval. She is very concerned, loving, compassionate, and protective of you. She can pick up your anxiety for sure. She is as relieved every time you get a clean test result, as you and your husband are. She is very tied into you—most fourteen-year-olds would have a hard time admitting or even realizing how dependent they are on us.

It sounds like a consultation with a family therapist for the entire family would be a great way for everyone to be heard and to share their anxiety about the present and the future. The present we have some control over, but there is uncertainty no matter how much you reassure her that you are okay. She may worry about what happens if you need chemotherapy again. She may resonate with how it was for her when she was nine years old. She may be feeling frightened and overwhelmed now and minimizing this situation to protect herself as well. I am happy that she is so close to her dad and that she is comfortable talking with him about the possibility of your death. She needs to process and express her worst fears and to feel that you won't break in half if she shares that with you directly.

I would **script** it for both you and your husband this way: "Abby, as a family we have been through some challenging situations and times, the number one being that I am battling cancer again. I know I am not myself and do the best that I can to deal with the uncertainty of this, but this is really taking a toll on all of us. You know how Dad shares everything with me, right? It's okay for you to wonder and be scared about me and how that is affecting you now and in the future. I need help myself with this, maybe the same help I had five years ago from a wonderful therapist. This time I think we can all benefit, to air ourselves out, not hold back to protect anybody. I think this is a good thing. It's not good to hold it all in. Abby, maybe you are feeling angry and frustrated sometimes and are being protective of me? I don't know, I just want us all to be honest and move forward."

I think that's the next step and a move in a direction that will be helpful for the entire family.

A Story of Hope

Louisa May Alcott once said, "What do girls do who haven't any mothers to help them through their troubles?" Hope Edelman has spent a lifetime finding the answers to that question. She lost her mother as a teenager, and through her writing, has connected with many other daughters and mothers like herself. She has written powerfully about the legacy of mother loss in her books, *Motherless Daughters and Motherless Mothers*. I talked to Hope about mothers and daughters.

Hope, you lost your mother at the age of seventeen. How has that profound loss affected the relationship you have with your daughters and the type of mother you are today?

Like most motherless women, I live with the awareness that I could be taken from my children at any time, without any notice, and this definitely percolates up into my conscious choices as I raise them. I try to make each moment count, to build good memories of times together, and to teach them what they need to know to manage without me—within reason—as they grow. That can mean anything from knowing how to cook their own breakfasts to knowing how to fill out applications by themselves. Does this make me an engaged mother, or an overanxious one? Probably a little of both. I'm also an inveterate cataloguer of family photographs and memorabilia. I don't want them to grow up wondering what we did as a family in 2004, or what their first words were, or what I looked like when I was thirty, just in case I'm not here to remind them in the future. Writing my memoir is part of this too, I think. They'll always have a printed record of what I was thinking, and what I've learned.

—Hope Edelman

I also talked to Emme, a spokesperson for the National Eating Disorders Association (NEDA), author, plus-sized model, and one of *People Magazine's* fifty most beautiful people.

Emme, how has growing up as a teenager who experienced the sad loss of your mom at the age of fifteen impacted your relationship with your daughter?

I spend as much quality time with my daughter as possible... making homework fun, thinking of the little things that I wish I had my mom for, special little notes in lunch bags, snuggling in the morning before the day begins, remembering to remain calm and to LISTEN more than lecture (this one is hard for me but I keep on trying).

—Emme

CAN'T SAY NO

Dear Arden,

This weekend I am taking my fifteen-year-old daughter, Chloe, to summer camp. Before she leaves, she wants a massage and a facial, along with a manicure and pedicure and new clothes. I also have to buy her shampoo, soap, and other necessities and supplies. The problem is her dad lost his job and we are living on one income. I put aside money to cover the cost of supplies and to pay for the gas to drive her there, but I can't afford any extras. She blew a gasket when she found out and started screaming at me about what a terrible parent I am. She says I am being mean and cruel. She really thinks all I have to do this week is get her ready for camp. Sometimes I think she just sees her dad and me as walking wallets with car keys. I am tired of having to go without because of her needs.

Chloe is behaving as if she is totally unaware of the stress and pressures that you and her dad are feeling. You and your husband need to have a talk with her and be real about what you can and cannot afford. She will feel upset, annoyed, disappointed, and angry. Remind her that in light of this change, you all have to make some sacrifices, and hopefully this will be temporary until Dad gets another job. For the time being, it's about being kind, especially to a dad who is hurting and making the best of it, and feeling grateful for what you do receive.

In the meantime, Mom, I don't want you to become a martyr who feels angry and resentful of Chloe. Sometimes when we have bent over backward and given our children too much, it is more in response to what she expects and not what she needs. She will act and feel deprived. Please be patient, and don't backslide or go out of your way to indulge her.

For now, acknowledge how difficult it's been for all of you to downsize, and how emotionally and financially taxing it will be to live on one salary. It's a helpless "I have no choice" kind of feeling. You also may feel guilty and want to keep everything as it was before for Chloe. Instead of focusing on what you can't buy, be grateful for the things you have and the bills you can pay: rent, mortgage, property taxes, the utilities, car payments, food, gas, and other miscellaneous expenses.

You need to cultivate an attitude of gratitude and resourcefulness, starting with yourself. "Yes, it's too bad we can't buy those things, but let's see if we can hold a tag sale, or a clothing swap. Maybe we can learn how to sew." Let Chloe know how lucky you feel that she can go to camp, and that she did not have to miss out this year. Celebrate what you can do for her and what you can do together. Take walks on the beach, sing songs in the car, bake cookies, teach each other French. There is plenty to enjoy in life if you look for it.

A BIG MOVE

Dear Arden,

My husband recently received a big promotion. It is the opportunity of a lifetime for him, and as a result, we will have to relocate our family. My youngest, Erin, is fourteen and will be entering high school, but it's my oldest child, Ava, who concerns me. She's seventeen and she's set to start her senior year in a place where no one knows her or what she can do. In her old high school, she was very beloved and popular. Everyone knew who she was, and she took a leadership role in many extracurricular activities. What can I do to help ease their adjustment to a new place? My daughters, especially the oldest, are crushed. They think we are ruining their lives.

Congratulations to your husband. It must be such a life-affirming experience for him to be recognized in his career. And it also sounds like a life-altering experience for your daughters. Mom, it's a good thing you are so tuned into your daughters; that will be a life-saver for them. Your fourteen-year-old is starting high school with a new pool of kids. She will have a period of adjustment, as any teen moving from middle school to high school would. She needs to join and get involved in as many extracurricular activities and clubs as she can. This will give her plenty of opportunities to make new friends.

It's your senior daughter that I am more concerned about right now. Ava is feeling angry, resentful, and upset. Along with having to face the stress of college applications, essay writing, standard-ized tests, and visiting potential colleges, Ava is leaving behind some of her BFFs and BFFLs and maybe a boyfriend. You are going to have to view Ava's anger as an expression of how devastated, hurt, disappointed, sad, and scared she is at the thought of leaving all that is secure, happy, and familiar behind. It must feel to her like a brutally random, premature departure, one that she did not choose for herself.

Give yourself and your daughters a good six months to adjust and acclimate to the new surroundings. You don't have to be happy or like it, you just have to acclimate. Ava will resist, but if she is resil-ient (and I have a feeling that she is), she will join new activities and find a niche for herself.

Initially she will feel awkward and probably ask, "Why am I here? Why did this have to happen to me?" Here's where it's imperative to maintain her connections with her old friends, who can and will help her through this major change.

Share my advice with Ava and tell her that I know a lovely family with two daughters and two sons that relocated from Los Angeles to New York and decided to vacation with their L.A. family pals. The older teens maintained a connection through Facebook, texting, emails, and IMing. Both families continued to visit each other for many years. It became like an extended family for all of the children.

Another family I knew moved at least nine times throughout their daughter's and son's development. They are not army brats. Dad kept on advancing his career and moving up to better his family. Both of them are well-adjusted, adaptable, resilient, flexible, great conversationalists, and very intelligent young adults.

Both moms from these families were pivotal in helping to facilitate their families' adjustments by taking into account how their children felt, by coming from a place of compassion and understanding, and reassuring them that it would take some time for them all to create a sense of familiarity and security.

With Ava, reassure her that much excitement is in store for her. If your daughter is applying for early action, she will hear from some of her top-choice schools in December. She may decide to hold off until January through May, when she will be anxiously waiting to hear from all the other schools she applied to. Spring rings in with decision-making time, what college is a good fit, and shopping for a dress for the senior prom. She will be heading off to college sometime in August. Who knows who she will bump into there? Ironically, this transitional experience will help prepare her for college, when it comes time for her to adjust to a new school setting, roommates, and new classmates. The best news is that she will be starting where they are and will be more on an equal footing.

TUG OF WAR

Dear Arden,

My fourteen-year-old daughter, Ginny, constantly plays her dad and me against each other. If I tell her, "No, you cannot go to the mall today with your friends," she goes directly to her dad to complain, and the next thing I know, he is driving her to the mall! It drives me crazy! She has always been Daddy's little girl, and he has never been able to say no to her. I, on the other hand, get stuck with being the disciplinarian and the bad guy, and I am getting sick of it. How do I get my husband to stop caving in to her every wish and demand and work with me instead of undermining my authority?

Ginny couldn't possibly pit you and your husband against each other if you both spoke to each other more often about how to handle her. Sorry, Mom, that you feel undermined. Your husband, it appears, works around you rather than with you in a partnership. Take a good, healthy look at yourself. Are you coming on too strong, perhaps alienating your daughter and your husband? Could they be afraid of you? I just want you both to sit down and be very honest with each other so that Ginny will be handled with fairness, consistency, and flexibility, with appropriate limits and boundaries.

Circumstances, such as having lots of homework, may dictate whether it's timely for her to go to the mall. Dad simply may not have all of the details that you do. Sit down, listen to each other without interrupting, with no finger-pointing or raised voices, and come to some understanding of each other's positions and feelings. Once you both have some clarity, then you *both* can speak to Ginny in a united front.

Kids normally go from one parent to the other. They are great at lobbying and figuring out how to get their needs met, by hook or by crook, and not thinking past the moment.

For now, you and your husband need to create a tribunal, a think tank, which will serve your daughter's best interests. A family works so much better when everyone is in the loop.

IT'S A WAR ZONE

Dear Arden,

My ex and I have gone through probably one of the most spiteful, nasty, ugly divorces on record. I am very embarrassed now for the way I behaved. My three children were very affected. I have physical custody, but my ex has the kids every other weekend and can see them during the week as well. He was not Father of the Year, but I admit he is better now since he misses the kids: Melissa, fifteen, Ally, thirteen, and Brooke, eleven. Melissa is fed up with me and her father and has screamed she'd rather live with my sister, Josie, in New Mexico. That's about a five-hour flight from where we live! Ally tolerates us, and Brooke loves her Daddy and misses him terribly. I think she is more angry with me for making him leave. Ally is very careful and quiet and holds a lot in. It's a mess.

I am trying to pick up the pieces of my life. My ex and I are trying to be civil now that the court proceedings are over. That was so horrible for my kids to have to talk to a court psychiatrist about what it's like for them and how much they were affected by living with two children (their parents) who were constantly at each other. The psy-chiatrist shared with me and my ex what the children said. I admit I felt so guilty afterward. I even think my ex was not proud of himself as well. I am feeling a bit lost and know I have to find some way to help my kids. Any suggestions?

I am so relieved that you and your ex are taking stock of the situation and ownership of all of your hurtful and angry accusations thrown at each other. You are both making efforts and trying to be more mature and responsive to the children. There is nothing like guilt sometimes to set us straight. You are trying to see the bigger picture, and that's a good thing. I have a feeling that you are very capable of making the best out of a precarious situation, and with good, caring, compassionate direction you will be able to pick up the pieces of your life.

I'd recommend talking with a therapist for the family. Each of your kids was very affected. They are all hurting. Your middle child must also be feeling between a rock and a hard place. She is the quiet one, the one who does not want to get involved or take sides. Wow, what a position to be in. Your Melissa has had it and craves some peace and harmony. Your sister must be a calming presence and a place of refuge for your daughter. All of your children are still dependent, but your youngest sounds very attached to her dad and may be blaming you and holding you responsible for making Daddy angry and for his leaving the home. I am assuming you and your ex have apologized to the girls? If not, I would suggest each of you talk to your daughters. Just to clarify, your ex can do this on his own time; you don't have to do this as a couple.

So your **script** can go as follows while you speak to each of your daughters individually in the presence of the other two: "Brooke, I am so sorry that you had to be put through all this pain. I was out of control and looking to get even and spite Daddy. I know it was not very adult-like, and for that I am ashamed and embarrassed. Daddy and I could not live together any more; it had nothing to do with you. I love you and want to start over. Daddy and I are trying very hard to get along, not to get back together but to be better parents, putting your needs first.

Melissa, I expected too much of you. I was not fair, saying all sorts of negative stuff about your father, whether yelling at him or in my private grumblings to you. You are my daughter who is a teenager, not my girlfriend. I don't know what I was thinking. Maybe that's just it; I was not thinking, just very overemotional and reacting. I'm trying. I hope you give me a chance and don't run off to Aunt Josie in New Mexico. I don't mind a visit if you want to see your aunt, but I want you to come back home. Will you think about that?

Ally, sometimes I don't realize how hard you try not to take sides. You try to be fair and hear all sides—that's one of your qualities—but I think you have been working overtime and that's not fair. I know you have plenty going on in your life with middle school, your friends, and homework. You did not need your parents to air their dirty laundry in your face.

Melissa, Ally, and Brooke, for all of this I am so sorry. What do you all think about going to someone who can help us talk about what has happened to our family and how we all feel? I for one am going to go to get some help for myself. Maybe it can be the same person. If any of you want to say something, I promise to listen and not interrupt."

Leave plenty of time for each of your daughters to respond and just listen to them. Try to respond, not react, and come from a place of love and calm. Even if they say very little, that's okay; you have planted some very powerful seeds and created a golden opportunity for the family to begin to reconnect and move forward.

A LEGACY OF LOVE: MODEL MEN

Our tween and teen daughters benefit from nurturing male role models throughout their lives. These men play significant roles in how our daughters feel about themselves. They can offer our daughters unconditional love, respect, and stability during challenging times and can share in their joy, triumphs, and accomplishments.

One such special man in my life was my Uncle Larry. He was like a surrogate dad to me. When I was twelve, my parents separated for six months. My mom, two brothers, and I moved into Uncle Larry's home. My Uncle Larry treated me with respect and gave me attentive listening ears. He was a man who loved me unconditionally. He let me get very close to him, question him, and challenge him. He showed me a patience and kindness that stays with me to this day. Over the years he encouraged me and took great interest in my education, chosen profession, and all the effort that went into becoming a better me. He was the prototype of the family man, devoted to his wife of sixty years and his children. He had a strong work ethic and an insightful steel-trap mind.

Oddly enough, it was my uncle's nurturing nature and the charismatic traits of my father that attracted me to my future husband, Larry. I know it's too much—they even have the same name! Larry struck me as warm, attentive, and strong.

He is ambitious, hard-working, and the prototype of the model man. As a dad, my husband Larry was and still is a family man who loves his children with a sweetness and tenderness that's touching. Our children, Todd and Samara, feel very secure in his love.

As a result, our daughter expects men to treat her with respect. Samara identifies with her father's strong work ethic and compassion. Her dignity, sense of worth, confidence, and self-respect are directly linked to the relationship she has with him.

Don't ever underestimate the impact, influence, and power that solid, caring male role models have on your daughter's life. Whether they are fathers, uncles, brothers, boyfriends, husbands, or sons, the good men in our lives offer us strength, stability, and lots of love.

UNLUCKY IN LOVE

Dear Arden,

My daughter, Lauren, has grown up watching me date one loser after another. One was a drunk, one was verbally abusive, etc. I'm so afraid that she is going to take after me and inherit my bad judgment and bad luck in the men department. How do I teach her to do better than me? I want her life to be better than mine. I don't want history to repeat itself.

You can start by being the role model that Lauren needs you to be. I hope you are currently not dating a "loser." You are her example, Mom, and you need to start being a much better picker and screener. Take a peek at why you are dating the wrong kind of guy. I am concerned about how you're thinking. Why would you put up with a drunk and a verbally abusive man?

Mom, I feel you need major infusions of self-worth, self-esteem, and confidence. You need to start feeling that you matter. You need some positive self-talk. Say to yourself: "I am a person who matters. I deserve to be treated with consideration, sensitivity, kindness, intelligence, and compassion." Write this down on Post-it notes if you must, and stick them on surfaces throughout your home. Mirrors are good places. I think it would be very good for Lauren to see that her mom is making an effort to raise her standards and her circumstances. As a result of this self-love and self-care, you will wind up attracting a much better kind of guy. In life, how we feel about ourselves is manifested in the world. So think and be self-respect and confidence. Like yourself, love yourself, and accept all that is special and unique about you. I have a feeling Lauren recognizes all these wonderful qualities about you; she is acquainted with your best traits. Now it's time for you to see this in yourself. Once you do, others will too.

NO LONGER SINGLE

Dear Arden,
After being a single mom for many years, I have been dating a man for the past year. I think I have found the love of my life. The problem? My fourteen-year-old daughter, Brianna, is dead set against my remarrying. She's never had to share me with anyone before and is very protective of me. How do I reassure her that this change is going to be good for the both of us?

The good thing is that she is expressing her dismay. It's much better that she gets it out than holds it in and says nothing. Make no mistake, we know where she stands. It's one thing to date, quite another thing to tell Brianna that you are getting married. It becomes so final for her. Now it's brought to her attention that she has to share you, share her space, and make a major transition that she has not chosen. She's afraid she is going to lose her mom to her new stepdad. Your daughter feels threatened and dethroned. Give her reassurances that she is still number one with you. Once she gets used to the idea, include her in some of the wedding plans (e.g., addressing invitations, buying your dress and her dress, choosing a reception hall or other venue). Does he have children too? Keep that in mind, because that will have an impact as well.

It's been just the two of you from the start. Make sure you both still enjoy special alone time together, "just us girls," for the rest of your lives. All the best of luck; you deserve it!

By the way, I was much older than your daughter when my mom started to date again; I was twenty-three. My mom dated for two years before she met George, my stepfather. They dated for six years before they got married, and I was so overjoyed for her that she had someone special in her life. Thirty-one isn't the same as fourteen, but your daughter will get there someday.

SIBLING RIVALRY: IF CAIN AND ABEL WERE TEENAGE GIRLS

Dear Arden,
Our daughters were born two years apart. Our eldest is very capable, responsible, and mature. She has never given us a moment's trouble.

She gets excellent grades, is a competitive runner, and has just enrolled in her college's pre-med courses. Our youngest, on the other hand, does not know what she wants to do with her life, but insists on competing with her older sister every chance she gets. She claims that our oldest is the family favorite and compares everything both girls receive, down to Christmas and birthday presents. It has caused much stress and strife at home.

It's very normal for there to be sibling rivalry, especially for your younger daughter. Your oldest is a tough act to follow. She casts a big shadow. I think it's more of a challenge having two children, close in age, and of the same gender. Your task is to help your younger daughter shift from comparing herself to her sister to working on herself and being the best person she can be. More often than not, this is not accomplished by comparing herself to others but by finding her own distinct and personal brand of excellence. Right now your younger daughter is so busy watching, emulating, comparing, and feeling jealous and envious of her sister that there is little or no room for her to see how very special and unique she is. She needs to run her own race, at her own pace.

Yes, your older daughter has probably known she has wanted to be a doctor since she was a little girl and is on a fast track. Your younger child is like most kids. They go to college and wear lots of different hats before they can figure out who they are and what they would like to do. You need to help your younger daughter find her passions, her loves, and what engages her and screams her name.

CHAPTER 6

School

---

*"My mother never gave up on me. I messed up in
school so much they were sending me home, but my
mother sent me right back."*

—Denzel Washington

Gail came into my office, furious with her thirteen-year-old
daughter, Amelia, who had been a solid B student and had suddenly started to fail a few classes. She started by venting about
all the things her daughter did to "waste time" when she could
be studying. Then she listed all the things she would take away
from her daughter until she got her grades back up. When
there was a pause in her tirade, I took the opportunity to calmly
ask her a question: "Do you think punishing your daughter by
taking away all the things she likes to do is really going to motivate her to do better?"

I explained to her that punishing her daughter could be
counterproductive. "Maybe your daughter is struggling with
a learning disability, or maybe she's under so much pressure,
she can't perform." The reasons for her daughter's sudden
and spectacular failure would never be known unless Gail dug
deeper and took the time to ask. I told Gail to approach her

daughter gently and compassionately. That was the only way she could begin to unravel what was happening at school.

After home, school is likely the place where your daughter spends the most time, but it's not always easy to keep up with what's happening there. She could be having a problem with a teacher or a peer or a class, and you might not find out until things get really bad.

TOO DISTRACTED TO STUDY?

Dear Arden,
Whenever I check on Ivy, my fourteen-year-old, to see if she is doing her homework, she always has her Facebook page open and is in the middle of several chats. How can she possibly be doing her home-work? I couldn't focus like that!

Mom, I am so with you. I would observe Samara in high school and say, "How can you focus when you are IMing, texting, talking on the phone, watching *One Tree Hill*, and listening to your iPod?" "WHAT?" she'd say. "I can't hear you!" Only recently has she admitted that she was distracted.

Welcome to the age of the Internet. It has gotten so entrenched in tween, teen, and young adult culture that it is the norm. Ask Ivy, "What would it be like for you and your friends to do your home-work in silence?" She'd probably look at you like you were from another planet.

Forget about it—Facebook and all that goes with it is here to stay. Our girls just don't want to miss out on anything that spells S-O-C-I-A-L, and for their generation, this is it.

Today, my daughter is a focused and organized college student. She likes to listen to music because it's soothing and relaxing for her. Every kid is different. As a mom, I try not to sweat the small stuff, unless her grades are suffering and her homework is left undone or incomplete. I save my concern and worry for bigger issues.

DRAWING A BLANK

Dear Arden,

My daughter, Willow, studies so hard for quizzes, tests, and oral presentations to the point of exhaustion, only to come home with grades that are just fair. I asked her, "Do you think the problem is with how you study and maybe that affects what you remember?" And she answered, "I blank out sometimes. No matter how hard I try, it just doesn't come back." She gets great grades on her papers. Do you think she is nervous or anxious? Could that be getting in her way?

Absolutely, Mom. Willow could have it all stuffed in her head, ready to spout it out, and poof! All gone. Before a test or an oral presentation, she will work herself up and feel lots of tension and anxiety. She then tightens up on the spot and is unable to perform. Emotionally she "flees" the scene and disconnects.

What we need to do, Mom, is to help her connect and find herself again. I find that deep breathing and a guided visualization are helpful. Let's say she has an oral presentation; she can imagine herself in front of the class rehearsing what she is going to say and practice in front of a mirror at home, where it's much safer. There is something about the emotional and physical security of home that she can bring with her to the class. Let her wear something of yours, Mom, maybe a lucky pin, scarf, or sweater. Before Willow presents, she needs to breathe deeply and imagine herself confident and proud, having the courage to perform, and performing. Each time she does, she will build more of a "can do" attitude.

PRIVATE SCHOOL OR BUST

Dear Arden,
I have told my fifteen-year-old daughter, Tabitha, that if she brings home one more failing grade, I will pull her out of public school and put her in private school. She has too much potential for me to let her fail. I know that I let my daughter walk all over me. Whatever house rules and curfews I set, she ignores. I am ready to send her to private school, and she knows it. My mom was very strict with me and sent me to parochial school.

I think you remember what it was like for you as a teenager. Did you feel punished and restricted, the need to be the people-pleaser? Tabitha sounds like the flip side of you, free-spirited but to an extreme. It's fine for her to express herself, but within reason and with respect as well. A fifteen-year-old is going to test your limits and boundaries, but here you are struggling with what's age-appropriate and where to draw the line. I feel for you and your struggle, but threatening to send your daughter to private school or parochial school is just that, a threat. Tabitha will not take you seriously because you never seriously enforced such threats in the past.

Maybe a smaller school setting could work better for her, but you both need to sit down together and figure it out. I think that you have been overindulging your daughter and trying to make up for what you didn't get emotionally from *your* mom. Perhaps you are still holding a grudge against your own mom. Think about what it was like for you. That might help you. It usually has when I was at a crossroads with my own daughter. Rather than come from a place of anger and resentment, elevate a bit and come from a place of understanding and love. You have the power to make it different for your daughter, to be a more eagle-like mom, able to see the bigger picture.

SUDDENLY POPULAR

Dear Arden,

My fourteen-year-old daughter, Claire, used to be very shy and reserved. During middle school, the lack of close friends was painful for her. She got picked on a lot and was rarely invited to any parties. When she got to high school, she blossomed into a very pretty girl and found herself popular for the first time in her life. Now she has friends—lots of them—and they call and text her constantly. I can hardly keep up with her. She is understandably very excited and distracted with her new social status, but her studies and schoolwork have taken a back seat to her partying and socializing. I hope this is just a phase, but what if it isn't?

In middle school, your little flower was taking root, and her inner and outer beauty was hidden from the outside world. The middle school years can be so awkward and uncomfortable. Then all of a sudden, she feels more and more comfortable in her skin, and like flash photography, the flower that is your daughter bursts forth on the scene! Everyone is noticing.

As moms, we bite our fingernails when our daughters are picked on and fade into the background. Claire's newfound freedom must be a welcome relief to you both. Claire feels like she is on the upswing, and she is. It's not surprising then and hardly unique that her social calendar is in the foreground and her academics are in the background. You need to help her find a balance and help her manage both so she can have it all. Make sure she knows that you are only looking out for her and want the best for her. You don't want to rain on her parade or be a killjoy, but as her experienced parent, you need to help keep her feet on the ground, be aware of any possible pitfalls, and not let all the attention go to her head. Trust that protective "TUG" that you are feeling. Here's a **script** for what you can say to her: "Claire, I am so happy for you that you have so many new friends and a very full social calendar. Sweetheart, I am only looking out for you and want what's best for you. It's really hard to balance popularity and your studies. Please don't take this the wrong way. Don't let all the flattery place you in a position where you are forced to compromise yourself, your ideals, and values. Please use your head, run anything by me as you always have, and have some trust and faith in me. I won't let you down or steer you in the wrong direction. I want you to continue to grow and stretch your wings, but not to the point where you may get hurt physically or emotionally. This includes your achieving below your potential or giving up activities and friends you used to love just to stay popular."

Remind her of who her true friends are, the ones who stayed loyal and true before she was "discovered" by her peers and became popular. And don't let her ditch any family obligations for her new friends. Continue to put an emphasis on the characteristics and qualities that make her shine as an individual—such as a strong sense of right and wrong, courage, or creativity.

UNDER PRESSURE

Dear Arden,

Last night I found my sixteen-year-old daughter, Danielle, up at two-thirty in the morning, surrounded by papers and open books, trying to write a paper and study for a test. She was crying, "I just can't do it all. I'll never be able to finish this by tomorrow." A high achiever with excellent grades all through grade school and middle school, she is taking AP courses in high school. She is a yearbook editor, she competes on the swim team, and she plays French horn in the orchestra. I think she is overdoing it, but she tells me this is what she has to do in order to make it into a good college, and she needs to do more, not less. Her father and I are very proud of her, but she seems so anxious and stressed out all the time. I worry that she is not getting enough sleep. She's a perfectionist, but she doesn't seem to be having much fun. In fact, she seems miserable.

Danielle's high expectations are leaning to the superwoman side. She is pushing herself way too hard and ignoring her limits. I am concerned about burnout, which could sneak up on her once the workload starts to pile up. AP classes are very prestigious, demanding, and time-consuming.

Drive, drive, drive, press, press, press, push, push, push. The work is neverending. Soon the demands she is making on herself start to pile up and overwhelm her. Junior year is stressful enough. Not only are you required to take all those standardized tests, but you are also in the process of exploring colleges that could be a good fit for you. Oh, please make some time to relax, young lady. This is very hard advice for a focused teenager like yours. Any extra time Danielle has will probably be spent catching up on her sleep!

That said, there is so much buzz among her peers, teachers, and family about what goes into the making of an "ideal college candidate." This is especially true in tenth to twelfth grades. Students today are expected to hit the ground running—and not just race, but fly. Overloading on AP classes, clubs, sports, and activities to be more competitive means not dropping anything and doing more, not less. Honestly, colleges appreciate a well-rounded and bright applicant, but as with auditions, who knows what they are looking for this year? As her mom, you need to be aware of when she is over the top. One patient of mine started to cry to her parents that it was all getting to be too much. She was taking many AP classes, running track, and in student government. She was so afraid of disappointing her parents and track coach that she kept herself running all day long. She expected the world of herself—and felt the pressure to do it all.

She knew she was not going to become a professional athlete. Her head coach, however, had very different ideas. What she really wanted to do was focus on her AP classes and spend more time with her girlfriends and her boyfriend. She wanted a more "balanced and normal and active social life." It took a number of months for her to work up the courage to tell the head coach and her parents. She didn't want to disappoint anyone, including herself. Immediately after making the decision to cut back on meets and to run for fun, she felt so much lighter and relieved. She knew immediately that she had made the right move.

I think this is the direction your daughter needs to take as well. Sit down with Danielle and read this question and my answer together. I hope the two of you can come up with a solution. She sounds like a smart girl, and so do you.

Over Her Head

Signs your wonderful, high-achieving, perfectionist daughter is way over the top:

1. Crying in the morning that she doesn't have enough time to breathe.
2. Stressed out over the smallest of things.
3. Becoming an insomniac because she is so overtired and sleep-deprived that her mind doesn't stop racing.
4. Shows noticeable signs of obsessive-compulsive behavior (i.e., washing or disinfecting her hands several times a day). No matter how hard she labors, nothing is ever right or good enough and she agonizes about what she can do or has produced.
5. Often a people-pleaser to an extreme, losing sight of what's in her best interests.
6. Regularly pulls all-nighters and studies until two-thirty in the morning when school begins at 7:40 a.m.

Creating a Healthy Balance

Guidelines for a healthy mix of school, activities, and a social life:

1. Works to achieve a balance between school work, extracurricular activities, a part-time job, and a fun and playful social life.
2. Gets sufficient sleep and rest. Teenagers need at least eight to nine hours of sleep per night. According to the

latest research, most teens perform optimally with ten hours of sleep.

3. Makes plenty of time for laughing and downtime, where you need not get anything accomplished. This is all about being, not doing, and letting your mind float.

4. Makes time for family. Soon enough, it will be time for her to go to college. She needs to make the most of her last two years at home.

5. Imagines and anticipates what college and dorm life are like.

6. Is true to herself.

7. Doesn't have to be constantly achieving and winning in order to feel good about herself.

TEACHER TERROR

Dear Arden,

Our daughter, Gillian, is caught in a personality conflict with a very domineering teacher. He criticizes her, berates her, and puts her down in front of the class. Our confident, hard-working girl is starting to look down and stammer—and this used to be one of her favorite subjects!

Advise your daughter to consult her guidance counselor. The guidance counselor can offer advice and speak to the teacher if need be. If the harassment continues, she can ask to be transferred out of the class, with your support.

I have zero tolerance for bullying of any kind in a school. I explore the topic of bullying in greater depth in Chapter 8. It's more complicated, of course, when the bully in question is a teacher. Depending on the school's policy, Gillian might be able to switch to another class or she might have to stay put. If you aren't taken seriously, it might be helpful to consult an attorney. Hopefully it won't come to that. There are many talented administrators who work with their staff and student body to create a harmonious and respectful school climate.

Try these steps, Mom, and see what happens. I don't want your daughter to stammer and avoid a class she loves because a teacher becomes a dark cloud over her being.

NO HOMEWORK

Dear Arden,
My twelve-year-old, Tori, just decided to stop doing her homework. She's polite to her teachers and to us, but she refuses to try. Her teachers say that she hands in tests that are completely blank. Her avoidance of certain subjects (anything to do with writing and reading) is driving us nuts!

At first glance, she seems to be behaving in a contrary and passive-aggressive manner, but she is polite about it. I feel there is more to this than meets the eye. You need to be a bit of a detective and consider any variables and possible triggers. Has she been doing all her homework and taking tests up to this point? Did anything happen to make her suddenly frustrated with schoolwork or homework? Does she have a new teacher or subject to study? Has she always struggled with test-taking or reading or writing?

I think an educational and psychological evaluation may give you, your daughter, and her teachers some insight into her resistance and reluctance to do her work. The academic workload gets more challenging in the sixth grade. Perhaps Tori has fallen between the cracks? She may have processing or learning issues that need to be diagnosed and addressed. I know many tweens and teens who receive special accommodations in school, like having extra time to take a test or going to a resource room for reinforcement. They also benefit from tutoring in the home.

It sounds like Tori has given up, and that's a shame. As her parent, you are her most loving supporter. It's up to you to get her the help she needs.

A STRAY MARK

Dear Arden,

My thirteen-year-old daughter, Shelby, usually comes home with A+s and As on her report card. You can imagine my shock when I sat down at her eighth grade graduation ceremony and opened up the program and noticed her name was not on the honor roll. Then I found out from her teacher that she had stopped doing her lab homework for two months and was given a B-. I was livid! I couldn't believe she had let her grade drop so carelessly like that. When I confronted her, she said lab was "sooo boring" and she thought her lab grade would be averaged in with the rest of her science grade. Turns out she was wrong. I am so upset right now. The ceremony was two weeks ago, and I am still steamed about that B-. How can I punish her?

Is this one of the first times your little A+ tween has acted out? You have a golden opportunity to sit down with Shelby and share your concerns. In the scheme of things, eighth grade is not high school, and college admissions don't look at that year, so it's a great opportunity as a "transformative teaching moment" (see Chapter 1). You need to view this as a workshop where you don't have to punish her for her mistake in judgment.

I would **script** it like this: "Sweetie, you will have boring subjects, teachers, and experiences throughout your life—I hope not too many—and I hope in the future you feel comfortable enough with me to run some of these irritating, frustrating situations by me before making a decision. I can help you. There could have been other options instead of not doing your work."

Rest assured that if you handle Shelby with a more relaxed, understanding, and nonpunishing approach, she will be less likely to act out again.

GOING FOR HER GED

Dear Arden,

Instead of taking her SATs, my sixteen-year-old daughter, Jen, says she wants to get her GED and graduate from high school early so she can take college classes and maybe travel and study abroad. I feel like she's going off the grid and jeopardizing her chances for a successful future. Isn't the GED for pregnant teenagers and high school dropouts?

Not anymore, Mom! Nowadays, kids can get their GED if they want to hit college—and grad school—earlier. At college, she can enjoy being more independent in a less structured environment. (For more information, see Maya Frost's book, *The New Global Student*.)

Lots of college students spend a semester abroad to immerse themselves in a foreign culture and language. College graduates with study abroad and work abroad experiences do have an edge in job and internship interviews and grad school applications. The downside? She will miss out on one-of-a-kind experiences like prom and homecoming, plus the graduation ceremony with the rest of her grade.

It's not the traditional route, and it's not embraced by many, but it's definitely a viable alternative. Jen must be very focused and independent to make it work. It sounds like she has lots of options that she needs to consider and discuss with you, her educators, and college students who have done exactly what she's contemplating. She needs to gather more information before reaching a decision from a position of strength and confidence.

CLASHING OVER COLLEGE

Dear Arden,

My husband went to an Ivy League university and is dead set on our daughter, Erica, applying to his alma mater. She has her heart set on a smaller, less traditional college where she can work off-campus for academic credit and create her own major. He openly derides her choices at the dinner table and says she is throwing her life away and wasting his money. I think his comments are hurtful, but he just brushes me off. Then he retorts, "What would you know about it? You didn't even go to college." It's true my parents couldn't afford for me to go, but I managed to work hard and have a career. Whose decision is it?

My, my, isn't your husband the provocative one! I can just envision him verbally running circles around you and your daughter. So how do we enlist him to be supportive of Erica, who is just trying to figure out which college would be a good fit for her, and where she can make the best use of her time? Hey, it sounds like she has a good head on her shoulders. Is he aware of that? That's something most parents would appreciate. Your husband sounds angry and sarcastic, and that's too bad. I think we need to disempower him by shaking our heads at how pathetic he sounds and just let your daughter go about her business. A show of strength by both mother and daughter here will disarm him.

When he derides you for not knowing much because you did not go to school, remind yourself with self-talk, "I have worked long and hard to have my career. I'm smart and have self-worth." Put some Post-its up for yourself, write this in a journal, and let it become your mantra. It's great for Erica to hear you as well. It's important that she sees her mom can no longer be metaphorically pushed under the truck and that you are taking a proactive, life-affirming, assertive, positive stance with your husband.

If you and Erica don't take the bait, he will be forced to quiet down. In the meantime, be your daughter's strongest supporter and advocate, visit the schools *she* likes, and if your husband refuses to go, tell him, "Stay home. We are going no matter what." Let's throw him off a bit and see what happens. You sound like one very fine, smart, devoted mom. Don't let him wear you down.

NO COLLEGE PLANS

Dear Arden,
All my life I dreamed of my daughter, Vanessa, going to college.
We sent away for brochures and visited colleges on road trips. I put
money aside in a college fund for her. I grew up in a large family and
not everyone who wanted to attend college could go. I am deter-
mined to make sure my daughter doesn't suffer from the same lack
of opportunities as me. Yesterday, she told us that she might not
want to go to college. College is not for her, she says, and she wants
to take time off, maybe travel, she wasn't sure. We had a huge fight.
She finally said she would consider taking a few classes at the local
community college for a year or two if I let her take cooking classes.
This is not what I envisioned for our daughter's future at all. Can I
force her to attend college? How do I convince her that taking time
off is not the way to go?

This is a tough one for you, Mom. As parents, we so want our
children to succeed, to become more than us, and to enjoy opportunities that we missed. You have a tremendous emotional and
financial investment in Vanessa going to college. It's disappointing
to hear she doesn't want to go. It sounds like she needs to wander
and begin to find her way. You and your husband can help her. She
is seventeen going on eighteen and in search of who she is, her
purpose, and what would make her feel happy. She is experiencing
the world outside the safety of her home. You two must have done
a good job if she feels secure enough to want to leave the nest.
Think of it that way, Mom. Fighting will get you both nowhere, and
I don't think you really want her to go to college under duress.

Despite graduating six months earlier than the rest of my class,

I found I had cold feet concerning college. My mother put it plainly when she said, "Well, if you're not going to college, then go get a job." I had worked at part-time jobs since I was fifteen, but somehow the thought of a full-time job made me weak in the knees. I remember sitting on our steps for a few minutes. "You know, Ma, maybe I will go to college." She nodded and said she thought that would be best for me. Honestly, I was really scared. College sounded so big, so daunting to me, but a full-time job absolutely terrified me. The choice was clear.

Now, I am not suggesting she get a job just yet, but let's see if you can get to her fear, maybe about growing up, that is surely there. For now, a junior community college is an excellent alternative where she can take some cooking classes and maybe a few additional subjects to get a taste of it. She can do a bit of traveling as well. Let her know she has a month off from December to January, and another break from May to August. That's plenty of time to travel. I think that's the direction I would take if I were in your shoes. I think Vanessa's just testing you and obviously knows how much you care.

BATTLING STEPDAD AND DAUGHTER

Dear Arden,
I feel like I'm in a constant tug of war between my daughter from my first marriage and my second husband. He is much stricter than I am and expects the kids to behave in a certain way. My sixteen-year-old daughter, Carly, has gotten into some trouble over the years, nothing major, but she's had to switch schools three times due to failing grades, smoking, and skipping class. It feels like he is always

watching her and waiting for her to mess up. He thinks I am too soft
and that I have to give her consequences for her behavior.

It has become a constant source of friction between us and we
fight all the time. My daughter responds to his yelling and threats
by openly defying him, talking back, and staying out later and later.
The other day I caught her taking $20 from my wallet. She admitted
to taking the money, but said she really needed it, and her allow-
ance was too small. My husband hit the roof and demanded that
I punish her. He told her if she didn't like it, she could get a job or
move out.

I feel like I am being forced to choose between my husband and
my child. Her father died last year, and she was very close to him. I
feel that if we forgive her and demonstrate how much we love her
and care for her, she will settle down.

I feel for you and your family. Your free-spirited sixteen-year-old is
all over the map. Something in her is not being addressed. I think
his name is Daddy.

Carly is screaming her rage and pain through her failing grades,
smoking, skipping classes, stealing money, and staying out late.
I am not justifying what she is doing, but perhaps your husband
does come down too hard on her. Unfortunately, that puts you
between a rock and a hard place.

The death of your daughter's father needs to be factored in and
addressed BIG time. Has she grieved the loss, does she speak about
him, has she changed dramatically? Is she acting more moody, bel-
ligerent, and depressed? How did her father die? Was he ill for a
long time or was it sudden? When did all of this acting out begin?
Did it coincide with his death?

Moving from school to school has been an attempt on your

part to help her, but I think what's more in order is the following: you need to ask her if she has any clue about what is driving her to behave so out-of-the-box. She may blame your husband. She may say her stepfather doesn't care. You can weave the topic of her father into the conversation and see if this helps to soften her anger. For instance, "If Daddy was still alive and here, how different would it be for you, dear?" I think this is at the crux of her acting out. At least this is a place to start.

Carly's behavior has screamed in a negative way, "Pay attention to me." She may not realize it—she thinks she wants to be left alone to do her own thing. Believe me, there is still another side of her that needs to know that her mother loves her and cares about her and will help her get to the bottom of what's troubling her.

Your husband needs to back off for now and have faith in you. Hopefully he will come around once he gains a deeper understanding.

COLLEGE REJECTIONS

Dear Arden,

Our daughter, Miranda, is crushed that she was not accepted into her first, second, or third choice for college. She is taking the rejections personally. She was certain she was going to be accepted, and now she wants to drop her plans to go to medical school and become a doctor. She shrinks whenever anybody asks her about college. How do I explain that these things happen sometimes?

Ah, I feel so badly for your Miranda. Being rejected from her dream schools must hurt. She's seventeen, Mom, and you know there will be even more rejections that she will have to face in life, whether she likes it or not.

Samara is a musical theatre major, now in her senior year at Manhattanville College. Since she was seventeen, she has been auditioning for roles in plays and musicals. When she gets a call back, she gets so excited and imagines and dreams that she could get what she has worked so hard at—specifically, being recognized, appreciated, and validated for her voice and acting prowess. If she does not get into a play or gets a lesser role than she had hoped for, she feels broken-hearted, hurt, and very upset. I listen to her with deep compassion, and it cuts through me like a knife when she says, "Mom, I wanted this part so badly, I just wanted a chance. I deserve to be given a chance to prove I can do it." Eventually I say, "It sucks. Who knows what a casting director is looking for? It's hard not to feel rejected and not take it person- ally." She really hears me and, with each experience, she is better able to deal and make lemonade out of lemons. I further say, "If someone hands you a 'gift' that really is not a gift at all, you can give it back and not take it personally. It's just their opinion."

Good timing and being compassionately attuned to our daugh- ters is where it's at. Let's face it: it's tough not to get what you want, especially when you have worked so hard. Give Miranda a day or two, and then help her focus on the other schools.

I would **script** it for her as follows: "Sweetheart, you have worked so hard. Sometimes we don't get the recognition that we deserve. That doesn't mean we have to stop trying to succeed. Maybe you can start in another school and then reapply and transfer into one of your chosen schools."

It's so competitive out there. We need to give her some hope and a reason to hold her head high.

What Does Your Daughter Want You to Know?

When we ask our teenagers, "If you could write one chapter in a parenting book that every parent would have to read, what would it be about?" the majority of them answer that they want their parents to truly understand them. This is a tip that every parent can implement and use. I think they do this by asking open-ended questions. Some questions are:

"What is your favorite YouTube video? Why?"

"What videos have you watched today?"

"Why do you think Facebook is so popular?"

"What do you do when you go online?"

—Vanessa Van Petten, youthologist, founder of www.radicalparenting.com, who uses peer counseling to help teens change their lives for the better.

CHAPTER 7

Peers

"Friendship is born at that moment when one person says to another: What! You too? I thought I was the only one."

—C.S. Lewis

It's ironic that the word "peer" is often defined using the word "equal"—as in a person of equal status or background—given that the interactions between teenage girls can be anything *but* equal or kind or sincere. It's not rare to see one girl dissing another at a party, gossiping about friends, or kicking someone out of a group. Among tweens, who can be notoriously fickle with their friends, it's even worse. For a tween or teenage girl, it's really very simple. You want to be accepted, but you also want to be admired and liked. You want to look good.

There are various ways girls try to set themselves apart to be seen as cool. Party invitations, boyfriends, and material possessions from clothing to cars all can work as status symbols. All the one-upmanship can be enough to make a mother cringe. At this age, the opinions of your daughter's peers can carry more weight than your own. It can be excruciating for you to stand on the sidelines and watch as your precious daughter adopts and adapts new attitudes, postures, and behaviors. Buying a new pair of earrings is one thing, however, and ditching your best friend from kindergarten is quite another. But even if you can't pick your daughter's friends, you can still influence her decision-making. Be there to comfort her when she feels rejected. Pick the right moment to talk. Know when to step back and let her take her lumps. Remain alert, especially if the only place she meets new friends is the Internet.

Our daughters have a right to choose for themselves who they like and want to be with, but we don't want them to treat anyone—especially themselves—with disrespect.

There are valuable lessons to be learned from friends and peers during these years, from being a true friend to learning how to stand up for yourself. Moms can help, but they have to be careful not to project old injuries and slights from their own adolescence. What happened to you may not be happening to her. After many years, the memories of put-downs and rejections from former friends can still sting.

TWO PEAS IN A POD

Dear Arden,
I let my eleven-year-old daughter, Dana, go to the mall with her friends yesterday, but when she got dressed for school this morning, I nearly screamed. She looked exactly like her best friend, down to the hairstyle, the clothes, socks, and shoes. They even wore the same color of lip gloss and shade of nail polish. How do I encourage her to be her own person, and not a clone of somebody else? Honestly, they could have passed for twins!

Some girls have one very very special BFFL that they pal around with twenty-four/seven. It's something about struggling with identity for sure, but it's so much more fun when you have another person to swim with in the pool of tweendom. Can you remember that far back? I do. I had that one friend who, if my mom would have permitted it, would have been sleeping over all the time. Or think of it this way. When your daughter was little, she wanted to be like Mommy. This is not that different. She is moving on similarly, just with her peer. It's a safe form of experimentation that's very phase-driven.

Some of this copycat behavior is about popularity and being recognized. Believe me, they think that they are standouts as well. I know, complicated, but very typical and normal.

Once they are in high school, our daughters seem to grow more comfortable in their skins and become more of themselves. This includes developing their own style of dressing. Samara would look back and comment about the pressures in middle school and how much better it was in high school. Now she comments about the social pressures and conformity in high school and how much more loose, laid-back, and fun it is in college. Hindsight is the best insight for sure.

Dana's specialness and unique way of being and dressing will emerge as she grows more comfortable and confident in who she is. Just take a few steps back and try to relax.

B IS FOR BOSSY

Dear Arden,
My daughter, Presley, is very bossy. Hearing her talk down to her
friends makes me cringe. Truthfully, we all are a little afraid of her,

including me. I am afraid she is going to lose all of her friends if she continues to be so overbearing and obnoxious. Is there a cure?

I know so many girls, especially between the ages of eleven and fourteen, who boss their friends and families around. Like you, their concerned mothers warn them, "You are going to drive your friends away." Like your daughter, they roll their eyes when their moms approach this touchy subject. They resent being told what to do. They know it all. They have little or no patience. Well, maybe they will drive their friends away and learn the hard way.

More likely, Presley probably has a few saving graces. Is she dramatic? A former patient of mine blossomed and mellowed once she joined the Drama Club at school. It's a constructive way to channel her need to be seen, matter, and be known as special. Who knows? She may get a great part and make some talented and artistic new friends, as my former patient did.

When you say you all are afraid of her, what power does she hold over you? Has Presley been overindulged? Mom, this will take a while to undo. Standing up to her and retaking the reins, setting some respectful limits and boundaries, is the way to go. She will buck for sure, but perhaps that's what she really wants and needs from you.

Seriously, the "cure" for bossiness, if there is one, is to be around kids who won't take or tolerate any bossiness or nonsense from her.

STEPPING IN

Dear Arden,
I overheard my fifteen-year-old daughter, Julia, crying in her room. I knocked on the door and asked, "What's wrong?" She told me that

she and her friend Erica, also age fifteen, had been Skyping. "Mom,
Erica said, 'Julia, you are obsessed with your boyfriend and you're for-
getting about me. Stacy, Felice, and Ari feel the same way I do.'" Julia
assured Erica that she is still her BFFL, but Julia's upset and thinks her
friends hate her. I couldn't get through to her. Once she calmed down
she said to me that Erica was such a drama queen, and she asked if
I thought Erica was telling the truth about her other friends feeling
the same way. She was very agitated at the idea that the group was
rejecting her. She didn't know what to do or who to believe.

All of the girls have known each other since middle school. I am
so upset, I feel like calling Erica and putting her in her place. Erica
doesn't have a boyfriend. I know she's jealous of Julia, always wants
what she has. Erica has been pushing her around for years, and it
always ends with Julia crying and apologizing.

I'm not sure if it's best to intervene, step back, or just let the dust
settle between Julia and Erica. Julia and I are fairly close, and she
shares a great deal with me. What would you do if you were me?

Girls and their friends can have flare-ups one moment and in the
next be BFFs again. This gets much more complicated, however,
when they are moving from their tweens to their teens. Girls can
get possessive and jealous, especially when a boyfriend is added to
the mix or a new girl is added to the group.

What if I tell you that this is very familiar to me? Many times
Samara was the butt of some of her girlfriends' jealousy, and one
friend would pit her against all the other girlfriends. I would suggest Samara speak to her other pals and get one-on-one feedback
to check out the validity of the one stirring up the pot. Generally it
was the drama queen, maybe a wannabe, who was upset, not all of
the girlfriends. Julia needs to run this all by her friends.

The pain that we feel for our daughters being treated unfairly, pushed around, and bullied can drive us to act before we think it through. Hold off for now on intervening and calling Erica. I think your focus is going to be on building up your daughter, encouraging her to think, use her better judgment, develop her gut, and take the initiative to deal with Erica's bullying behavior. Don't do her work for her, but do support her in standing up for herself (see Chapter 8 on bullying). I would have a talk with Julia and **script** it like this: "Jealousy among friends is not unique, but a really good friend is also happy for your successes and cheers you on. Erica is becoming less and less of a BFF. You must be feeling tired of all the drama; it's so draining. It seems that you are usually the one who apologizes. I know I have said a few times that I have had enough of Erica, and questioned what kind of friend she is to hurt you and push you around. I ask that you think about your friendship with Erica over the years and weigh the benefits and the limitations."

Here's a good strategy: know your daughter's friends and boy-friends from the time they meet in grade school, through middle school, high school, and college years, or whenever she happens to meet them. This will give you an opportunity to develop a connection with each of them. Having an open door to sleepovers and visits, inviting them to special holiday dinners and gatherings, and being warm, engaging, and interested in your daughter's friends is key.

CRYBABY

Dear Arden,
My daughter, Dylan, has a friend who cries at the drop of a hat, especially when my daughter disagrees with her or won't do what

she asks. How can I get my daughter to see how manipulative her friend is?

Oh, boy, one of my pet bugaboos is friends who guilt-trip. Her friend's crying may be a cry for attention or a way to ensure she gets her way. If your daughter doesn't want to encourage this behavior, she has to stop giving in to Ms. Misery. Your daughter has to remain firm and let her friend see that when she behaves like that, she will get nowhere.

It's not necessary for Dylan to play the parent or therapist in order to maintain the relationship. She can try distracting her friend, but if that doesn't work, then Dylan needs to think about what kind of friend this person is for her—and if *her* needs are being met in the relationship. Different friends meet different needs in us. Maybe seeing less of this friend will be enough to send a message to the girl.

RUNNING WITH AN OLDER CROWD

Dear Arden,

My daughter, Riley, is thirteen and a half. She recently started hanging out with the wrong kind of friends. Until now, my daughter has been a good student, but these kids could care less about school and grades. She is starting to neglect her school work, dressing like a sixteen-year-old and showing too much cleavage, going online way too much, and texting until her fingers are falling off. The involvement of the girls in the group with older boys makes me nervous and I worry about her premature exposure to drugs, alcohol, and sex. I am feeling protective. I pride myself on being a mom in the know.

How do I bring this up to her without turning her off? I don't want to jeopardize or sever a relationship that has been close and loving until now.

Mom, I love your attitude and approach. You're thinking about the bigger picture—you're becoming an aerial parent. Stay calm, keep your cool, and trust your gut (TUG), that tug you experience that pulls you inward.

But let's get to the problem. Riley may be heading in a direction that's way over her head. There is the potential for serious trouble.

Girls are in such a rush to grow up. I sure was; how about you? Between the makeup and the provocative fashions these days, a girl can look so much older than her biological years, especially if her skirt is too short and she is showing too much cleavage. The fashion industry is marketing sexualized clothes to kids ages twelve and up and making approximately 10.7 billion dollars per year. Eight- to twelve-year-olds have been calculated to have 43 billion dollars in spending power! The attention Riley gets from boys, and girls, reinforces her new look and her pseudomature behavior.

Our objective here, Mom, is to create an environment where you can spend more time with your daughter doing activities she likes, and the two of you can spend quality time—and quantity time—alone. Yes, I know she just wants to be with her peers, but trust me, even though she won't admit it, she still wants to be with you too. While having fun together, you create opportunities to talk spontaneously with her about what's going on in her life with her new friends. You can go shopping, get a manicure together, or take a family vacation.

You sound like a savvy mom. Using your humor will go a long

way with her. Text and share some plans with her. I am sure she will be surprised and delighted.

FRANTIC ABOUT FACEBOOK

Dear Arden,

My husband got my fourteen-year-old daughter, Whitney, a laptop for her birthday, and now she's always on it. She is constantly chatting online and checking her Facebook page and the pages and statuses of her friends. She even has her cell phone set to receive updates, and her phone is constantly beeping and buzzing, even during meal times. She gets upset if she finds out she hasn't been invited to a party or sees pictures of her friends doing stuff without her. Sometimes I wonder if her being on the computer is a good thing if all it does is make her feel even more inadequate and excluded. I want to set limits on how much time she can spend online, but every time I suggest it, she screams and cries and says I am ruining her life and she will have no friends.

The Internet has transformed the way our daughters relate to each other and maintain their friendships and social ties. Checking in used to be done with a phone call or a passed note. Now it's done with a click. You can check out someone's profile to see what they've been doing, who they've have been hanging out with and talking to, and so on. No matter how old our daughters are, it's tough to deal with a neverending stream of visual and verbal updates, along with possible exclusions and rejections. Of course Whitney would want to be part of a good time. Toward the end of middle school, the need to be accepted and included by peers reaches its peak. At fourteen, can we slow your daughter down? We can try, but she is going to resist, have many meltdowns, and guilt-trip you like your mother never did.

When Whitney is obviously feeling down, say to her, "Honey, I can see this is difficult for you. It would be better for you not to see all of this stuff, but you can't resist, right? Let's call your closest friends for a sleepover here or hang out at the mall." You are bringing out a box of alternatives for her, giving her healthy distractions and ways to reconnect to her friends offline. It's amazing how resilient our daughters can be if handled with tender, loving care.

It's no easy feat to help process our daughters' pain. Keep in mind that this is all a part of growing up and helping Whitney to deal with life's realities. Truly, she'd know about the goings-on, parties, and plans without the phone, the Internet, or Facebook. Haven't you noticed that most tweens and teens are very tuned into what's going on around them socially? They have a built-in antenna that sticks out of their heads and a set of eyes and ears to pick up signals. Mom, listen to your favorite music and take a few breaths yourself. You've worked hard—you deserve it!

THE QUEEN BEE STANDS ALONE

Dear Arden,

My fifteen-year-old daughter, Kennedy, just found out that one of her "friends" is telling everybody to not invite her to a party this weekend. A mutual pal happily dished all the details. Can she confront the girl? Ignore the snub? Crash the party? Throw her own party? Leave town for the weekend? I so want to rush in and help. I can't stand to see her so unhappy and hurt.

It's so awful to see our daughters in pain. It stirs up "Mom to the rescue" fantasies and sometimes it screams for a call to action. You need to ask your daughter who this relational bully is. Is she a former friend? Would she have any reason to feel jealous or threatened? Did something happen at school to cause her to turn? Maybe this gal needs to be center stage. She's behaving as if Kennedy is going to steal her limelight and thunder.

If Kennedy is still invited, she needs to go to the party with her "real" friends who support her. Her presence at the party makes a statement that may neutralize this queen bee's aggressive attempts to influence others and tell her what to do. This is a statement about standing up to the relational bully. A bully is put in her place when others in the silent majority don't give in to her demands, confront her, or just work around her. Your daughter and her pals can talk about a unified strategic action plan.

Remember, most bullies are cowards. Left on their own without a court of wannabes, they are vulnerable and powerless. The latest research paints these bully girls as needy, attention-starved, and love-starved. It's pathetic that they go about "making friends" by using coercive tactics or forcing themselves on their peers. It's a surefire way to drive any smart, secure girl far away for her own protection.

LOST IN A FANTASY WORLD

Dear Arden,
My eighteen-year-old daughter, Cody, spends most of her time online. She is always in her room on the computer. She has no real friends—not the kind you can meet and hang out with, anyway. All

of her dearest friends are online. Some of them are much older than she is and hail from cities around the world. She chats with them every day on Skype. Next month, one of these guys is passing through our city and I overheard her tell a friend she was going to meet him at the airport. She confides in them and tells them intimate things she would never share with us. When I try to talk to her about it, she says that she knows them, that they are her "true friends." Is this normal or safe? I grew up in a small town where everybody knew each other. This is completely foreign territory for me.

I can appreciate your concern. My biggest apprehension is where are all of her local friends? Why is she spending so much of her time on Skype? How old are these online friends? The fellow coming through and stopping over, who is he? Honestly, some of them could be decent, honest people, but I'm from Brooklyn, New York, and I am of the mind that your eighteen-year-old's safety and welfare could be at stake.

Cody sounds very naïve and gullible, maybe sheltered. Sexual predators can spot a vulnerable girl from miles away and know just what to say to her to coax her out of her protective shell. A lonely girl with fantasies of meeting her "prince" online makes an easy target. Is your daughter starved for attention, love, and acceptance or insecure about her looks? A stranger can flatter her and tell her how beautiful she is—and that only he can see the beauty in her heart. For a female who feels stuck at home, the offer to escape and travel could be too exciting to refuse. Once she steps outside of your home and into his car or residence, she is no longer safe.

Mom, you need to lend your brain to your daughter, so that she can develop a better sixth sense. Until that happens, Cody needs your nonjudgmental, kind, and protective feedback to guide her through some very tempting but troubling invitations. She needs to learn how to listen to her instincts, intelligence, and common sense, especially with new, unknown online "friends" who would like to meet her! Again, I am the kind of person who does not throw caution to the wind. I trust my gut, and you had better as well. If something sounds too good to be true—"we fell in love on Hot or Not!"—then it probably is.

We need to work on your reengaging your daughter and getting her to leave her room and step away from her laptop. She needs to feel she is making a difference, that she is important and special—and not just because her friends on Skype tell her so. She needs more age-appropriate concrete experiences, such as community service, to pull her out of herself, let her flex her wings, and boost her self-confidence and self-esteem.

There are two books by Gavin De Becker that I highly recommend—*The Gift of Fear* and *Protecting the Gift*; both were given to me by a former patient who was a rape victim. De Becker's books will open your daughter's eyes to unsolicited promises, manipulative lines, common tricks and lies, and other examples of bad-guy tactics.

CHAPTER 8

Bullying

"Courage is resistance to fear, mastery of fear—not absence of fear."

—Mark Twain

Every day, one hundred and sixty thousand kids miss school because of bullying. They may seem depressed or reluctant to go to school. They might complain of feeling sick, suddenly forget something at home, or hide in the nurse's office. They'll do anything to avoid being ridiculed, poked with pencils, tripped, shoved, threatened, or having their hair pulled. Their belongings might start disappearing or turn up broken or damaged or defaced in strange places.

The game continues when the bully or bullies provoke the victim to react, lash out, or fight back. Frequently, any reaction from the victim only serves to fuel and empower the bully's efforts even more. As a result, the victim may be sent to detention or suspended, not only a target of the students but a fixture and eyesore on the radar of teachers and administrators. School becomes a place of torment.

What's really sad is that home might not be much of a refuge either. At home, the victim can be flooded with texts,

IMs, emails, and phone calls. Unwanted posts, cruel or unflattering photos, and mean comments can pop up on Facebook, MySpace, and other social networking sites. Often there's a spike of activity over weekends and during holiday breaks and school vacations. For a victim, having a cell phone and computer can mean hearing a bully's insults, put-downs, and threats twenty-four/seven. The comments·from others you used to consider your friends—or at least not your enemies—can be devastating and more hurtful than any physical injury. What used to take place in front of other students in a school cafeteria, locker room, bathroom, or hallway now has the potential to play out in front of a much larger—and anonymous—crowd, with an audience numbering in the hundreds and thousands.

It's the type of psychological warfare that can break our children's spirits. Physical wounds may heal, but the emotional fallout of bullying can damage and fester for years, like pieces of shrapnel lodged under the skin. Each insult, each gesture pushes the shrapnel deeper into the wound. What started as one bully, or three, can easily turn into a mob of tormentors keen on the sport of humiliation. Worse, former friends and classmates can turn into a silent climate of indifferent bystanders.

Few situations can raise a parent's hackles and protective instincts like bullying. As mothers, we need to be aware, proactive, and appropriately protective of our children.

The Facts About Bullying

- The National Center for Education Statistics reports that 25 percent of all students say they are bullied on a daily or weekly basis. For children with disabilities, that number jumps to 85 percent.

- Bullying can happen in any grade but is most severe from grades seven to nine.
- Nearly 43 percent of sixth-graders were bullied during the 2007 school year.
- One in twelve students stays home from school because she is afraid to go to school.
- Roughly 865,000 teens, or 5.5 percent of high school students, report staying home from school at least one day per month because they fear for their safety.
- Compared to their peers, kids who are bullied are five times more likely to be depressed.
- Bullied boys are four times more likely to be suicidal. Bullied girls are eight times more likely to be suicidal.
- Thirty percent of all child suicides can be directly related to bullying.
- In a survey of American middle and high school students, 66 percent of bullying victims believed that school professionals responded poorly to the bullying problems that they observed.

CARRYING A HEAVY LOAD

Dear Arden,

Yesterday I saw that someone had scribbled "SLUT" and "HO" and "BITCH" all over my daughter Jayden's backpack with permanent marker. When I picked up her clothes off the floor, I noticed that the back of her shirt had been cut with a pair of scissors. I tried to ask her what happened, but she just sighed and said flatly, "It's nothing. It's no big deal." Her reaction shocked me. She wasn't mad at all.

Whoever is responsible for defacing Jayden's' belongings and violating her personal rights needs to be called on it and confronted. This needs to be reported pronto, and let's see how the school administration deals with the situation. If you do not get a swift response, connect with a lawyer. That will get the ball in motion. My concern is for your daughter, who understandably is minimizing their outrageous behavior, perhaps out of a fear of any backlash from her harassers. I am so sorry that she has been subjected to this. I don't want Jayden to come to any more harm, emotional or physical, than she already has. I am sure you feel the same way. Talk to your daughter directly. Share this **script** with her: "Sweetheart, you have to be feeling frightened and helpless with all of this verbal abuse and unwanted physical contact and defacement. You are being violated. This is unacceptable. You don't deserve this kind of treatment from anyone. I think you are trying to push this all aside. This is too much for you to deal with alone. Your dad and I are here for you, and we will all figure out what's our best course of action."

This is not the norm; this is severe bullying and sexual harassment. Sexual harassment is unwanted and unwelcomed behavior of a sexual nature which interferes with your daughter's education, safety, and welfare. School policy prohibits such behavior. Sexual harassment can take many forms: graffiti on desks and bathroom walls; touching, groping, or grabbing of body parts; ripped-up or pulled-off clothing; sexually suggestive jokes, rude gestures, and leering; defacement of your daughter's belongings with sexually degrading comments; spreading sexual rumors; degrading comments about your daughter's form, body, appearance, and reputation; unwanted sexual propositions or overtures; forcing her to perform a sexual act, make out, or expose herself; or attempted or actual sexual assault and rape.

This type of harassment can happen after a girl breaks up with a boy, or starts dating a boy, or has sex with a boy, or talks to a boy in front of other girls. Such was the case of Phoebe Prince, a teenager from Hadley, Massachusetts, who hung herself after weeks of being tormented at school and online by students who called her a slut. The day she died, Phoebe had been harassed in the library and the auditorium. During her walk home, someone had thrown a can at her from a passing car. Her case led to the passage of anti-bullying legislation in Massachusetts and resulted in the prosecution of six teenagers, who faced criminal charges for harassment, statutory rape, and stalking.

PUSHED OUT OF SCHOOL

Dear Arden,

My eighth grader, Piper, is begging me to switch schools. For the past two years, she has been teased and tormented daily. She told me she didn't want to go through another four years with the same bullies. She was crying really hard and said, "I just can't take it anymore, Mom. There isn't one day someone isn't laughing at me or shoving me or poking me with pencils." We believe in standing our ground and not giving in, but she seems so miserable. Is this really an option or another sign that we let the bullies win?

You need to do what's in your daughter's best interests. Piper is begging for a change. Honor her plea. If she says she can't take it anymore and has reached her limit, believe her. Many parents of children who committed suicide later expressed their regret that they had not pulled their children out of school, homeschooled them, or transferred them to another school. Make sure she knows that she does not deserve this abuse. Then back her up by taking action. Ask her if she wants you to look into other alternatives, such as a private school, parochial school, or a different public school district. If she anxiously gives you the nod, then start investigating the alternatives. Do your homework on application requirements, due dates, and transfers as soon as possible. High school is a great time to make a change.

I know a gal who went from feeling like an ugly duckling in a public middle school to a swan in a private high school. She bloomed in a smaller, more intimate, and warmer school setting, where everyone knew each other. She became captain of the softball and tennis teams in her junior and senior years, excelled academically, and made lots of new friends. She was accepted into an Ivy League college when she graduated. Not bad for a teen who was made to feel that something was wrong with her. She left a toxic climate and moved to a much higher quality of air and conditions. I would start visiting other schools with her now. Give Piper the hope that things can be different and better elsewhere. It may not take that much to convince her at this point.

Leaving an unsupportive school is *not* a cop-out. Unfortunately your upsetting situation is not unique. Many "zero tolerance" school bullying policies are not enforced. Whatever happens, don't let your daughter suffer silently. File a police report if you must, keep track of the harassment, get her into therapy, and look for ways to bolster her self-esteem.

PRESSURED TO DATE

Dear Arden,

My fourteen-year-old daughter, Tatum, is nervous because a boy in her class keeps pressuring her to go out with him. She does not like this boy and has never encouraged him. She says she tried friend-zoning him, letting him know they would only be friends, but he won't take no for an answer. Despite her protests, he puts his arm around her and calls her his girlfriend in front of the other students. He jokes and winks with everybody that they are in a relationship, and this upsets her even more. What can she do?

Wow, is he pushing it! Some boys would have been terribly hurt and rejected by now. This young man appears impervious to her directness. Maybe he's just an immature guy who thinks she's playing hard to get.

Make sure Tatum really wants to be rid of him. If so, then I would **script** her refusal via a text or email and send it directly to him: "Joe, you are behaving disrespectfully to me and not taking me seriously. Do not, I repeat, do not put your arm around me or touch me. I am not your girlfriend and my friends know it. I am sure you will find somebody to go out with you, but that's NOT ME, GET IT? NO MORE. DONE!!"

As one smart eighth-grader, Lexie, said to me, "If that was me, I would ignore him. All my friends would know he's not my boy-friend. I would block him on Facebook. If he put his arm around me, I would tell him, 'Get your arm off me, I'm not your girlfriend.' If he followed me, I'd go to the principal and tell her he's stalking me." This spunky thirteen-year-old really could take care of herself. She was assertive, clear, and direct about her boundaries. She knew *exactly* what she would do if he overstepped the line. We want to get your daughter to the same place.

Cyberbullying: What You Need to Know Right Now

- According to a 2006 Harris Interactive poll, 43 percent of American teenagers reported experiencing cyberbullying in the past year.
- Girls are twice as likely to be the victims of cyberbullying as boys.
- Cyberbullying most frequently targets youngsters ages ten to seventeen.
- Thirty-five percent of kids have received threats online.
- Twenty-one percent have received mean emails.
- Eighty-five percent of twelve- and thirteen-year-olds have experienced cyberbullying. Fifty-three percent of them have been victims of cyberbullying.
- Ninety-three percent of parents claim a good, working knowledge of their children's online activities, but 41 percent of children say that parents are unaware of what they do online.
- Victims of cyberbullying are more depressed than victims of physical bullying.

A TARGET OF CYBERBULLYING

Dear Arden,
The other night I heard my fourteen-year-old daughter, Kayla,

cry out when she was using the computer. She was staring at the screen as if it had bit her. Some girls in her grade started posting mean comments about her after a boy stopped to talk to her. It turns out this boy just broke up with one of these girls, and her friends were furious with my daughter. The descriptions of what she deserved to have happen to her went on forever as I scrolled down to read them. I couldn't believe how explicit and graphic the language was! These mean girls had even made a list: "Top Ten Ways to Kill Kayla." She started crying and clicking and looking for any unflattering pictures of her they might have posted too. The school said there was nothing they could do about it, because it happened off school grounds and they have no control over what happens on the Internet.

This is such an outrage! Mom, get an attorney. If the teasing was on the basis of her race, religion, gender, or sexual orientation, then you may have a civil rights case. Depending on the severity of the abuse, some civil rights groups will work pro bono. They certainly have something to work with—these stunted girls have left a paper trail a mile long.

This needs to be nipped in the bud immediately. The longer this cyberbullying and harassment goes on, the more powerful the mean girls become. Jealousy between some girls can be so very nasty and cruel. Your daughter does not deserve any of this.

Many schools are already too overwhelmed with what's happening inside school walls to bother with policing what's on the Internet. In an effort to limit liability or damages, they've adopted a policy of just not getting involved. In my eyes, this is a real disservice—and a way to encourage more intolerable behavior from a bully. A 2010 *New York Times* article highlighted how inadequate and varied schools can be in their responses to bullying. This is especially true of cyberbullying, where many times "the action" takes place off school property.

And it's not just Facebook or email. There are many, many ways to do damage. On formspring.com, users can ask provocative or insulting questions in front of an audience of the student's friends. A child might be put down or hit with the same insulting question hundreds of times, from "Why are you such a slut?" to "Why are you so gay?" On the unregulated 4chan.org, anonymous users can post photos for ridicule, sport, or comment, including nude or topless photos of ex-girlfriends. These sites have taken the place of graffiti on the bathroom wall, albeit one that's read by a large and jeering crowd online.

If your child's school is unresponsive or slow to act, then you, Mom, must be more sensitive and responsive. Too often parents frustrate the victim by telling her to just ignore it, rise above it, or to act like nothing's wrong. You are the mother and must let Kayla know that you are with her and care deeply about what happens to her. If she cries, don't tell her to grow up or to stop acting like a baby. Reaffirm her feelings and say, "You are having a normal response to a horrible and abnormal situation."

Let your lawyer advise you on what to do. Involve the police if you must. I know, it could backfire and inflame the situation even more, but honestly I feel so protective of your daughter, and lately too many really good, sensitive kids have taken drastic measures into their own hands and have hurt or killed themselves. Parents need to be extremely proactive and bang the drum really loudly. Give Kayla a big kiss and hug. Remind her that you are in her corner, that this is intolerable, and that you will not sit back and take it.

Could Your Child Be the Victim of Bullying?

☐ Does she jump every time a text message or instant message arrives?

☐ Does she appear worried, anxious, sad, or upset when using the computer or cell phone?

☐ Does she uncharacteristically avoid the cell phone and computer, and keep them shut off?

☐ Has she become hyper-vigilant about opening every text, email message, or IM; is she spending more time online to patrol?

☐ Does she shut off the computer or cover the computer screen when you enter the room?

☐ Does she appear distracted and unable to concentrate on schoolwork; have her grades dropped or plummeted?

☐ Has she become tight-lipped about school and friends there?

☐ Does she have frequent and suspicious activity on the cell phone; does the phone ring nonstop?

☐ Has she become sullen, moody, or withdrawn?

☐ Has she become edgy and agitated; does she cry or blow up suddenly for no apparent reason?

☐ Does she seem vulnerable, lonely, and isolated?

☐ Does she refuse to go to school?

☐ Does she complain of stomach and headaches?

☐ Does she suffer from loss of appetite or other food disturbances?

☐ Does she suffer from sleep disturbances?

☐ Does she refuse to eat in the cafeteria?

☐ Does she seem to not feel safe playing outside during recess?

IT HAPPENED TO US:
ONE MOTHER'S JOURNEY

On the first day of school they told her to go kill herself. From there, the taunting only got worse. When nobody complained about the bullying or stepped forward to stop it, the behavior escalated. By November, they were shoving my daughter in the hallways, knocking over her books, and pulling her hair. If they were successful in getting her to scream or yell or fight back, she would get sent to detention, mostly for her own safety. Even the teachers were scared to come forward. Then the death threats started coming, over the phone and on the Internet. My daughter's cell phone never stopped ringing. There were graphic descriptions of what they would do to her, with threats of rape and worse. I started taking notes in my journal just because I was so upset. As the bullying got worse, my daughter began to call and text me from the nurse's office or the restroom. Various meetings and mediations took place, but nothing worked. I took my daughter to the police station and filed a complaint.

I honestly thought that would be the end of it. We didn't know we had to collect evidence. Together we built a chronology, a thirty-page history of incidents and confrontations over nearly two years, with the school's response summarized below each entry.

No matter how unpleasant and ugly the truth may be, you can't shrug off what your child is telling you—you have to listen to her. You are the adult, so you know what's a real threat, what's dangerous, what's posturing. These kids left a trail of comments, pictures, and instant messages all over Facebook and MySpace. I printed up everything and made photocopies. My daughter and I had a code, so that if things got really bad and she needed me to come get her, I would suddenly drop by the school to take her to a doctor's appointment. She needed to know that she was not alone.

It was like Humpty Dumpty. She'd get knocked down at school—*literally* and emotionally—and I'd search for ways to build her back up. It was important for her to have interests outside of school that were positive and fun. The new experiences and friends supported her—the real, authentic her, and not the narrow, limited definition of who the bullies wanted her to be.

At the end of the school year, she felt so hopeful that we decided to move. We never regretted our decision for an instant.

If Your Child Is a Target of Bullies

1. Keep a record of all incidents in a separate notebook, journal, or file, complete with specific dates and

times. That includes insults, IMs, confrontations, and teacher responses. Do not write down anything in this journal that you would not be willing to share in a court of law.

2. Take screen shots of Facebook and MySpace pages and make printouts. Copy and paste IMs and chats into emails that show the date and time.

3. Keep your child focused on reporting what happened, instead of reacting to it. The more details she can supply, the better. Note the bully's clothing, comments, and actions. Bullies never think they're being watched or reported.

4. Communicate with the school in writing. Keep copies of all correspondence and emails. Summarize each phone call, and jot down details—date, time, etc.

5. Follow up with administrators when they say, "I'll get back to you," or "I did not know that."

6. Familiarize yourself with the school's ethics code and policy.

7. Systemic change can take years to achieve. Find ways to nurture your child's spirit and build up her confidence and self-esteem now.

8. Be a presence at the school. Volunteer or join the PTA to get inside school walls and see what's happening. Talk to the security guards and staff.

9. Bullying is very isolating for the victim. Surround your child and yourself with good, kind people. Do not struggle with this alone.

10. Google your child's name online periodically or use Google Alerts to check for any suspicious activity.

PORTRAIT OF A BULLY

A bully operates from a deep-seated need for power, attention, approval, and acceptance. Extremely insecure and needy, this person learns to thrive on negative attention and, in a very driven way, looks to control and dominate others with aggression. Sometimes it's doing what has been done to him or her. The teasing, picking fights, making fun of another's appearance, and name-calling often feel like a reenactment. The bully may be a victim of aggressive behavior at home by a parent or a sibling who is significantly present in his or her life. In reenacting what happens at home, the bully identifies with the strong aggressor and rejects the victim, who is perceived as powerless and weak.

This is not child's play. Studies have shown that a history of bullying can lead to criminal behavior. According to the organization Fight Crime: Invest in Kids, 40 percent of school bullies had three or more criminal convictions by the time they turned twenty-four.

What spews forth from the bully's imagination often has a spiteful, vindictive quality to it. These folks don't just want to get even; they want to stay on top. Most bullies are cowards, afraid, and are terrified of being rejected. They need a stable of yes girls (wannabes) or yes boys around them to bolster them up. If they feel they are rejected by another peer, they will act and retaliate viciously. They feel entitled to behave this way, but underneath their domineering arrogance is a very deep need to be accepted and loved.

Parents who recognize that their child needs help will have to do some heavy lifting in therapy and at home. A child is not born a bully. Bullying is a learned behavior. In some families, one parent dominates, belittles, and criticizes, while the other parent may be submissive, enabling, and subjugated.

The most difficult bullies to treat are those who show behavior that is extremely sadistic, cruel, and mean-spirited. They get off on inflicting pain on their peers and those they deem "lesser" beings. These individuals have no conscience, no guilt, and no remorse for deeply violating the rights of another person. They lack sensitivity and empathy for others; they don't care about the impact of their behavior, which is sociopathic and pathological, and many times criminal.

Ask a bully why they do it and they'll tell you, "Because I can. Nobody stops me." They might say, "Because it's fun. She deserves it." Or "Everybody laughs. It's so cool." Some kids will do and say anything for the chance to be popular. Others become bullies because they themselves don't want to be bullied or have been the victim of bullying.

If this sounds like your daughter, you need to get some professional help.

PROFILE OF A VICTIM

There is no single identifying trait or defining behavior for a victim. Some of these children are randomly singled out, honestly for no particular reason other than for sport and target practice. Others do stand out. They may be perceived as too skinny, too short, too tall, too clumsy, too dumb, too smart, too nerdy, or too overweight. A victim may have rejected a bully's offer of friendship or refused to partake in bullying activities. It's so arbitrary. One thing is clear, though. Once a potential victim has appeared on the radar of a bully, he or she will remain there until the bully stops or is stopped. The bully will tease, ridicule, belittle, and intimidate this unfortunate soul until he or she gets the reaction he wants.

The bully gets off on provoking and getting a rise out of his/her victim. They like throwing off their victims. Unfortunately the victim generally takes the bait and either fights, flees, or gets paralyzed. This is not a pretty sight.

I have worked with a number of victims of bullying in my private practice. One that comes to mind was a fifteen-year-old female, Gianna, who was verbally abused face to face, cyber-bullied, and physically pushed around at her school and in her neighborhood by two girls her own age. Apparently they were looking to befriend her and went about it in a very mean-spirited way. Gianna did not want to be their friend and was paying a very high price for her avoidance of them. She kept this from her parents until it was over the top. Once her parents found out, they did what any good, caring parents would do—they went to the principal. Mom and Dad's protests fell on deaf ears with the school administration. Before they could hire a lawyer, their daughter overdosed with two bottles of sleeping pills. Luckily her stomach was pumped and she survived, but the emotional and physical damage was brutal beyond belief.

The mom contacted me, and before I even saw her daughter, I advised her to get Gianna out of the school and, if possible, put her up with her aunt in another part of the state that they all lived in. Within a few days, she was attending a much smaller public school, living in a safer environment with her mother's sister, and feeling so much better. The painful emotional work with me lay ahead, but she could face it now that her mind, body, and spirit were safe. She loved her new school, made friends, and sprang back to herself. She had a very hard time forgiving herself for the overdose and swore she did not mean to kill herself. It was just that she had to stop the pain. Mom and Dad felt so guilty for not intervening sooner. Yes, it's so important to be aware of your child's well-being, but how do you do that when your daughter is acting like everything is okay, and doesn't want to share because she is rightfully expecting a backlash?

(P.S.—Gianna is doing great in college and has formed an advocacy and support peer group for kids who have been bullied.)

Kids who find themselves the targets of bullies may already be socially isolated, hurt, and trying to withdraw from the world. They may not know how to be assertive or stand up for themselves. They may be shy, quiet kids whose desire to stay in the background and go unnoticed makes them easy prey. Other likely targets are kids who are depressed, anxious, needy, sensitive, tearful, and distressed. Youngsters with special needs, such as those with Asperger's, autism, or learning disabilities, frequently find themselves the targets of bullying. After prolonged bullying, victims may start to feel like they "deserve the treatment" and expect to be pushed around. They may have a bullying and intimidating parent who terrorizes at home and reinforces the message that they deserve to be mistreated and abused.

Both bullies and victims are internally driven by insecurity and anxiety. Under the right conditions, a victim can turn into a bully. According to the U.S. Department of Justice, in two-thirds of school shootings (in which the shooter was still alive), the attackers were victims of bullying: "In those cases, the experience of bullying appeared to play a major role in motivating the attacker."

SCARED OF WHAT COULD HAPPEN

Dear Arden,

I am afraid for my eighteen-year-old daughter, Ashley, who recently come out as a lesbian. We live in a homophobic world. I brought her up to be true to herself, and I support her no matter what, but what if my daughter is not received as a human being, with feelings, thoughts, and beliefs? What happens if she is taunted, teased, harassed, and bullied in college or on the street? She felt safe enough during her college orientation, but who knows? There are some very disturbed people out there. She is young and feels invincible. She thinks I am being ridiculous and overly protective. Am I?

I understand your concern, Mom. Given the history of antigay violence and bias crimes in this country, you have every right to feel protective. This hate can be internalized, as we witnessed with the suicide of Rutgers freshman Tyler Clementi in September of 2010. Clementi jumped off the George Washington Bridge after his roommate secretly videotaped him in a sex act with a man and broadcast the footage online. He was one of six young men who tragically killed themselves in 2010 after being targeted and bullied for being gay or being perceived as gay. The suicide rate for gay students is four times the national average.

I think the more Ashley is aware of and educated about the realities of discrimination, prejudice, and hate, the better protected she will be. Most bias perpetrators are between the ages of fourteen and twenty-two. She could become proactive at her new school and join an activist club or group to work on educating her fellow students. Here in Rockland County, we have a wonderful group at Volunteer Counseling Services called Change Project that celebrates diversity and gay pride. To me, this is no different than the struggle for women's rights and the civil rights movement in the sixties. The emphasis is on equal rights under the First Amendment no matter the race, creed, or color, and I will add gender identity and sexuality to that as well. For you, I suggest joining PFLAG, a group for parents of LGBT (lesbian, gay, bisexual, transgender) teens to show further support for your daughter.

For now, Mom, take a breath. I admire how you love your daughter and how secure she feels in it. She sounds strong in herself, but she is only eighteen after all and has not seen much of the world. Soon enough, she will learn to how tell who her real friends are and experience both acceptance and rejection firsthand. Reassure her (and yourself) by sharing with Ashley that if anyone or any situation feels dangerous, uncomfortable, weird, or strange to her, to please share it with her new pals, the disciplinary people in charge, and especially her mom.

Rainbow Alert

- A 2005 Harris poll found that 90 percent of gay and lesbian teens admitted to being bullied in the past year.
- According to a 2009 survey of 7,261 middle school and high school students by the Gay, Lesbian, and Straight Education Network (GLSEN), nearly two-thirds of gay students feel unsafe in school due to their sexual orientation.
- Nine out of ten LGBT students reported being bullied.
- Approximately 32.7 percent of LGBT students missed a day of school in the previous month because they felt unsafe.

> • Nearly a third of the students who reported an incident said that the school staff did nothing in response.

PROTECTION STARTS AT HOME

Dear Arden,

My daughter, Lola, is just about to enter the dreaded middle school years, when mean girls rule the school and bullying hits its peak. What can I do to protect my daughter from becoming a victim? What can she do if any unwanted teasing starts? I know that bullying makes folks feel powerless, so how can I shore up my child? I would hate for a situation to snowball into something bigger.

The lessons for teaching tolerance and acceptance of difference begin at home. Lessons in kindness, respect, and gratitude start in humble places: the kitchen table, the backyard, the living room. The lessons revolve around simple things: sharing a bedroom, negotiating time in the bathroom, watching the TV in the den, who sits next to the window in the car. As a parent, you are Lola's' first teacher. We teach our children about patience, self-control, and tolerance for frustration through our actions as mothers and fathers. Our children pay close attention to how parents behave, react, and treat each other and their children.

Every day you show Lola how women can expect to be treated with kindness and respect. This can only happen if you are crystal clear and working hard to be a kind and respectful person in your dealings with your own family. Observing and learning how to negotiate differences of opinion through listening, empathizing, compromising, and cooperation can lead to a higher level of understanding. Family members agree that there will be times when we don't have to see eye to eye—we can agree to disagree—as long we work on respecting each other.

Just to set the record straight, anyone who knows me knows I am not a pushover. Being kind is not about letting someone walk all over you, especially your partner or your children. This is how we demonstrate to our daughters how to expect to be treated by others and how to treat others in a respectful fashion so that if and when she finds herself in a position where there is potential to be bullied, verbally threatened, and physically harmed, she will feel in her gut the unfairness, the unrighteousness, the cruelty, and know that this does not have to be tolerated. This is part of the process of empowering our daughters.

You need to check in with Lola daily, especially when she begins a new school, and even more so if it's a middle school. Here's a **script**: "Honey, tell me how it is for you at your new school? Who do you sit with at lunch? Tell me about your new friends, your teachers, etc." Open-ended questions are extremely crucial to see how your daughter is adjusting and how she is being received.

RESPECT stands for...

R   regard for self and others
E   empowerment through healthy self-expression
S   self-esteem and worth
P   passion and the potential to become all that you are meant to be
E   empathy
C   compassion, cooperation, and compromise— three C's
T   Tolerance for others, zero tolerance for any verbal or physical act of aggression

Once your daughter admits that she has been teased or bullied, the next step is to ask her what she feels or thinks is going on. You need to get her read and take on the situation, and her feedback.

This is invaluable because she so needs to be heard, listened to, and understood. Ask her: "Honey, do you have any ideas of how we could nip this in the bud? How long has this been going on? Do your friends know about this? Are other kids being bullied? What do your friends do when they see that you are being teased and bullied?" Once you get some feedback, then the next step is to see how your child wants to handle the situation and the bullying. You may be surprised to hear that she has an idea of how to begin to protect herself. Maybe she already has taken some small steps. Lots of kids don't report bullying to a parent immediately.

Let your daughter run some ideas by you and tell you what she has tried so far. Work with her to come up with options, alternatives, and solutions. When she can figure it out and take the lead with your help, she feels empowered. She also feels that her parents have faith and trust in her perceptions and judgment. Some parents enroll their child in karate, kickboxing, kung fu, or self-defense classes. The purpose is not to encourage fighting but to build up their daughters' self-esteem and confidence.

It's also important to teach your child self-talk skills. Instead of exploding and letting the bully provoke her, your child takes a deep breath, and says to herself, "She is trying to lure me in, don't fall for it. Don't give her what she wants!" Then she can walk away, disempowering and neutralizing the bullies' hold on her.

When dealing with face-to-face bullies, there is a great mnemonic you can use: HA HA SO.

H is for seeking *help* from an adult or other kids.

A is for *asserting* yourself. You can say, "Quit spreading rumors about me. It's mean."

H is for *humor* to neutralize and take the air out of the bullies' bravado and balloon.

A is for never walk *alone*, and always be with someone. The bully loves to swoop down when you are walking home by yourself.

S is for bolstering *self-talk*, such as "This kid's got big problems. I'm a good person with lots of people who like and respect me."

O is for realizing that *owning* your reaction to the bully will only serve to make her try even harder.

When the going gets really tough, and the bullying escalates (and this you will know by talking daily with your child), then it's time to involve the teacher. If the teacher does not see anything in the classroom (because bullies generally are cowards and do their work when no authority figure is around), then I suggest that your child enlists the help of a friend in class to corroborate her story. If that does not work and the bullying continues, then you move up to the assistant principal or the principal. Say that you have spoken to the teacher, who does not see that bullying is going on, and you need additional help. Often principals are protective of their teachers, so you are showing that you have made the attempt to communicate with the teacher and are now going through the appropriate channels.

Bottom line: you need to be an educated and aware parent from the get-go, Mom. This involves teaching your child to be her own advocate and enlisting others to help her. Good citizenship, character building, and consideration and kindness toward others are the way to go. It takes so much courage to challenge and change what does not work.

> "I think it's very important to create an open and safe environment at home in which your child feels comfortable talking about her life and bringing up issues at school. Parents

will need to initiate the dialogue and ask questions. Children need to know that you are listening and supportive. If we can empower kids to "say something when they see something," and become allies for the person being oppressed, I believe incidents of bullying would decrease rapidly. It's having the courage to speak up in the face of injustice."

—Professor Hannah Fox, cofounder of Big Apple Playback Theatre and originator of "Keep The Peace!", an anti-bullying program.

CHAPTER 9

Dating

---

*"I'm glad I have a few more years. I'm not ready
for them driving, dating. I'm not ready for any of
it. Our plan is to just have a really, really great
relationship with our children, so when they hit
that time that they don't want to talk to us, we've
instilled some good values already because it will be
too late as they're walking out the door."*

— Angelina Jolie, on her children's future dating

Dating issues are among the very first adult decisions your
daughter will ever make. *Do I like this person? Do I feel comfortable with him? Will I see him again?* And they can be nerve-wracking moments for parents, who hope their daughters can
steer away from trouble as they're venturing forth to meet new
people. Dating can be an awful lot like walking into the deep,
dark woods for our daughters. There in the wilderness, your
daughter will have the opportunity to use her intelligence,
her wits, and her instincts and compassion. In encounter after
encounter, sizing up one stranger after another, she will learn
she cannot trust every traveler she meets along the journey, and
that she needs to keep a close eye on the company she keeps.

TOO YOUNG TO DATE?

Dear Arden,
My twelve-year-old daughter, Brittany, wants to go on group dates
with her friends. Do I let her? At what age is it okay for girls to date?
These days, it seems to be younger and younger.

The magic, age-appropriate word here is *group*, as in group dates with her pals. These are coed middle schoolers hanging out with each other at the mall, the movies, or having a bite to eat at a fast food restaurant. You're right—twelve is the new thirteen, or even fourteen at times. As a seventh-grader smack in the middle of middle school, the sense of belonging to a peer group outside of the family's protective sphere becomes tantamount to feeling accepted, validated, and special. It's the first mini-break away from the family, aside from sleepaway camp.

One way to handle this is for you to become more involved in her social life. You become a bit of a shuttle service, as she asks, "Mom, could you take us here?" or "Mom, you can pick us up now?" You listen to her and her friends' loud and enthusiastic conversations in the background. You take it for what it is, a beginning, a stretching, a mini-adventure. It's absolutely okay for Brittany to go.

Guidelines for Group Dates

1. Talk to your daughter about safety. A good rule of thumb: "Stick with your pals and don't wander off on your own." Transient people who come in and out of a mall can be of questionable character. Remember, security cameras

are installed for monitoring stolen goods, not stolen children.

2. Teach her that she can say no to any and all uncomfortable touching.

3. Set an agreed-upon time for pickup. Picking up the kids from the mall or movie theater presents a golden opportunity to meet her new friends. At twelve, you have plenty of influence over what she thinks and does. She so wants your blessing and approval, no matter how embarrassed and awkward she may appear.

IS THIS PUPPY LOVE?

Dear Arden,
My fourteen-year-old daughter, Stacy, got involved very quickly with a boy who's seventeen. He seems nice enough, but I think they're moving too fast. He told her he loved her after one week of dating and bought her an expensive necklace.

I think you are spot-on, Mom. This may feel like puppy love to Stacy, but this young man is way too needy, clingy, and possessive. Your fourteen-year-old might think it's romantic, but she is too young to be seeing a seventeen-year-old. I don't like the way this feels to me. You too, right? So what do you do here? If you encourage her to break up with him, she will cling to him even harder. You're in a tough place.

When it comes to protecting our lovely daughters, we need to be eagle-eyed and vigilant. I side with caution. Let Stacy feel comfortable enough with you so that she continues to share the details of her romance with you. Meanwhile, you keep on planting little seeds of doubt in her mind. Look for those golden moments and opportunities to steer the conversation to what she can expect when boys and girls date.

Hopefully, as you continue to plant these conversational seeds and your ideas take root, Stacy can begin to gauge whether this is what she really wants in a relationship. This will take patience and time on your part.

A relationship can start innocently enough, as a crush or infatuation. This is especially true for girls who are fourteen and younger; they may have different boyfriends every week or month in school. As your daughter matures and develops a greater need for attachment and intimacy outside of the family, she may look for a more "full-time" boyfriend, hopefully one who is more in tune with her needs and wants.

THINKING AHEAD

Dear Arden,

Our fourteen-old-daughter, Lucy, a middle school student in eighth grade, really wants to have our blessing to begin to date. She says there's a boy in the high school who asked her out. I asked how old he is, and she said he's sixteen, and his name is Kevin. I know Kevin and like his family. Now, I am not one of those head-in-the-sand parents. I know all about oral sex and the girls who do it. I teach at that high school. If we let our daughter date Kevin, an older and experienced young man, are we encouraging her to have sex early?

I would ideally encourage Lucy to date someone her age in middle school, but it sounds like Lucy and Kevin probably are already at least one or more steps ahead of us. I love that Lucy wants your approval and blessings. She's a respectful daughter.

Please don't jump up and down when I give you a qualified yes. A fourteen- and sixteen-year-old are very hormonal and curious, but don't forbid Lucy from dating Kevin. That would be a major mistake, because she will see him behind your back. She is being so responsible by running this by you. I would have a talk with Lucy. Here's a **script**: "Lucy, I would prefer your going out with someone your own age. However, you can go out with Kevin provided that I help you set some age-appropriate personal limits and boundaries for you both. Let me help you with this, Lucy. I know this sounds a bit corny, but Dad and I will 'lend you our brains' and help you have a keen conscience that will guide you to think before you impulsively act out. Imagine having a self-protective thermometer and barometer, so that you can measure the temperature and pressure of any sexual situations that will arise. You need to stay alert and know when to pull back or simply say, 'No thanks, Kevin.'"

I have a feeling your daughter will go along with the script because she will be thrilled that you are cooperating with her dating Kevin without giving her a hard time. It's a wonderful thing to have your daughter be upfront with you and it sets the precedent for her coming to you because of your helpfulness and approachability.

WHY DIDN'T HE CALL?

Dear Arden,
My daughter, Nicole, eighteen, is a college freshman on break. She is pacing around the house like a tiger that just got let out of her cage.

She looks so unhappy. I ask her, "What's wrong, Nicole? You don't seem like yourself." Well, she starts to bark at me, "I'm fine, Mom, just fine." I persist because she looks so miserable. "Nicole, please tell me, honey. Maybe I can help?" She sighs, "Ugh, guys are so ridiculous. This cute guy asked me for my number a few days ago. We go to school together. He could have Facebooked me or IMe'd, but he asks for my number. Okay, so I give it to him. So now, do I hear from him? Noooo! What gives?" She adds, "He seemed really into me..." "So call him," I tell her, and she says, "No way, Mom! There are rules. You don't just do that. I'll seem too desperate." Help me out here, Arden. I just don't get it! Are there rules?

Oh, boy, I can see that times have not changed too much. I can remember waiting at home by the phone for that call for a date. At least with the cell phone, teens these days can have the freedom of leaving home and living their lives while they wait for that call! Unfortunately, they can also see whether the guy tried to reach them or not. When he doesn't call, it's a major annoyance, a distraction, and a possible rejection. It's perfectly natural to wonder, "Can't he at least text me? What's the big deal?" These are all very valid questions.

In the meantime, moms must realize that dating is a far less formal activity than it was in their heyday. Thanks to cell phones, meet-ups are more casual now and on the fly, with lots of teens opting to hang out in groups or clump together. They might start off planning to go to the movies, but end up watching a video or playing video games or stopping for a pizza instead.

As to whether Nicole wants to call him or text him, that's her call. I asked several teenagers what they would do, and they said that they would text something like, "What's up?" Not from an angry place, just very casually, as if they were passing each other on campus. She can try that. He will get the text, so there's no excuse for not answering. I spoke to a few teens who found this option better than calling, and not so desperate-sounding. Some of them spoke from experience. As one girl said, "Guys can be so excited at one moment and then get all weirded out and need their space."

So for now, it's touch and go. Nicole may need to wait until break's over. It's so much easier and more natural to get together when they run into each other on campus, can see each other's faces and reactions, and decide to take a walk or visit each other's dorms. And there's a lot less pressure too.

SAME-SEX SMOOCH

Dear Arden,
I caught my fourteen-year-old daughter, Bailey, making out on her bed with her best friend. She said she was just curious. She added that at parties all the kids make out with each other, it's no big deal—girls and boys, girls and girls, and boys and boys. They make "a cuddle puddle," which sounds to me like a group hug that just keeps on going, or groping. Could my daughter be a lesbian? I started crying because she is an only child and I really wanted grandchildren!

Bailey seems to be experimenting for the moment. It's not uncommon for both straight and gay teens to become very, very close with their BFFs. They have sleepovers and stay in the same bed and can see each other morning, noon, and night. They borrow each other's makeup and clothing and share their deepest secrets and intimacies about themselves.

Teens have strong internal sexual longings that drive them. With gay and lesbian youth, some researchers propose an early genetic predisposition; others see it as a combination of nature and nurture. I have worked extensively with gay and lesbian youth coming out. There is so much questioning and puppy-love crushes before they are even comfortable emerging.

And if Bailey is a lesbian, you'll have to be mindful that she is internally questioning how she is feeling. Some teens are quietly aware of their attraction to the same gender as early as middle school. By the time they reach high school and college, they may have come out. Even though there is so much more cultural, peer, and familial acceptance these days, it is still a sweaty and anxious internal process to step up, step forward, step out, and come out.

For the time being, let's not box Bailey in and just let her be. Step back a bit and see her wing-flexing as an adventure in discovering who she is. Your thrust is to be open, flexible, loving, and unconditionally accepting of your incredible daughter. She will love you for it!

WALLFLOWER

Dear Arden,

My daughter, Eden, is almost seventeen years old and has never been on a date. (I tell myself she's not in full bloom like her other girlfriends.) I see her girlfriends talk about their boyfriends or guys in general, and she just sits quietly in the corner. She is adorable, shy, sweet, and kind but I fear she is losing step and falling behind. Sometimes I try to reassure myself that she is just an "emotional year" younger, but other times I see the pain on her face and fear that she is becoming a solitary outcast. I remember what it was like to be a third wheel when I tagged along on my older sister's dates. I love my daughter. Is there anything I can do to nudge her forward?

It sounds like Eden has not fully found herself yet. Every teenager flowers into a full-bodied rose at her own developmental pace. Perhaps you were a late bloomer as well? Her self-conscious and shy demeanor is what's holding her back. It takes only one friend to help pull her out of herself. Does she have a pal who is more forward and gutsy? If she does, I would encourage Eden to make plans with her. The two of them can go get their nails done, take a Pilates class, go to the beach, or go on a family vacation. The other thought is that she could do some volunteer work and some community service. That's a surefire way to meet other teens. She can join a youth club at a YMCA and become active in the youth groups at your place of worship. I have a feeling that in another year, when she's launched into college, she will have many more opportunities to meet a whole new set of friends and roommates.

HATES HER DATES

Dear Arden,
I don't like the boys my sixteen-year-old daughter dates. Sometimes I think she is just trying to shock her father and me. Her father yells, "Do you think you could find a guy without tattoos or body piercings, Christina? Why do you have to bring home these losers?" Then the situation turns into one big shouting match.

Sounds like Christina doesn't want to be set up with who you both think is best for her. She feels criticized, judged, hurt, and angry that her conscious choice of male dates is being solely based on their appearances. Teens are very sensitive to their parents' opinions and seek their approval, and want to be understood. Even though you may think she is acting in a rebellious manner, and maybe she is, she wants to be respected by you both.

I think we need to start from scratch. Rather than attack her choices, share with her what makes you nervous or anxious about piercings and tattoos. Does something negative come to your minds? Do you think Christina is not safe, that something could happen to her? Perhaps Dad is acting out of his need to be protective of his daughter. He unfortunately is going about it in such a way as to drive your daughter away. Maybe biting your tongues a bit and allowing your daughter not only to date these fellows but showing some interest in meeting them will help calm you all. You may be very surprised that underneath all the tattoos and body piercings is actually a nice guy, albeit one with an unconventional appearance.

A PROPER INTRODUCTION

Dear Arden,

My husband is very old-fashioned. He insists that our daughter Kelsey's dates come up to the house to meet him before they go out. She shakes her head—"No way!"—and says it's too embarrassing. She's sixteen and doesn't want anyone to meet her dates until she knows "they're cool." Who's right? Since she plans to live at home during her first few years at college, we need to figure out what's acceptable protocol now.

Your husband is not old-fashioned as much as curious. He wants to have the opportunity to meet her dates and get first impressions of them. Dads can feel left out of the loop and a bit protective; after all, Kelsey was and may still be Daddy's little girl. If you try to explain this to your daughter, she may balk and roll her eyes, "Geez, you have to meet every guy, even the ones I think I'm not interested in yet? Ugh!"

Here's a hint: the guy Kelsey does bring home is the one she likes. Dad, you will have lots of chances to say hello and shake his hand. Hopefully you will get the opportunity for more contact and target practice later. (Just kidding!)

As your daughter gets older, you will have set precedents that show her just how much her parents care about her safety and welfare. Who knows? She may even realize that you both are just looking out for her, and she may feel appreciative that you love her so much.

So let it go for now, just a bit, and keep a casual tab on her social life.

NO BENEFITS

Dear Arden,

I recently found my fourteen-year-old daughter, Darcy, crying in the bathroom. She was hysterical. She said she had been fooling around with this older boy who told her that he loved her and was seeing only her. It turns out that he was a player, and he was dating and hooking up with other girls on the side. Then he told her he just wanted to be "friends with benefits." When she started crying, he told her she was being "a big baby" and "lots of older girls do it."

Awww, what an introduction to sexual contact or, as your daughter calls it, "fooling around." Darcy had no idea what she was walking into—it was a setup from the start. This fellow sounds very practiced at what he does. He knows what to say to get what he wants.

There are guys who openly flirt with other girls and ex-girlfriends, hoping the girls will turn on and attack each other. These dudes get a huge ego boost from the thought of girls fighting over them. Physical fights between girls have become a common sight in high school hallways and restrooms, with girls pulling each other's hair, screaming, scratching, and hitting each other.

So many of my fourteen-year-old patients in high school felt so flattered the first time senior boys paid attention to them. It gave them a special status in high school, made them more visible and popular. It's easy to see how your daughter could feel flattered by the attention of an older boy. Certainly this can backfire, and it sounds like it already has. Darcy was vulnerable, and she naïvely believed that their connection was real and exclusive, until she found out he was a player and was hooking up with other girls.

Mom, comfort your daughter and let her know, as she understands all too well now, that he was using her as he would any other girl who lets him. Give her a hug for being gutsy and confronting him, because this is no small thing for a fourteen-year-old! Tell Darcy that she deserves better treatment and that she will learn from this painful lesson. One simple way to see who is lying and who is telling the truth: notice what a person does, not just what he says, and give yourself enough time to know a person. People can be on their very best behavior for the first few weeks before showing their true colors. They will say a lot to get a girl to like and trust them. Encourage Darcy to be more selective next time—to pick a guy who won't pressure her to do and be something that she is not. Tell her to do the choosing. Caution her to watch where she swims and to keep a close eye on who is swimming around her.

SECRET CRUSH

Dear Arden,

My fifteen-year-old daughter, Becky, has a crush on another girl who is pretty, popular, and very straight. Recently she told this girl about her feelings, but this girl turned her down and told her she is not interested. My daughter expected the rejection—this girl is a cheer-leader, with a boyfriend on the football team—so I don't know why she decided to come out this way. Do you? We live in a small town and a confession like this is social suicide.

Mom, does Becky watch the hit TV show *Glee*? I hope she does and that she saw the episode in which Kurt, a gay male Glee Club member, starts to flirt and come on too strongly to Finn, a straight male Glee Club member. Finn got so upset with Kurt and let him know so directly, more than once. If your daughter happened to see this, she would have witnessed Kurt's sense of deep hurt, rejection, and anger.

Kurt knew that Finn was straight, but it just didn't seem to make any difference to him. He had a crush on Finn. He was des-perate for a boyfriend. My heart was in my mouth while watching this—it was easy to see what was coming next. Ouch! You may reflect, "Becky did the same thing. Why didn't she protect herself more? Why did she shoot herself in the leg like that?" You can ask why, but then you have to try and figure out what you can do to soothe your daughter's bruised heart and soul.

I recall the conversation Kurt had with his father. No matter what Dad said or how he said it, his son felt so wounded. When Kurt sobbed, "When am I going to have someone special in my life?" Dad reassured him of how special and lovable he was and told him that it would happen one day. It was a powerful teaching and learning moment. Your daughter had such urgency to come out and find love. She was clouded and fueled by tremendous overwhelming anxiety. She really was not thinking about her impact.

Mom, watch this *Glee* episode with Becky. She will get it and understand, and you will recognize that your validation of her specialness, for the moment, will put salve on a deeply complicated wound. Does your small town have a rainbow-friendly group or club for her? If not, perhaps she could start one. For starters, open up her world and go online with her to look into PFLAG (Parents and Friends of Lesbians and Gays) and GLSEN (Gay, Lesbian, and Straight Education Network). Becky needs to feel and see that she is not alone, that there is a wonderful and friendly assortment of people out there just like her, who just want what most people want—someone to love them outside of their parents, friends, and extended family.

SEXY PROFILE

Dear Arden,

I was shocked to discover that my fifteen-year-old daughter, Melody, posted a profile on a popular dating website. In the photos she is posed very provocatively and lists her age as twenty-one—and she looks it. I immediately ordered her to take down the profile, but she just laughed at me and said she would put it back up again. I am so afraid for her! What if she decides to meet one of them and he turns out to be a pervert or a creep? Some of the men who responded to her profile were in their forties, close to her father's age. Her father and I are divorced. He is a successful businessman and recently remarried. Between his business ventures and his new young wife, he rarely has time to see our daughter. When she does visit him, he is very cold and remote.

Mom, I am so sorry to hear this. Generally at fifteen, daughters can be a bit hormonal and boy-crazy for guys her age and a few years older. But Melody is seeking out the attentions of older, wealthy, professional men. This prototype is a dead ringer for your ex-husband. Most likely, she is copying what she thinks her father finds worthy of his time in his sexy, young wife.

Melody is a child playing a dangerous and adult game of dress-up. Putting herself out there as a sexually desirable and mature woman is risky business. No doubt her new look is garnering plenty of attention from strangers. Ironically, she feels heady and power-ful but is also putting herself in grave danger. She is way over the edge and can get hurt or worse. She is being particularly provoca-tive, derisive, and rebellious with you.

Please talk with her about the dangers of posting intimate photos of herself on a dating site. Some pictures can linger in cyberspace for years, even after you take down the profile. Talk to her about how individuals can misrepresent themselves on the Internet. Melody could be seduced, manipulated, kidnapped, or placed in some very dangerous and compromising positions and situations. Sexual predators are a very real, dark, and scary reality of her rich fantasy life online.

I don't think she fully understands what she is doing. The sad-dest part to all of this is that if Melody was getting more than a few crumbs of attention from her father, she would probably still be testing the boundaries, but not so provocatively.

You will need to monitor her computer and cell phone usage, especially social networking sites like Facebook and MySpace, along with her IMs, texts, and Skype chats. Keep a close eye on her whereabouts and her comings and goings.

Enlist the help of her sisters, friends, and cousins. They know what's going on and will immediately see how vulnerable and exposed your daughter is. You can ask a trusted female adult friend, teacher, doctor, or nurse to speak to Melody as well. If all else fails, an intervention is in order. Sometimes, these online personas can take on secret lives of their own and set a girl on a path to becoming a runaway or a prostitute. If you suspect that a line has been crossed and that she is sexually active as a minor, you might want to take criminal action against her adult suitors. At the very least, you can email the dating site and inform them of her real age. If she has been having unprotected sex, she will need to be tested for STDs, as some of them can result in infertility or cancer. Right now, she might not imagine a day when she wants to have children of her own, but as her mother, it's your job to hold out the promise of such a happy ending for her.

TOXIC LOVE

Dear Arden,

My daughter, Amber, is a freshman in college, and she is deep in the throes of her first serious relationship. One day she's ecstatic and blissful and the next day, she is edgy, out of sorts, teary, and explosive. Yesterday, I overheard her sobbing in her room and apologizing to her boyfriend on her cell phone. When I walked in, she wailed, "Jake just broke up with me! He thinks I cheated on him, but I didn't. I went to a party and I talked to my friends. No big deal. Yes, my ex-boyfriend Kyle was there but I didn't do anything. Now Jake is accusing me of wanting to go back out with Kyle. He is so jealous. I love him, but he is driving me crazy and now he wants to break up because of something I didn't do! I just want him back, Mom, how do I get him back?" Over Christmas break, she actually talked about taking a semester off from college so she could move into an off-campus apartment with him.

This is a really challenging one! Okay, so Amber has a very jealous and possessive boyfriend. It sounds like he has trust issues and a temper. How does his lack of trust make her feel? Is he so squeaky clean? I wonder. Why does he have to make your daughter be the cheater?

I am detecting a lot of red flags here. Can Amber maintain her connections with family and friends, including boys? That is so very important. Does he demand that she spend all of her time with him? Does he have a Jekyll and Hyde personality—can he be loving one minute and angry and abusive the next? Has she given up activities she used to love in order to be with him? Does she work too hard at the relationship and come down hard on herself? Is she in a panic all the time, trying to soothe him or please him?

Sometimes the thrill and passion of a first love—and the thought of losing it—can cause people to act obsessively. As one person vies for control of the relationship, the accusations and ultimatums can really escalate. It's not uncommon to hear cries of "You don't love me!" or "If you really loved me, you would do this!" Your daughter's boyfriend may be feeling insecure about himself or mirroring and imitating unhealthy behavior he's witnessed at home. If his parents had a tempestuous or abusive relationship, it may be hard for him to break free of these patterns. Or maybe he likes to pick fights with your daughter and throw her off balance. This kind of drama can be very addictive. As the relationship swings from highs to lows and back again, there are many breakups and the reconciliations. This is heady stuff for a teenager. Amber may think to herself, "He must really love me to go off the deep end this way." If he has threatened to commit suicide or hurt himself, she may be feeling even more tied to him and responsible. It's up to you, as her parent, to set her straight.

By the way, guys are not the only ones who can go over the top. I have witnessed many drama queens over the years. One nineteen-year-old I know seemed to be quite normal until she got a boyfriend on one of those dating websites. If she is with him, she's fine, but when they are separated from each other, she screams at him on the phone, throws temper tantrums, and accuses him of flirting with her friends. If he doesn't respond to her texts right away, she shows up where he works to find out why. It's a shame she is so bossy and controlling of him. He seems like a nice enough guy, but I don't think he will put up with her behavior for much longer.

If you suspect your daughter is in an abusive relationship...

- Validate and respect your daughter's feelings, boundaries, and confidentiality.
- Listen to her concerns and fears in a nonjudgmental way, and keep the lines of communication open.
- Recognize that she loves him and feels responsible for him.

- Realize that she feels torn between staying and leaving. If you pressure her to leave, she may boomerang right back to him.
- Understand that she views aspects of the relationship as positive. For instance, she may see his jealous rages as proof of his passion and love for her.
- Gently point out any discrepancies in the relationship. For instance, he has to know her whereabouts at all times but refuses to tell her where he's going.
- Let her know that she can come to you and ask for help at any time.
- Resist the urge to take charge of her life, as that will only support the idea that she is incapable of making decisions for herself.
- Don't threaten to cut her off from the family or issue her any ultimatums.
- Express your concern for her in case he becomes violent.
- Contact a local domestic violence agency for help and support.
- Be there to help her if she decides to leave him and help her come up with a plan for her escape and safety.

FORBIDDEN LOVE

Dear Arden,

My sixteen-year-old daughter, Natalie, was in a relationship with her soccer teammate, Beth. The girls told everybody they were "best friends" to throw off suspicions, but they have known they were in love with each other for a few years. Now Beth's parents (who are very conservative) have forbidden their daughter from having any contact with Nat. I was shocked when I found out the true nature of Nat and Beth's relationship, but I can see how much my daughter is suffering. She's hurting, angry, and sad. She feels she has lost her best friend in the whole world and is not allowed to talk to her. What can I say to comfort her?

It feels like this is still very fresh and raw! Perhaps Beth's parents had no clue of their daughter's leanings and sexuality. Temporarily forbidding Beth from having any contact with Nat is their overreaction based on shock and anger. But forbidding the girls from seeing each other will not change Beth and Nat's attraction and deep connection. Beth may go along on the surface for fear of angering her parents, but eventually the girls will see each other again behind their backs.

Are they still soccer teammates? Are Beth's parents threatening to take her off the soccer team and change her school? Will they be shutting down her Facebook or taking her cell phone away? I sure hope not. It will serve no purpose; if anything, quite the opposite. When parents demand and force a severing of a relationship, generally it boomerangs in their faces.

I can imagine your daughter is hurting, devastated, frightened, and confused. Your being more concerned about her welfare at this point speaks volumes about the quality of the connection you have with your daughter. Tell her, "I am here for you, Nat, to listen, to be there in any way that you need or want me." Reassuring her about how much you value her, how much she matters, and how much you love her—no matter what—will be incredibly validating.

She will need all the support she can get. Since she and Beth were hiding out for the past few years, they must have known that certain people would react very strongly against them and to the news of their professed love. I am so sorry that she has to go through this. This is where tolerance is not enough. She will need to feel acceptance and compassion from you and her friends. Beth and Nat need to figure out what their next steps are. Perhaps when things calm down, they can run some ideas and thoughts by you.

SCARED FOR HER SAFETY

Dear Arden,
Now that my daughter, Amanda, is eighteen and out and about in the world, she is studying, working, and traveling independently. She is meeting and dating new people. Even though I am not with her, or even living close by, how can I protect her and keep her safe from the threat of date rape and other forms of sexual assault?

Among teenagers, date rape is the most common form of sexual assault. Here are some cautionary measures Amanda needs to take seriously to responsibly educate, empower, and protect herself from such a dreaded assault.

The Wrong Kind of Guy Red Flags

1. Too controlling. He tells you who to be friends with, or how to dress, or he tries to control other elements of your life.
2. Emotionally abusive. He insults you, puts down your accomplishments, and acts sulky or angry when you think for yourself and initiate an action or idea.
3. Acts superior. He does not see you as an equal, either

because he is older or because he believes himself to be worldlier, smarter, and more experienced than you are.

4. Jealous. He gets jealous for no reason.
5. Intimidating. He openly sneers at you and belittles your efforts.
6. Can't take rejection. He is unable to handle sexual or emotional frustrations without getting angry.
7. Talks negatively about women. A red flag for misogyny.
8. Drinks heavily and abuses drugs. He tries to get you drunk or berates you for not getting high with him, sometimes before having sex.
9. Physically violent. He becomes explosive and turns suddenly violent—striking, slapping, shoving, or kicking you, or dragging you across the floor.
10. Has a fascination with death. He is fascinated by death and weapons.
11. Bullies. He enjoys being cruel to animals, children, or people he can easily push around.
12. Suicidal. He threatens to commit suicide if you want to break up with him or leave him. This is a very manipulative form of emotional blackmail.

Date Rape Statistics

- Among teenage rape victims, date rape (also known as acquaintance rape) is the most common form of sexual assault.
- Six out of ten rapes among young women occur *in a familiar place*—at home, in a relative's home, or in a friend's home.

- Roughly 44 percent of rape victims are under the age of eighteen.
- Sixty-eight percent of young women who were raped knew their attackers.

FOR YOUR DAUGHTER:
PROTECTING YOURSELF

1. Remember, you have the right to set sexual limits and boundaries and to communicate those limits as well. Sex must be mutual and consensual.
2. Be assertive. No means no!
3. Ask around about a new date and check his background.
4. For the first date, arrange to meet him in a public place. Notify others of your plans and whereabouts. Give details of the date to a friend who can check in on you later.
5. Be careful of whom you invite into your home. Remain cautious when entering someone else's home. You might think you're having a chat and just hanging out, but he may misinterpret your invitation to go inside as an invitation for sex.
6. Alcohol and drugs can impair your judgment and your partner's judgment. Many rapes go unreported because teens are afraid they will get into trouble for using illegal substances like drugs and alcohol. Stay sober and remain in control, especially on a first date.
7. Take your own car and bring enough cash to get home in case of an emergency.
8. If you're going to a party and you're not familiar with the

host or the neighborhood, don't go alone. Go with a group of friends.

9. Learn how to take care of yourself. Take a self-defense course, kick-boxing class, or martial arts class.

10. Trust your gut. First impressions are the most powerful. Cut the date short if your date is too aggressive or creeps you out.

11. College students need to take special precautions. Don't go to a party alone or walk on campus alone after dark. Wait to go on a date until you know him well and feel comfortable around him, especially if he's a senior. Be vigilant. After all, there is only one special you, and you need to be intelligent and protective of yourself.

If You Do Find Yourself in a Potential Date-Rape Situation

- Stay calm and assess the situation, then act quickly.
- Try to yell, get away, and scream for help.
- If necessary, attack forcefully with your elbow. It's the hardest bone in your body.
- Buy time with talk. Keep talking to distract him. Derail his idea of seduction by making yourself appear less attractive and appealing to him.
- Remember, giving in is not consent. Do not blame yourself for the assault if you've been overpowered.

SOS, PLEASE SOMEONE
HELP MY DAUGHTER

My daughter, Justine, is sixteen. She is a smart, well-read, and respectful young lady who has been through too much. I feel so guilty that Justine witnessed her father's verbal and physical abuse of me. He did not physically hurt her. I made sure of that. But I know she was emotionally scarred. You will be happy to know that I divorced her father when she was ten years old. She has visitation with him, which has not ever pleased me. She loves her father and prefers not to talk about his past violent behavior.

What concerns me is how she could have chosen to be with her first boyfriend, Tommy. I get very bad feelings about him. I don't like the way he puts her down and belittles her. She is constantly making excuses for his actions. He drinks—I know lots of teens do, but I believe he does to an excess, like my ex did. He does poorly in school, doesn't work, and expects my daughter to foot the bill. Her close girl-friends have fallen by the wayside. I don't think they like him, and honestly I think he doesn't mind.

The other day, Justine's eyes were bloodshot, not from drinking but from crying. I saw fingerprints on her arms and scratches on her neck. When I try to talk to her, she gets protective of him, angry and defensive. The most she says is that he has a temper. This is too close to home for me. What can I do?

This sounds like a reenactment, a replication of Justine witnessing the verbal and physical abuse you were subjected to from your ex. I can imagine Justine trying to help and protect you when she was a child. At times, however, when she was confused and feeling disloyal to her father, she probably rationalized, excused, and minimized her father's outrageous behavior toward you. Now she is unwittingly minimizing Tommy's negative and violent behavior. It sounds like she is covering up for him and is trying to save him (her old childhood wish to save her father).

You are right that she is tolerating abusive treatment from him. Relationship violence with an intimate partner can be brutal. I advise tweens, teens, and young adults to run away as fast as they can from any boy or man who displays the characteristics I talk about in the section "The Wrong Kind of Guy Red Flags" earlier in this chapter.

Please sit down with Justine and let her read my advice to be aware of the wrong kind of guy. Refer to the "Toxic Love" section earlier in this chapter and the "Black and Blue" section in Chapter 10.

I also suggest that both you and Justine go for family counselling. There is much to be addressed that will help open your daughter's eyes to what she is doing and putting up with. She doesn't deserve this treatment, and I feel that you need to steer her in the direction to realize that. She may resist, but just let her know how much you love her and want what's best for her.

CHAPTER 10

Sex

"Telling a teenager the facts of life is like giving a fish a bath."

—Arnold H. Glasgow

It happens time and time again. Mothers come to me or write to me in a panic because they've found out something about their daughters and sex, something that shocked them. Maybe they discovered condoms in their daughter's underwear drawer. Or maybe they saw some sexy text messages between her and her boyfriend. Or maybe it was something less subtle, like stumbling across your daughter's porn collection on her laptop.

I always ask, "Have you talked to your daughter about sex?" The answer is often some version of "sort of." When it comes to sex, there is no "sort of." Sex is not a vague, abstract quality. It's tangible and real. In my experience, most moms educate their daughters about the practicalities of the birds and the bees, but many shy away from talking about any values and emotions involved.

None of us really wants to think of our teenage daughters as sexual beings, but the statistics here are clear. The vast majority of kids will lose their virginity during their teenage years, and a significant number will do so before the tender age of fourteen. In fact, within that young age group, girls are more likely to become sexually active than boys. Not only do we have to talk to our daughters about sex, we have to do it early and often. It's a wake-up call for us moms and a true test of our connection with our daughters.

For many parents, there is an imaginary dividing line between "before sex" and "after sex." Before sex, your daughter was a sleeping beauty, waiting to wake up, but you can't expect her to keep her eyes closed forever. She's going to turn on all the lights so she can finally see what she's been missing.

The sexual landscape is electric with opportunities to connect, and charged with emotion and passion for your daughter. That beep on your daughter's cell phone could be a text from her boyfriend or a potential hook-up: *are you there? can you meet me?*

Here's the deal, Mom: teens are waiting longer to have sex, but they are experimenting with oral sex and anal sex at much younger ages. Teens may not be "doing it" as much, but they are definitely thinking about it, watching it in the form of porn, and experimenting.

The majority of young people have sex for the first time at age seventeen and get married in their mid- or late twenties. That puts young women at risk for unwanted pregnancy and sexually transmitted diseases (STDs) for nearly *a decade* before marrying. And since the average age for cohabitation and marriage is going up, the wait could be even longer than that.

Latest Statistics on Teen Sex

- According to the Guttmacher Institute, nearly half of all fifteen- to nineteen-year-olds in the United States have had sex at least once.
- By age fifteen, only 13 percent of unmarried teens have ever had sex.
- By age nineteen, seven out of ten unmarried teens have engaged in sexual intercourse.
- Nearly 60 percent of sexually experienced female teens had a first sexual partner who was one to three years older. Eight percent of sexually experienced female teens had first partners who were six or more years older.
- More than three-quarters of teen females report that their first sexual experience was with a steady boyfriend, a fiancé, a husband, or a live-in partner.

IT HAPPENED TO ME: "WHY DID I DO IT?"

Quinn, a seventeen-year-old senior, recounted to me in a therapy session how she regretted giving oral sex, or BJs (blow jobs), when she was younger: "I was so young and stupid. I was fourteen, a freshman in high school, and I wanted to be popular. I made friends with a few girls who were just like me. I highlighted my hair, got into cheerleading, and became fast friends with all of the male athletes. I was really flattered by their attention, especially the seniors. My parents were so clueless. I had parties at my house. It was so easy to get alcohol. I smoked pot and drank. At 'rainbow parties,' I put on a particular shade of lipstick—all the girls did, just different shades—and we competed to see who could get a penis deepest in her mouth and leave a ring of color farthest from the tip. The boys competed to see who could get the most colors. It was so funny then. Giving a BJ seemed natural; all the cool girls were doing it, so I did it too. I did not feel like a slut. I did not get emotionally involved with any of the guys. It was not sex, I couldn't get pregnant. I had no idea about 'saving it' for someone special. I really didn't think that far. Now I see how dumb it was. It was all about fitting in, but I felt lost and uncertain.

"If my parents had known what I was doing, they would have been furious with me. I really did not talk with them and they just didn't get it or get me, for that matter. I guess I was really angry with them for not caring enough. I know I would have fought them if they held me more accountable, but I think it would have been better for me. I now hold myself to a different set of values. Yes, I still smoke pot, but not like I used to, and I don't give casual BJs any more. Those days are over. That's so not cool. I am so lucky that I never got herpes or some other STD."

Mom Alert

Be mindful, not every girl is giving a boy/young man oral sex, no matter what your daughter might be thinking or saying to herself and you.

After speaking to a number of moms in my practice, working with some younger teenagers that were on the surface making it appear that having oral sex was "just like kissing," I was determined to get to what's really underneath this urgent, anxious, impulsive, reckless acting out. Our daughters feel driven to be popular, seen as cool and fitting in on the surface. However, once I dive in with them, they start to sound very confused, embarrassed, and uncomfortable and start to wonder what really drove them. Tween and younger teen girls want to please, especially boys. They are very insecure and anxious about asserting themselves, especially around something sexual. When exploring together, they reveal that they can be easily coerced by a guy saying "It's no big deal" or putting his hand to her head and directing the action. Even if your tween/teen daughter says no, how strong is her no? Is it a NO, said with assertion? That's a lot to ask of our younger girls. The bigger issue here is about being taken seriously, firstly by herself, and secondly by the boy/young man. It's so important for your daughter to see and consistently observe that you take yourself seriously, that you have self-respect and are treated by the significant men in your life with high regard. As moms, we have a tremendous impact on our daughters.

"THAT'S NOT SEX!" OR IS IT?

Many teens don't think that oral sex or anal sex is really sex. To them, sex is vaginal intercourse and vaginal intercourse only. Some teens engage in oral and anal sex, thinking it's a way to stay virgins. Kids also opt for oral sex because they don't have to worry about pregnancy.

But the truth is that you *can* contract sexually transmitted diseases through oral, vaginal, and anal sex—and pass them to your partner. Tissues may tear during anal sex, leaving partners more vulnerable to the transmission of bodily fluids and sexually transmitted diseases through the blood, and putting young adults at far greater risk of contracting HIV and AIDS. The ignorance of proper hygiene during anal sex can also result in a urinary tract or a vaginal infection.

It's also possible for people to contract STDs such as genital warts (HPV) and herpes through skin-to-skin contact, without penetration, just from lying naked next to each other. Herpes can be transmitted during unprotected oral sex. Every year, roughly 30 percent of new herpes infections are transmitted through oral sex, when a partner with oral herpes transmits the virus to his or her partner's genitals. The opposite also can happen: herpes can be passed from one partner's genitals to the other partner's mouth. In rare circumstances, it is possible for herpes to be passed to the rectum and other parts of the body, especially if there is broken skin and an infected sore or fluid. Also in rare instances, herpes can be passed to the eye and trachea. People with herpes can be contagious without showing any symptoms of the disease and can spread the virus unintentionally.

The Facts on STDs

- About four million teens contract a sexually transmitted disease every year.
- One in two sexually active youths will contract an STD by age twenty-five.
- Although fifteen- to twenty-four-year-olds only represent one-quarter of the sexually active population, they account for nearly half of the 18.9 million new cases of STDs each year.

- Human papillomavirus (HPV) infections account for roughly half of the STDs diagnosed among fifteen- to twenty-four-year-olds each year.
- According to the Kaiser Foundation, more than one-third of new HIV infections in the United States occur among people between the ages of thirteen and twenty-nine.

THE TRUTH ABOUT HPV AND CHLAMYDIA

Human papillomavirus, or HPV, accounts for nearly half of all sexually transmitted infections among fifteen- to twenty-four-year-olds. HPV can be asymptomatic (that is, it produces no symptoms) and spread through skin-to-skin contact and sexual contact. If not detected or treated, certain strains of HPV can lead to cervical cancer. In 2006, the U.S. Food and Drug Administration approved the vaccine Gardasil for use among girls and women ages nine to twenty-six in order to prevent infection with the types of HPV most likely to cause cervical cancer.

The number of new chlamydia cases is so high among teens that it has been called a silent epidemic. Chlamydia is a common bacterial infection that is easily cured but hard to detect since it is asymptomatic. Seventy-five percent of women who are infected with chlamydia show no symptoms. Chlamydia is most prevalent among persons ages fifteen to twenty-four, with the majority of new cases in young adults in their teens and also the age group nineteen to twenty-four years of age (79 percent).

Only an estimated 30 to 45 percent of eligible young females were screened for chlamydia in 2003. If a young woman contracts chlamydia in high school or college and it goes undiagnosed and untreated, it can eventually result in endometriosis, infertility problems, and sterility. The *American Journal of Public Health* reports that 15 percent of women who are infertile cannot conceive solely because of an untreated STD. Forty percent of untreated chlamydia cases lead to pelvic inflammatory disease (PID). The disease can progress and go undetected for years; it can be heartbreaking for couples hoping to start a family later in life. Symptoms may or may not be present. Sexually active females need to request individual tests for chlamydia, gonorrhea, syphilis, and other STDs at the gynecologist's office or in a clinic, since tests for these infections are not always part of a routine office visit. This is especially true if your daughter has been having unprotected sex. If you are not sure which tests to request, simply inform the doctor that your daughter has been having unprotected sex and the doctor will determine which tests to administer.

THE THONG SONG

Dear Arden,

When I was putting the laundry away in my fourteen-year-old daughter Elizabeth's underwear drawer, I discovered a tiny, black lace thong with a bunny pom-pom on the rear, a very sexy push-up bra, massage oil, a vibrator, and a box of condoms. The "outfit" didn't bother me so much as the vibrator and the condoms. I confronted her about it and asked, "Why did you buy condoms?" and "Do you have someone in mind that you are going to experiment with?"

Her answer: "Mom, I want to be prepared, I don't have a boyfriend

yet." I asked her, "Do you know any girls having sex?" She answered, "No, I don't know anyone, Mom."
We have had the birds and the bees talk, but honestly I was not prepared for this so soon. Maybe having talks about being with someone special has encouraged her to think too much about sex? She does get a lot of attention from boys, especially older ones. I don't know if I can believe her. She may have a boyfriend and be embarrassed; then again, she said she does not. Isn't she being precocious to be thinking ahead? This is all so confusing to me.

This is a tough one. Think back to when you were talking with her. Did you pick up any nonverbal cues (see Chapter 1)? Was Elizabeth looking away from you, rolling her eyes up to the ceiling? Was she upset with you? Did she become defensive? I am not picking up any anger. She didn't even sound surprised or startled that you found her stash so easily. I'm surprised she didn't hide it better. Maybe she wanted you to find it. If she has experimented at all, she has picked up some preventative messages to protect herself from an unwanted pregnancy or STD. She has certainly made her way to a Victoria's Secret type of store, has had health class, and probably has spoken to some of her sexually active peers. It sounds like she may be having some sexual contact.

Elizabeth's image of sex is all about what she's seen, which is not surprising given how oversexualized our culture is and the depiction of teen sexuality in the movies, in magazines, on television, and porn on the Internet. The painful reality is that girls two years younger than your daughter are engaging in oral, anal, and vaginal intercourse.

It's never too late to anticipate and be prepared. Share with your daughter this **script**: "Honey, I am feeling very confused and anxious. I have a feeling in my gut, the TUG that something's up. It's almost like you left this stuff around for me to find and you want to tell me something. Whatever it is, if it is anything, I promise not to be mad with you. If you are doing anything with a boy your age or older, like sexually experimenting, be aware that there is great potential for your being used, taken advantage of, terribly hurt, and devastated." She may look at you like you have ten heads, but that's okay. Elizabeth really could be struggling with this, and she may be feeling guilty about what she's done.

Use a TV program geared for a teen audience—there are so many these days—as a springboard for discussion about girls who rush into sex. Make it a transformative teaching moment while you choose the right time and place by spontaneously emphasizing the value of waiting for that special someone. Elizabeth may frown a bit and not like what you are saying, but that's okay. Do your best to slow her down.

Be wary of unsupervised parties with older teens present. I know a few kids whose high schools begin in eighth grade. Drive your daughter to her destinations and pick her up. Know where she is going and whom she is seeing. Do I sound a bit protective? You bet I do! Be a tiger here, and "lend your brain," whether she likes it or not.

PORN TO BE WILD

Dear Arden,
Recently I was changing the sheets on my thirteen-year-old daughter Emma's bed when I noticed she had left her laptop open. As I tried to close it, an XXX-rated porn film came bursting to life on the screen. The sexual action was so explicit and frenzied, I felt sick. Is this what she's

doing when she goes into her room and closes the door? I am beside myself. I have two other children, a twelve-year-old daughter and an eleven-year-old son, and if I could stumble across it, so could they. I wonder if she watches it alone, or with friends. How could I have missed this? I have always tried to respect my daughter's privacy, but now I think I will have to start spying on her and monitor what she's doing.

Porn is everywhere. You can watch it on cable TV, or on a DVD, but for Emma's watching to go unnoticed, she'd have to watch porn on the computer. And if she has a computer in her room, that means she has twenty-four-hour access to XXX-rated action whenever she wants. We have an extremely overexposed, overstimulated generation of tweens and teens who think they have to be doing something exciting all the time or else life is one big bore! Lots of today's teenagers don't understand the point of idleness. They don't allow themselves time for reflection or quiet contemplation. Instead, they look externally. They haven't figured out yet how to make use of those precious and gorgeous moments that don't have to be full of activity. Porn can be the perfect drug—and on a laptop or DVD, it's portable too. Thrilling, titillating, and extreme, it screams of forbidden fruit. Like any drug or compulsive activity, watching porn can become very addictive.

My concern is that porn distorts our perceptions of sex and women. It's a very narrow and dark peephole into sex as entertainment. The attitudes toward sex that are prevalent in porn are not healthy or accurate. Women are objectified and treated in a very degrading way. This is not something I want my daughter to watch or emulate. You might tell her that you can't watch porn without distorting your own self-image and hurting yourself. That's the approach I would take if I were you.

It's good to be a secret agent sometimes, Mom. You have to assume and expect and maybe be a bit suspicious for your daughter's own good. Rather than stumbling into the porn, as you have done, as moms we need to do a daily Internet spot-check and look into our daughter's world. As we are feeling our own TUG, we need to teach our daughter to develop and use her TUG. Some of this will be through role-modeling. Some of this is an extension of "If it doesn't feel good, don't do it or let anyone else do it to you. If it feels over the top, if it's making you feel anxious, stop, reflect, and look within." It may sound like a lot, but that's the work involved in teaching and educating our daughters to be proactively protective of themselves.

Create an opportunity to talk with her that is not face to face. Imagine you are taking a walk with Emma, coming from a place of calm and love. Here's a **script** you can use: "Emma, I am curious, what have you learned from watching porn? What did it show you about sexual relations between men and women?" She may shrug her shoulders and not look at you, and say, "I was curious. I won't do it again." You can reply, "Emma, I am not mad, and this is not a lecture. I just want to educate and inform you about the purpose of porn. It's a multi-billion dollar industry that is ruining the sex lives of millions of people. Boys come away with a very distorted view of women and sex and intimacy after watching hours of porn. And girls do too. I want you to be aware of how damaging porn can be to yourself and your future relationships with males."

You're keeping your message short and simple (see Chapter 1). Give your daughter plenty of time to respond and please don't interrupt once she starts to talk. She may ask you some "Why can't I?" questions, and that's a good thing. Not to worry if she doesn't. You have planted a seed by being very responsive and not reactive.

You may be very surprised by what you hear and what she may anxiously share with you now or in the future. Just give your daughter plenty of time to respond. Mom, it's so worth the effort to share your expertise and be her "brain trust."

I recall a fifteen-year-old female patient sharing with me a conversation she had with her mom in the car about porn. Her mom explained that porn sends out the wrong messages about sex, especially to guys—that it's casual and all about using the woman. My patient felt embarrassed, and said, "Mom, stop, I know all about this." Her mom didn't stop talking, though, and later my patient admitted to me that before the talk, she *had* thought that sex was like the sex she had seen on the Internet. As she expressed to me, "I am grateful my mom went out on the limb."

HAVING "THE TALK" WITH YOUR DAUGHTER IN MIDDLE SCHOOL

One enterprising mom seized the moment during a relevant Oprah segment about how to have "the talk" with your eleven-year-old daughter. (The girl's mother and a pediatrician were also present during the segment.) Mom insisted that all four of her daughters—ages sixteen, fifteen, thirteen, and eleven—come upstairs to watch the show. Then she locked the door and asked her captive audience if they had any questions for her.

At sixteen, Lila replied that she already knew "all this stuff" from her fifth-grade health class and her seventh- and eighth-grade sex education classes. She learned the most from a close girlfriend, who was the youngest in her family and had benefitted from having older siblings. Lila felt it was important not to go over an eleven-year-old's head. She said it was okay to talk about kissing, but parents needed to take it slow or else it would get too uncomfortable.

Lila recounts, "My mom tried to have the talk with me when I was twelve, and I got so emotional, overwhelmed, and angry that I stormed off." Now in high school, Lila realizes how television glorifies anything sexual. "It's not real," she pointed out.

Sarah, fifteen, chimed in, "It's not cool to copy what you see on TV. You need to make your own choices."

Thirteen-year-old Jessica smiled upon hearing this, but stayed quiet, while the youngest, Becky, announced, "Hey, I'm not even listening."

Take your cues from your daughter to glean, by degrees, how ready she is. A twelve-year-old does not need to hear too much information that could scare or overwhelm her, but a fifteen-year-old will be more familiar with most of what you express and will be capable of following you and forming her own opinions.

THE EXTENDED-PLAY VERSION OF "THE TALK"

Consider and discuss the following points over the course of your daughter's sexual development:

1. Reinforce that she doesn't have to do anything if she feels pressured or uncomfortable. She might think she has to be cool and go along, especially if she's with an older boy who expects she will. Many females perform oral sex on their

male counterparts with the mistaken notion that it's "cool and safe and not sex at all." Guys can take advantage of this.

2. Focus on teaching her how to be on guard against risky and dangerous behavior, such as unprotected sex.

3. Try to discourage your eleven- to fourteen-year-old daughter from dating anyone on a one-on-one basis until she is at least fifteen or older. Research bears this out: the younger your daughter starts dating, the sooner she will be in a physically intimate relationship.

4. With your eleven- to twelve-year-old, you can water down the details of the talk. After she gets her period and matures, you can share more. Play it by ear, so you don't overwhelm her.

5. Please don't worry. Sharing information is not encouraging her to act on it, and you can state that upfront. In fact, the more you and your daughter talk about these concerns, the more she'll delay being sexually active. Research bears this out too.

6. From ages fourteen to nineteen (or sooner, depending on her physical, emotional, and intellectual maturation), explain the difference between true romantic love and a "hormonal surge." Having sex to "get it over with" or because you're curious is never a good idea. You will lose out on having an intimate connection with a person you care for deeply.

7. Try to stall her by emphasizing that sexual contact is most fulfilling when it's shared with a special person and you feel a true connection.

8. At sixteen to seventeen, if not sooner, she may approach you responsibly with the following: "Mom, I am having an

active sexual relationship and I want the Pill because I don't want to get pregnant." When you can hear again, remind her to use condoms to prevent the transmission of STDs.

9. If you think you can slow her down, you can try, but don't be surprised if she insists, "Mom, make an appointment with your doctor or clinic, I don't care. You can come in after I talk with her, okay?"

10. Take ten deep breaths—yes, like Lamaze!—and count backward before taking her to her first gynecologist appointment.

11. Be thankful that she is coming to you and that she is behaving in a forthright, mature, and responsible manner. She is being upfront, nothing sneaky or secretive. It's all a bit hard to process, isn't it? Remember, this is not an easy subject for parents to handle.

12. Follow up with her by asking, "Do you think you're ready? You really care about him that much to step it up?" And if she answers you, "Yes," then don't brush her off. Instead say, "You can't blame me for trying to discourage you, right? You are precious to me."

As caring parents, we keep talking and don't throw up our hands, especially if we feel that TUG that our daughter is not taking care of herself and is way too casual and uncaring. We continue to educate and inform (see Chapter 1) and try the best we can to protect her from herself. We hope she hears our "take care of yourself" message somewhere in her head and developing gut.

Do share your concerns with her about the Pill and tell her that it's not a lifelong solution for contraception, especially if there is a history of breast cancer in the family. Tell her that, for now, you suppose the Pill might be the best recourse for a teenager who does not want to get pregnant, but her partner still needs to use a condom to protect them both against STDs. Remind her that many times partners don't even know that they are infected with an STD and unknowingly infect their sexual partners. The more sexual partners a person has, the greater the risk for contracting an STD.

"This is your chance to be young," you can tell her. "Don't rush it." If she says she can handle it, reply: "You don't know what you're in for—having sex *intensifies* a relationship. You don't think so? Just ask your friends who are sexually active. They'll tell you. You'll feel more possessive of him, especially if he is your first love. You'll expect him to text you constantly and if he does not, watch out!"

Having worked with my share of young and passionate females, I have seen too many meltdowns up close, and it's not a pretty sight. Not all girls act like this, but there are enough examples to give you serious pause. "I am so mad at him, he's so immature, we fight too much, I hate it! We're breaking up again! Forget it! We are back together." You get the picture.

From age eleven to fifteen, a girl is still too young to get herself tied up in knots this way. Say to her: "Group dating is fine. You like a particular guy, that's super, but please no one-on-one's or solo dates just yet." Hold her off for as long as you can. Your hormonal fifteen-year-old will protest mightily and buck at the restrictions, but you still can try. I know one young lady who hotly debated her parents on this topic as if she were testifying before Congress. Only afterward did they realize that she was speaking hypothetically—and that she didn't even have a boyfriend yet! Don't get into a showdown or battle of wills with her. Stay calm, be reasonable, and do the best you can.

Let her know that you understand her normal passion and needs, that you were once a teen as well. Most importantly, tell her that you are supportive of her but may not agree with her decision just now. Remind her that you also need time to process and figure out where a more mature relationship for her is headed.

"IF YOU LOVED ME"

Nina, a patient of mine, was fifteen and dating a sweet guy. She said that they had discussed having sex, quite rationally, I might add, and that she needed to get birth control. I suggested she wait until she was a bit older. She insisted she wanted to have a session with her mother and me to discuss it.

Mom was having trouble processing her daughter's words and feeling disconnected; the conversation felt surreal to her, like an out of body experience. Hoping to slow her daughter down, she tried to encourage her daughter to think by challenging her: "How would the two of you know that you love each other? You both are so young. Are you sure you know what you're doing?"

Nina answered calmly, "Yes, we have discussed all of this. We love each other, the relationship is special, and we are ready." What a determined young woman she was!

In the end, Mom reluctantly agreed, probably right after Nina asked her, "Do you want me to get pregnant?" Mom made an appointment for Nina with the gynecologist, and Nina was happy.

Fast-forward to several months later: the sexual relationship was "okay" for Nina, but not great. Within six months, she had begun to regret her decision to have sex with her boyfriend and, in keeping with who she was, she told him so. She explained that she wanted to stop, she really didn't enjoy having sex, and she wanted to wait to have more until she was older.

He was furious with her. "How could you do this to me? Don't you love me? If you loved me, you wouldn't stop!" This went on for a month or so, until she broke up with him: "We agreed to give sex a try, but I changed my mind, and you're not listening to me. I'm tired of your pressuring me. This is not love anymore; it's lust. I'm not in love with you anymore. That's it, we're done."

Nina decided to wait until college. She did not want to have sex just because she was infatuated with a guy or curious about sex. She felt that if a person truly loved her, he would respect her decision and not pressure her.

True to form, Nina kept her word and did not have sex again until she was a sophomore in college. After dating a young man she cared for deeply, she recognized that she was ready for a more intimate relationship, and she was glad she had waited.

TOO MUCH INFORMATION?

Dear Arden,

Yesterday I learned that my fifteen-year-old daughter, Kiera, has had sex several times and does not want to stop or wait until she is older. I realize that if she really wants to have sex, I cannot stop her, and I am scared for her. She is still so young and unaware. She says she will not get pregnant, but there are so many other issues besides teen pregnancy that could hurt and derail her. Is it okay for me to direct her to websites like "Go Ask Alice!" and give her books? This is such a Pandora's box for us! My husband says those sites will "give her ideas" and encourage her to be even more sexually active. I'm trying to be realistic. Now that the door to physical intimacy has been opened, I don't think she will stop having sex just because we say so.

Mom, take a look at one fifteen-year-old's decision to have sex with her boyfriend ("If You Loved Me," in the previous section), only for her to regret that decision big-time. If you feel it's appropriate, ask Kiera to read it too. That may help to slow her down, or at least get her to turn down the volume. If not, the "Go Ask Alice!" website is a good place for *you* to educate yourself. It's an informative website put up by Columbia University. The students ask some very blunt questions and the answers are spot-on; however, it's really geared more to the college crowd. I think it would be way over a fifteen-year-old's head. Instead, refer Kiera to sites geared specifically for an audience of teens, such as Sex, Etc., a website offering sex education for teens (www.sexetc.org) and affiliated with Rutgers University's Answer organization. For tweens and younger teens, TeenHealth offers information on sexual health and development (www.kidshealth.org/teen). Of course, you will want to check out any sites yourself before recommending them to your daughter.

I've said this before, but it's so important that I'll say it again. Parents worry that if they give their daughters too much information, they will go out and act on it. My experience has been quite the opposite. Your daughter is simply very curious and wondering what sex is all about. Some of her friends are having sex, and she does not want to miss out on anything.

You need to ask Kiera if she has a steady boyfriend. If she doesn't, and she is hooking up randomly with guys she barely knows, she could get very hurt, physically and emotionally, or feel used. She may declare, "Oh Mom, get real, I can take care of myself! We use condoms!" But you and I both know that she is far more vulnerable than she realizes.

Resist the urge to fight with her, because that will only serve to drive her away from you. Explain to her that condoms are not fool-proof. It is still possible to get pregnant or to contract an STD with a condom; using one simply reduces the risk. Let Kiera know that she may not always be in control in these situations, that sometimes guys can get carried away. Remind her that date rape is the most common form of sexual assault among teenagers. She may not fully realize what she's in for or be able to stop him until it's too late. Lastly, tell her that you are there for her to help her figure out this stuff, even if she does not think she needs your help or input.

HER ONE AND ONLY

Dear Arden,

HELP! My daughter, Holly, is fifteen, and she is dating an eigh-teen-year-old senior. She thinks he is her one true love, and I am pretty sure she is having sex with him. Her grades have dropped, and she has lost interest in her schoolwork, friends, and activities. I sent her to live with relatives out of state for several months, but she only came home more determined and more in love with him than ever. I'm worried that he might break up with her when he leaves for college. How do I prepare her for the heartbreak? She will be devastated.

When most females start to have sex, they think it's a forever thing, especially if he is the first boyfriend. Sometimes, this love can be the real thing. It also can turn into the wrong thing, an obsession, very quickly. Teenage girls can be possessive and jealous creatures. They have been known to stalk rivals, viciously gossip against other girls, and fight for their man. Literally. Ask any teacher who's had cafeteria duty about the girl-fights at school. The number one reason these fights break out: *boys*. Sometimes girls behave like drama queens, breaking up and getting back together every week. When they feel desperate and despondent, they might even threaten to hurt themselves and say that they can't live without him.

You say Holly's grades have plummeted; her interests outside of her boyfriend have dropped off considerably. This sounds like obsession to me, an obsessed gal who only has eyes for her eighteen-year-old senior. She has lost sight of her track and her life. She sounds totally derailed.

Your solution to move Holly to the relatives, probably seemed like a great idea, but as you found out, it only served to make her more determined to maintain a connection with him. I am sure they were calling, texting, IMing, and Skyping the entire time.

As for what happens next, he may or may not break up with her. But the possibility is there, so you'll want to help Holly anticipate it. Preparing an angry, hurting daughter for the pain of her boyfriend going away to college is no small task. You will have to be very gentle and direct here. Put it to Holly in such a way that she feels supported by you but also give her an important reality check.

I need you to totally shift to an open position with a compassionate and empathic attitude.

Here's a **script**: "Holly, I made a big mistake sending you away from home. I don't know what I was thinking. I am sorry for that. I want to help you anticipate and prepare for the possibility that your boyfriend may be consumed with adjusting to college life and may have a hard time giving you the attention that you are used to receiving from him. Do the two of you plan to stay together and maintain your relationship?"

At this point, she may answer, "I think so, Mom, he may be going to a nearby college." That's when you can step in with this wise piece of advice: "Holly, now is the time to reconnect with your girlfriends. Getting back to your studies will put you right back on your track. I want you to succeed, and I am sure that your boyfriend wants you to thrive and succeed as well. Your job right now is to be the best student you can be, and I will go above and beyond to support you."

Life can be so uncertain for anyone, Mom. Once he's off, his world becomes so much larger, and indeed he may have little or no time for your daughter. If that's the case, let her know that reconnecting with her girlfriends is key. I have always said to Samara, "Try not to wrap your life around a boyfriend to the point of losing yourself. Value and cultivate your relationship with your girl and guy friends. Boyfriends may come and go, but some friends will last a lifetime." The message is to have a life outside of your current significant relationship and stay focused on yourself.

It's so easy to make our lives revolve around another person. As females, we are wired to be caretakers and to let go of what's important to us. Often what gets dropped by the wayside is what helps us sustain our emotional and spiritual health. There needs to be a balance. We want our daughters to have plenty of confidence, energy, and self-love. We want them to put themselves at the top of the list.

READY OR NOT? JACKIE AND TALIA

Talia was sixteen when she approached her mom, Jackie, and said she wanted to have sex with her boyfriend. Talia was curious. Mom tried to dissuade her.

She said, "Sweetie, you are too young. Wait until you are in love with a boy, and it will be very special." Talia agreed to wait.

Fast-forward to one year later: "Mom, I want to have sex and I need birth control." This time, Talia had a new boyfriend.

Jackie took a breath and elevated high above, and asked Talia, "Is he special?" and Talia answered, "Oh, yes, this is very different." So off they went for a prescription for the Pill.

As it turns out, Talia's judgment was much better the second time around. This boyfriend was so careful and considerate that he put water in the condom and squeezed it to make sure there were no holes in it.

I know most of us moms would be jolted by a request for birth control. We want our daughters to wait another year, or two or three. These days, seventeen is the average age of our daughters having intercourse. You wouldn't want her sneaking around behind your back or having unprotected sex, would you? Remember, we need to be approachable and cultivate a deep, trusting connection. Our daughters will continue to seek our advice and love for the rest of their lives. I suggest that we have to see the bigger picture in the context of the world our daughters are growing up in and experiencing. No matter how old they are, our daughters really appreciate our blessings and love.

STATUS UPDATE

Dear Arden,

Yesterday, our fifteen-year-old daughter, Allison, posted on her Facebook wall that she is "bisexual." In her info, she describes herself as interested in both women and men. I found it shocking she would share that with people. We don't think she needs to put that information out there. What if somebody sees it? What would they think? When we ordered her to take it down, she breezily pointed out that many of her friends identify themselves as bisexual too.

Between your shock at what people will think and being protective of Allison, it's enough to make your stomach twist in knots. I get how you feel. But it's not uncommon for teens to post on their Facebook pages that they are "bisexual," "gay," "bi-curious," "lesbian," "heteroflexible," or even "polyamorous." Many teens like to push people's buttons and be out there. This is probably a common practice among her circle of friends. Teenagers tend not to take life too seriously; they like to play with expectations. Allison is looking for acceptance and solidarity, not censure.

The problem is that she is fifteen going on sixteen and she is not thinking self-protectively. Kids who have nine-hundred-plus friends and who randomly friend people on Facebook could be asking for trouble. She thinks she is being honest. It sounds cool and so very open-minded. You think she is being foolhardy and reckless and don't want to see her get hurt. You can share that she might not get the reception she expects, but she will say, "I will simply unfriend anyone who insults me and block them."

Try to put your worries on a shelf and give her your heart, soul, and both of your ears. Allison needs to experience your unconditional love and acceptance of her.

Let's create a transformative teaching experience. Some open-ended statements would be a great conversation starter. Here's a **script**: "Allison, I am open to hear all about what bisexuality means to you and your pals." Let her share her feelings and thoughts. "Tell me about the importance of posting your sexual preference on Facebook." She will tell you for sure. Maybe she has wanted to all along and just did not feel that you were receptive. As you listen, pay very close and careful attention for any signs of backlash, where she may have had some nasty feedback and whom she deleted. Please do not give her your opinions or offer any advice for the moment. Just listen and create a safe space in which she can express herself and share everything and anything with you. Breathe through any anxiety you may be feeling.

Pick the right time and place to make this a casual exchange. Hopefully when Allison sees that you are trying so very hard, she will be and remain receptive and open to you. As parents, we can make our best interventions when our daughters really trust our judgment and the helpful place we are coming from.

BLACK AND BLUE

Dear Arden,
My sixteen-year-old daughter, Gia, has been dating a very popular athlete at her high school. She's always been a model student and

athlete, but the other day I saw bruises on her wrists and upper arms. When I asked her what happened, she pulled her arms away from me and yanked her sleeves down. She says that she and her boyfriend were just playing around and he got a little carried away. "You worry too much," she said. "I can't help that I bruise easily." I am really worried about her. He seems nice, but you never know.

Oh, boy! A few things come to mind, Mom. Your daughter and her popular, likable athlete may be experimenting with S&M or rough sex. The bruises on her wrists could be from handcuffs. As for her upper arms, he may be tying up her arms or holding her down. If they were "playing around," perhaps the ties were too tight?

It's clear that she doesn't want you to know about this. This obviously embarrasses her, and after all, you are her *mom*. If this is with her consent, that's one thing. But if she is letting herself be pressured to submit in order to keep him happy and to ensure that he remains her boyfriend, that's something else! If I were in your shoes, Mom, I would say something along the following lines to my daughter. Here's a **script** for how you can broach a conversation: "Even though you have reassured me that you bruise easily, you know how I am. I love you to pieces and I am uncomfortable about too much rough-housing. Gia, I don't mean to pry, but what exactly happened?" She may not tell you, but you opened up the box for a potential conversation that may be tabled and tried later. The good thing is that it's out there.

The second possibility that really concerns me is that this could be a red flag for the beginning of aggressive, abusive behavior. A former patient of mine was dating a football quarterback who used to "pin her down" without her consent. She'd tell him not to do it, but he thought it was one big joke! He kept on pushing her and eventually forced her to have nonconsensual sex with him a number of times. She didn't tell anyone, including her mom. It took a very long time for her to share this with me. And when she did, it was many years after it happened.

Mom, be vigilant and stay on top of this. Be observant and compassionate, and keep looking out for your daughter's mental, emotional, and spiritual health. Talk to Gia about a female celebrity who's topical in the news and media who has been physically and or sexually abused. I am thinking of Rihanna, the R&B singer who was physically abused by her then-boyfriend Chris Brown. Her swollen, black and blue face was publicized in magazines and newspapers and on television. Eventually, she stepped forward and became a young role model for females to take a stand against violence. This is a wonderful springboard for future discussions with Gia. You are teaching Gia that she does not have to be pleasing and go along with what her boyfriend wants and that if she is being pushed around aggressively, she does not have to take it. Our daughters appreciate our being observant and looking out for their mental, emotional, and spiritual health as long as we can be patient, calm, loving, and compassionate.

The Reality of Rape

- One in six women will be sexually assaulted in her lifetime.
- Nine out of every ten rape victims are female.
- Ages twelve to thirty-four are the highest risk years for rape.
- Girls ages sixteen to nineteen are four times more likely than the general population to be victims of rape, attempted rape, or sexual assault.

- College-age women are four times more likely to be sexually assaulted.
- Approximately 66 percent of rape victims know their assailant.
- Twenty-nine percent of rape victims are ages twelve to seventeen.
- Forty-four percent of rape victims are under age eighteen, and 80 percent of rape victims are under age thirty.
- Sixty-one percent of rapes are not reported to the police.
- Ninety-three percent of junior sexual assault victims know their attacker.
- Four in ten rapes take place in the victim's home.
- Forty-three percent of rapes occur between six in the evening and midnight.

IT HAPPENED TO ME: ANGEL'S STORY

After appearing in a segment for Parents.tv called "Preparing Your Daughter for Her Period," which was later posted on YouTube, I received a flood of questions, many of them from girls between the ages of twelve and fifteen. I had to wonder, why weren't they asking their own mothers? That experience really made me realize how much help mothers could use to connect with their daughters.

One of the emails came from a thirteen-year-old girl I'll call "Angel." Angel had reached out to me because she needed me to help her connect with her mom. During a vacation with extended family, Angel had been raped by her uncle, her mother's brother. He was drunk, and he came to where she was sleeping and ripped off her clothes. She begged him to stop, "What are you doing? I'm a little girl! Stop! Stop!" but her cries fell on deaf ears. Afterward, she was in terrible physical pain and needed stitches. Her best friend advised her to go to a gynecologist, and Angel asked her aunt to take her. When Angel returned home, she tried to tell her mom what happened but Mom refused to listen or believe her. Mom pretended it never happened. Her aunt continued to help, but Angel clearly wanted my help to engage her mother so that Mom could be emotionally available for her daughter and become the advocate and protector Angel needed her to be.

Many emails and phone calls followed. Angel was furious with her mom for being silent and avoiding her. She also needed her mom to make it better. I explained to Angel that Mom must be feeling helpless and guilty because she couldn't protect her.

To Angel I was "Auntie," her champion. I suggested that Angel's aunt could get the gynecologist's report and go to the police station with her. Angel told me she had saved her underwear from that terrible night. I was stunned and said, "Angel, he can be prosecuted on the DNA sample."

I asked her not to give up on her mom but to keep trying to get through. My courageous Angel tried and tried and finally one day burst out crying, "What kind of mother are you? You have to do something." Both Angel and Mom cried in each other's arms. From that moment on, Mom became protective of her and did everything she could to help her daughter.

I asked Angel to share all of our emails with her mom and she did. Her aunt obtained the gynecologist's report, and went to the police, and the uncle was arrested. A month later, Angel pointed him out in a lineup. Let me just describe how brave this thirteen-year-old was. The extended family was furious with Angel and her aunt. She'd get calls, "You are breaking up the family; you are a liar; he didn't do it." This continued right to the day of the trial. She nearly backed down.

I said, "You have come this far. I know this is awful, but for your healing and recovery, and for all the other angels he probably has raped or will in the future, you must do this! You didn't ask for him to rape you; you are an innocent. He has to deal with the consequences of what he did." She agreed with me and stood tall in her being.

With Angel's aunt, a female lawyer, and her mom present (and Auntie Arden there in spirit), her uncle was found guilty and sentenced to jail. She sent me a victory email, "I did it, I did it." She was overjoyed that it was over. "Oh, my Angel," I wrote back. "I am so proud of you. You are a person of courage who soars with the eagles."

During the entire process, Angel openly shared how dirty she felt. She would shower up to three times a day and relive the memory of the rape. I let her know that this was all part of her being traumatized (post-traumatic stress disorder) and no amount of showering was going to get rid of her feelings of being violated. I listened to her and comforted her. I explained to her that she was in the process of healing and recovery, which involved reliving and processing her life-altering attack.

She would ask me, "When will it go away, Auntie?" I told her, "Every day will be up and down. Eventually it will be in the background, and your life, friends, school, piano, and dance will be more in the foreground." She tried to understand. I said to her, "You will be the kind of woman who will tell her story with the hope of bringing other survivors out and offering them advice, direction, and hope."

Her uncle eventually admitted his wrongdoing and wrote a letter of apology to Angel. Her rage at him softened to sadness. She was glad for the validation and admission of guilt. She would pray and work on forgiveness, not at my suggestion, mind you—she just knew what to do and how to be. She was truly a remarkable young woman full of wisdom and faith.

I periodically hear from Angel, who insists that I tell her story, and I am being true to my word. She brought out my love, the protector and tiger in me, my passion, and my need for fairness and justice. I have a new niece and cheerleader in my life.

Her mom asked her to thank me for all of my help. I was very appreciative and grateful that Angel and Mom became even closer and have remained so.

Signs Your Daughter Might Have Been Raped

- She does not seem herself and stares off into space.
- She is overly sensitive, moody, and sullen, and suffers from unexplained crying jags and sudden bursts of anger.
- She appears depressed, sad, anxious, and lost, and may suffer from panic attacks or sleep disorders.
- She starts cutting classes, loses her focus, and has difficulty concentrating. She may take a medical leave of absence and drop out of school.
- She develops an eating disorder—anorexia, bulimia, or binge eating disorder. She shows others signs of changes in appetite, sudden weight loss, or weight gain.

> - She starts cutting herself secretly as a way to release her pain.
> - She may be needier and more dependent, resembling a little girl.

For moms to have an inkling of what rape was like for their daughters, I will share the following composite description drawn from my patients over the years:

> *He was attacking me, forcing me to have sex. I didn't want to. I repeatedly said "No, No!" He wouldn't listen. He felt entitled, like "I am your boyfriend, I expect this." I wasn't into it or him. I was afraid. I watched from the ceiling. I felt broken. I felt ugly, dirty, worthless, and needed to shower. I couldn't get rid of what I felt. I wanted to disappear. I lost control. I felt overwhelmed. The pain was too great. I had nightmares of being attacked, raped, chased. I started to cut myself. I lost my appetite. I stopped eating. I developed an eating disorder. I became anorexic. I purged my self-hate. I became bulimic.*

Rape is a fragmenting dissociative experience, no matter what age you are. One older former patient of mine asked me numerous times during the course of her treatment, "Arden, when am I going to get better and get over this rape? Will it take a lifetime?" My response: "Healing and recovery is a journey that takes as long as it takes." This particular gal worked very hard in therapy to reassociate, remember, repair, and reeducate herself. Over the course of six years, she came to therapy twice a week, shared her awful nightmares and her most cherished dreams, and eventually became a powerful advocate for other victims of rape and sexual assault. It was a long and arduous journey, but by the end, she was not just a survivor but a success.

LIFE INTERRUPTED:
SIXTEEN AND PREGNANT

Dear Arden,

My sixteen-year-old daughter, Gabby, just announced that she is four months pregnant. Yes, she has been provocative and rebellious. She dropped out of school recently. The father is a few years older than Gabby. I hate to admit it, but he is a decent guy. We talked about the options with her—pregnancy, abortion, and adoption. My daughter wants to have the baby, she has agreed to go back to school, and she and her boyfriend are discussing marriage. That's a lot of change for a sixteen-year-old to handle all at once. I never told Gabby this, but she's smart enough to figure out that I was only nineteen when I had her. I was a teenage mom too, so I know how rough it can be to juggle a baby with school, marriage, and growing up. My question is, how can I help my daughter be responsible but at the same time realistic?

History has repeated itself. You were a teen mom yourself, so you really do know and understand what your daughter is in for, don't you? This must all hit very close to home for you. Rather than beating yourself up, be there for Gabby with empathy and compassion. She will need your emotional support and guidance. I can tell that you are trying to be calm and accessible for your daughter. That needs to be your position and attitude so Gabby can come to you without fear of being judged or criticized. Let her know what it was like for you as a teen mom and what to expect. Her life is about to change in this huge and irreversible way.

It's so different now than it was sixteen years ago when you had Gabby. I don't know how supportive your parents were, but from doing many talk show segments on "babies having babies," I know teen pregnancy used to be a huge cause for embarrassment and shame. Today teen moms and their parents are dealing with their feelings out loud, not burying them so they can resurface in the next generation.

Have you seen the MTV show *16 and Pregnant* and its spin-off, *Teen Mom*? Millions of people have watched the struggles and tough decisions these teen moms face about adoption, marriage, school, work, and in-laws. Sitting down and watching these programs with Gabby will give her insights into the realities, challenges, and complexities she's facing. Spending this time with your daughter will provide you both with opportunities to bond and have a real conversation.

Mom, you can share what you remember about the excitement and fear of giving birth while you and Gabby are shopping for baby clothes. You can talk about what it was like to care for her as a baby while looking through photo albums. Talk to her about your early marriage, feeling overwhelmed, and your efforts to build a home and family. Understanding and forgiving each other's "mistakes" can help you heal and repair the rift between you.

Teen Pregnancy

- Ten percent of all U.S. births are to teens.
- Each year, close to 750,000 fifteen- to nineteen-year-olds become pregnant.

- Eighty-two percent of teen pregnancies are unplanned.
- Two-thirds of all teen pregnancies happen among eighteen- to nineteen-year-olds.
- In 2006, 59 percent of teen pregnancies ended in birth, 27 percent ended in abortion, and 14 percent ended in miscarriage.
- There were 200,420 abortions performed on fifteen- to nineteen-year-olds in 2006.
- Seven percent of teen mothers do not receive prenatal care.
- Teen mothers are more likely to deliver low birth weight babies than women in their twenties and thirties.
- As of January 2010, thirty-four states require that teenagers who receive abortions have parental consent or involve their parents in the decision-making.
- As of January 2010, twenty-one states and the District of Columbia allow minors to obtain contraceptive services without a parent's involvement. Both Texas and Utah require parental consent for contraceptive services in state-funded family planning programs.
- For the first time in over a decade, the pregnancy rate among American teenagers *increased* between 2005 and 2006, resulting in 71.5 pregnancies per one thousand females ages fifteen to nineteen.
- Teen mothers who have babies are more likely to get their high school diplomas and GEDs than their predecessors, but still lag behind their peers who delay childbearing to go to college.

CHAPTER 11

Body Image, Health, and Personal Identity

"Every time a woman passes a mirror and judges herself, a girl is watching."

—Gloria Steinem

Our poor daughters are laced up so tightly by expectations of how they "should" appear, dress, and be that they might as well be wearing corsets. Restrictive doesn't begin to describe it. "They all have the same look," complained one mother. "Skinny, with long, straight hair, and they all dress alike and wear the same clothes."

It's easy to feel inadequate and "less than" when you are flooded with images of physical perfection beamed directly from the television, illuminated on the movie screen, looking up from the pages of magazines, or staring down at you from giant billboards. The cult of celebrity, the cosmetics industry, the fashion industry, and the porn industry have fed our daughters a steady, streaming diet of images. Collectively, they tell our girls what they need to buy, wear, and do in order to be considered beautiful and desirable, when the simple truth is our girls are astonishingly lovely as they are.

As mothers, our work is cut out for us. We hope that when our girls look in the mirror, they like what they see. We try to be role models for our daughters, to provide living, breathing examples of self-love and self-acceptance. We have no advertising budget to broadcast our message—just a humble grassroots campaign of time, repetition, and hugs. We radiate love to our highly impressionable girls. We tell them that they are knockouts, spectacular masterpieces, and true originals. We emphasize how clever our daughters are, how creative, how resourceful, and strong, and quick, hoping that if we love them enough on the inside, they will reject and push away the oversexualized images that confront them on the outside. We try to relax the standards of perfection, loosen the laces on the corsets, and breathe.

Mom, telegraph to your daughter from the beginning that her body is unique and wonderful.

- People come in different sizes and shapes.
- Be mindful not to compare herself, or her body, to anyone else.
- Try to resist the cultural beauty myth of equating self and body worth with perfection.
- Her body is able to do amazing things—run, jump, kick, stretch, walk, bend, dance, hop, skip. Remind her that her body develops at her own pace.
- Her inner beauty shines when she is happy.

Thoughts from Emme

Emme is the spokeperson for the National Eating Disorders Association, an author, and a plus-sized model, and has been named one of *People Magazine's* "fifty most beautiful people."

What changes would you like to see in the media, TV,

radio, print, and Internet that would more realistically depict women and girls? Do you see any shift?

The Body Image Council (BIC) is looking to dig into enlightening the media along with the Girl Scouts of the USA and the GS Research Institute. Incredible information is coming out through the Girl Scouts' initiative in relation to negative media images, messages, and output affecting our young girls.

What I would like to see is more responsibility taken around the conference room tables, and more editorial filters in place, especially by those who know that what they say, show, and portray negatively affect our youth. Industry-wide changes need to take place to desexualize and tone down the images of young women and reflect a more age-appropriate scenario in ads, magazines, movies, and TV shows.

A HAIRY SITUATION

Dear Arden,
My eleven-year-old daughter, Morgan, just told me that girls her age and younger are having their body hair waxed or removed. I saw a recent Today *show segment on the subject and couldn't believe it. Some of these girls were as young as seven!*

It's shocking, isn't it? A girl who gets her period earlier (and this can happen as young as age seven), will have more hair at an earlier age. This is all about normal body development. As for the reactions of mothers and other peers, that's something else.

This needs to be about healthy body and self-image. As the mom, it's your responsibility to determine what's in your daughter's best interests.

If an eleven-year-old is fine with her "excessive" arm hair, leave it be and leave her alone. It's part of who she is. However, if she wants to get her arm hair waxed, pick the right time and place to talk to her. This could be in the car or just sitting together having breakfast. Let it be on the casual, friendly side. If it's possible, you need to get to what's underneath her need to wax. Just put out one open-ended statement to draw her out and get the conversation going. Try something like: "Tell me about what it's like for you to have more hair on your arms than you would like."

If she is older, say twelve, thirteen, or fourteen, you can ask her point-blank: "What is it about your hair that makes you feel uncomfortable? Has anyone teased or bullied you about the hair on your arms, legs, or face? Do they make fun of your mustache?"

Once you have asked her, then you and your daughter can make a decision based on what is in her best welfare. Mom, your message to your daughter needs to remain constant: you are special, beautiful, and unique.

Let your daughter come to you if she is feeling in any way embarrassed about her appearance. Please do not bring it to her attention. It's her body, and yes, you are there to guide her and keep her safe, but let her experience her own discomfort, if there is any at all.

A PIERCING QUESTION

Dear Arden,
My seventeen-year-old, Taylor, really, really, really wants to get

her navel pierced. She said if we don't let her, she's going to get her
tongue pierced too.

I want to be me, me, me! She sure is singing that song big time. Any teen will tell you that piercings are self-expressions. Of what, you ask? They are making an attempt to be different, to stand out. These days, many teens have pierced a different part of their body. Ask them why they do it and they'll tell you they like it, it's cool, sexy.

It sounds like Taylor has a mind of her own. At age eighteen, she can pierce without parental permission. It's not that far off. I think I'd pick my battles here. Ask her why a navel piercing. You may be surprised at her answer. Let her see you both seriously considering her request. She's asking, not doing, not sneaking behind your back. She's being up-front and direct. Praise her for that. Let her know you appreciate her running it by you. Let her see you are with her, not against her. If you don't, the power struggle will continue in other forms because she is struggling to find her identity and to think more independently. She is testing the boundaries through piercing.

If she is basically a good soul and not self-destructive, why not? Yep, I know she's not my child, she's yours, but it's her body. So think about it.

PLASTIC SURGERY

Dear Arden,
My daughter, Molly, is about to turn sixteen and really wants to get
breast implants for her birthday. She wants to have a Sweet Sixteen
pool party and show them off. Apparently, some of the girls in her

high school got plastic surgery for their birthdays—nose jobs, for example—and she doesn't know why she can't have it done too.

When a sixteen-year-old female is looking to make a serious change to her body, like breast implants, something's up with how she sees herself. Feelings of inadequacy, such as not being "big enough" or "sexy enough" may be getting in her way. What's more, Molly presents the idea like she is getting highlights in her hair and doesn't fully appreciate that it's surgery. It takes time to heal and adjust to a very different body and body image. Mom, be alert to the Western world's cultural distortion that tells us to overvalue appearance and body perfection. I have given many workshops and keynotes on the myth of the Barbie doll, the idea that you can't be too thin or too pretty. A vunerable tween or teen who sees very skinny models, actresses, and rock stars on TV and in magazines tries to fashion herself in their likeness in an attempt to bolster her fragile, developing body and self-esteem. Mom, be an advocate for your daughter. Molly needs to be educated to resist the cultural perfection pressure and learn to see through these distorted images. I would ask Molly to wait a few years, until she is older, and agree to revisit to see if she is still determined to get implants.

CHUBBY

Dear Arden,
My twelve-year-old daughter, Paige, wants to lose weight. She is chubbier and she has a different body type from her middle school friends, most of whom are very skinny, but I am not sure how to help

her. I don't want to put undue emphasis on her weight or figure, but at the same time I'd love to encourage some healthy habits.

I'm not trying to scare you, Mom, but off the top of my head, I can think of five anorexic teenagers I have worked with who were all put on diets in fifth and sixth grade. I am not saying that they developed an eating disorder right away. That came later, in ninth and tenth grade. By then they felt like their body and eating were out of control; they felt self-conscious. Most were teased by their peers. Many heard denigrating comments from their families, from "Why can't you stop eating?" to "Why can't you eat less?" and "Haven't you had enough?" As these girls got older, they all felt that something was terribly wrong with them and were stuck in a very black-and-white diet mentality.

Give Paige time to go through puberty and its aftermath. She may stretch out and lose her baby fat. In the meantime, I'm all for a healthy lifestyle, mindful eating, and having a joyful passion for life. You and Paige can make a list of fun things to do together outside of eating. Go to a play, take a walk, or swim at the beach. Sign up for a theatre group, art lessons, softball, and team sports. Explore her passions. I need you both to become less preoccupied with her weight and more focused on what her body and being can do in a positive way.

WHY CAN'T MY DAUGHTER BE LIKE ME?

Dear Arden,
My fourteen-year-old daughter, Peyton, is obese. I try to get her to exercise more and control her portions at meal times, but she just

sneaks off to McDonald's or Taco Bell after school. She refuses to eat any vegetables or any of the healthy meals I make at home. What makes it worse is that I am in excellent shape. I work out, go to the gym every day, and watch what I eat. I have the same figure I did in high school, and I run, bike, jog, and jazzercise. I bought her a gym membership but she only used it once. She walked on the treadmill for five minutes before ordering food at the snack bar. What can I do to make her lose the weight? Can't she see that I want what's best for her? To make matters worse, people don't even think she is my daughter.

Mom, I think you are trying too hard with her. Peyton is picking up your anxiety about her appearance, and she is doing her best to resist any attempts to change her. I don't hear how much you love her and appreciate her as a person. Perhaps you do, but it's not coming through. I hear and sense an inner drive on your part for her to be more like you. She may be feeling pressured that she has to meet your high expectations.

It sounds like you are taking great care of yourself. Continue to be a role model, but give your daughter some space. Her binges sound like they're escalating. What she's hearing from you is that something is wrong with her and she doesn't matter. Being a compulsive overeater is not something that changes over night.

I recall a mom who tried so hard, like you, to change her obese daughter, only to be met with anger and increased binges. I like the mindful approach. Teach her to eat when she's hungry and to stop when she's full. No diets. As for the gym, perhaps a female trainer can motivate her to walk one step at a time.

Try not to get sidetracked by what people think. It's how *you* feel about her that counts. Does she embarrass you? Did you expect Peyton to be more like you? Our attitudes can manifest in undermining and cutting comments made to our children. Some parents try to bribe their daughters into losing weight to fit into a bathing suit or a prom dress and say, "You look great now that you have lost weight." When you withhold from your daughter because of her larger appearance, and you are critical and judgmental of her, you need to make an effort to confront your bias, look in the mirror, and challenge yourself. You don't want to send your daughter the message that she is worthless, useless, and lazy. I can't say it enough—our daughters are so much more than their bodies.

Be appreciative that like any addiction, a food addiction is something that just does not go away because you don't like it or because you tell your daughter to stop and control herself. Food may be preferable to other substances, but the obsession, sneakiness, binging, shame, humiliation, and guilt that accompany it is absolutely draining for your tween or teen, especially when she has to deal with the looks of people who mean so much to her. Our culture is very weight-obsessed. A recent study showed that overweight kids not only face discrimination at school and in relationships, but they often come home to harsh treatment and withholding from their own parents. They turn to food to help them deal with their own internal demons and low self-esteem, as a way to self-soothe, fill a void, become numb, and stuff down feelings of pain, anger, rage, sadness, tension, anxiety, and panic. Medical complications (high blood pressure, Type 2 diabetes) and physical limitations often result.

Focus on what you love about Peyton. We need to shift how *you* see her in order for your daughter to make some modifications in her life.

TANOREXIC

Dear Arden,

My seventeen-year-old daughter, Sienna, has been using a tanning bed for well over two years. First it was bikini season, then it was homecoming, then it was cool to have a tan for Christmas, spring break, the prom. You can see where this is going. She looks good, but this getting out of hand. She went from tanning once a week to twenty times a month. She insists all she wants is a healthy tan and that she looks so much better with it.

Sienna is hooked on the notion that she looks better with a tan. This is very similar to having a substance abuse addiction to cigarettes, alcohol, or drugs. And it can be as dangerous. Consider this: tanning beds are now considered as great a cancer threat as cigarettes and have been placed on the World Health Organization's list of the most cancer-causing substances and habits, next to asbestos and arsenic. Using tanning beds before the age of thirty raises the odds of skin cancer by 75 percent. A twenty-minute visit to a tanning bed is the equivalent of an entire day spent at the beach.

Bring out the statistics and do a show-and-tell. Here's a **script** for you to share the following: "I know I'm your mother and you will say, 'Oh Mom, you always tell me I'm beautiful no matter what I look like.' Honey, I don't think you realize how carried away you are getting with wanting to have a tan 365 days of the year. I know you say, 'But, Mom, it makes me feel good.' Okay, but if it wasn't for serious skin cancer concerns, I'd say fine, do what you want. You've stepped it up so much this year. Can we please take a look at what else could be driving you to do this? Your health and safety are my number one concern."

She may say, "Oh Mom, you exaggerate!" That's when you point to the statistics again and say "Stats don't lie, honey," and continue to do a show-and-tell. Say to her: "You are so much more than your appearance. You are smart, funny, and a good, caring person. Let me help you focus on the fact that you are so much more than your body." I think this will give Sienna food for thought and hopefully begin to move her in the direction of loving and liking herself and her body.

EATING DISORDERS

The most poignant image of eating disorders and the havoc they can wreak is a harried-looking mom and her waif-like anorexic daughter walking into my office for a consultation. The mom looks overwhelmed, tearful, and guilt-ridden; her daughter looks exhausted and drained. Underneath, Mom is terribly frightened. Where did she, the caretaker, go wrong?

Eventually I ask both Mom and daughter, "What is her body screaming that both Mom and Dad don't hear?"

I have an image of a child holding her breath, turning blue, refusing to eat, eating like a bird, going on a food and hunger strike. She now claims to feel no hunger pangs and is victorious and proud of that. She can handle food and prepare it for others while not tasting a morsel. She has shrunk in size, weight, and years. She no longer has her period and has the body size of a tall eleven-year-old.

Subconsciously, she does not want to grow up; it's too stressful. The world was so much simpler when she was a little girl. She is now an ambivalent tween or teenager who fights getting help—her way seems easier. The eating disorder has served the function of drawing the parents in closer to her, especially Mommy. Sometimes the "little girl" becomes an all-powerful presence who uses food as a tool for self-control, body control, and as a means of controlling Mom as well.

Girls with eating disorders hunger to matter. They hunger for their parents' praise, recognition, approval, validation, and unconditional love.

If an eating disorder could talk, it would say, "My mom has an eating disorder or a disordered relationship to food. My parents are divorced and are at each other's throats; there is lots of toxic energy at home. My dad has a terminal illness. My mom is an alcoholic. My brother is chronically depressed. My mom is a perfectionist and so am I. I have a traumatic childhood that has been dissociated and repressed. I was raped or physically abused. There is a history of abuse and psychiatric illnesses in my family. There is a death in the family that we've never addressed or processed. Mom and Dad are too opinionated and controlling. Even though I am emaciated, I still see myself as huge and fat. I'm furious. I hate my body."

And so starts the educative and mindful process to introduce mothers to the world of their daughters' eating disorder, or Edna. "Edna" is the feminine form of "Ed," the masculine name that some eating-disorder specialists like me give to your daughter's eating disorder. I use it sometimes for a tween/teen/young adult to have an internal dialogue with herself. It makes the eating disorder come alive in my therapy session and I use that to help separate the struggling, suffering girl from a thought process that's strangling her being, presence, and essence. The longer Edna has been in charge of her mind, the more distorted her thinking, the more wasted away her body is, the more deadened her spirit.

I have explained to so many moms, dads, and daughters that for someone in the throes of this problem, she gets full quickly, because her stomach has shrunk. She is terrified of food and sees it as her foe. She has lost sight of all the wonderful aspects of nourishing and loving her body, fueling herself to reach her potential and fulfill her dreams.

Recovery is a very slow, unraveling, and painful process, with no quick fixes. She will resist. To heal, I try to educate both mother and daughter—sometimes individually, sometimes together, and sometimes with the whole family.

Fast Facts About Anorexia and Bulimia

- One out of every one hundred young women between the ages of ten and twenty is starving herself, sometimes to death. One percent of female adolescents suffer from anorexia.

- According to a 2005 study on youth risk behaviors by the Centers for Disease Control, 12.3 percent of high school students have gone without eating for twenty-four hours or more in order to lose weight or keep from gaining weight in the past month.
- The same study showed that 6.3 percent of high school students have taken diet pills, powders, or liquids without a doctor's advice to lose weight or keep from gaining weight in the past month.
- The study also showed that 4.5 percent of female high school students have vomited or taken laxatives to lose weight or keep from gaining weight in the past month.
- Approximately one to two percent of late adolescent or adult women suffer from bulimia.
- Four percent of college-age women have bulimia.
- Fifty percent of people with anorexia develop bulimia or bulimic patterns.
- Thirty-one percent of teenage girls are somewhat overweight.

WILTING

Dear Arden,

My daughter Beatrice, is fourteen years old, five foot three, and weighs eighty-nine pounds. She's an anorexic. She has not had her period for over a year. We have taken her to many specialists but get nowhere. She is now hospitalized against her will and is very angry. She is on intravenous feeding and is being forced to drink Ensure, a liquid supplement, because she refuses to eat solid food. She insists she is fat, there is nothing wrong with her, we are lying to her, and everyone needs to leave her be. Every day she gets weaker and weaker physically, but more and more stubborn and unable to see what she's doing to herself. She no longer purges and is monitored very carefully by the staff. Her dad and I are depleted and beside ourselves with grief and worry. The doctors say if she continues this, she could die! This is not even having an impact on Bea. We are trying with her therapy to get to the bottom of how all of this started. I am desperate for any suggestions.

You all are suffering. I know it makes no rational sense how your daughter could starve herself, purge the little that she has eaten, and still see herself as fat. As she wilts and shrinks in size, her brain's capacity to see how tiny she is gets more and more compromised. Your Bea sounds like many other young teens I have worked with in my private practice. She's stubborn, angry, very intelligent, maybe a high achiever intellectually, but a frightened little girl on the inside.

Yes, her power over her mind, body, self, and parents is being exerted through her eating disorder. Apparently, sharing that she could die if she keeps this up fell on deaf ears. The body is amazing and resilient. Once there is some momentum and she starts even regaining a few pounds, she will be moving further away from the danger zone. In the meantime, her therapist, nutritionist, and psychiatrist at the hospital will work with her.

Please take a look at my "mindful meditations" for moms and parents in Chapter 2. Too often parents of eating disordered tweens, teens, and young adults understandingly become so consumed with their daughter's illness and recovery that they forget about themselves. Burnout is not uncommon, and Bea needs to see that your life is going on and that you are taking good care of yourself.

Here's a **script** to reach your daughter that I hope helps: "Bea, dear, we are not giving up on you and are here to help see you through. No matter how angry you are with us for putting you in the hospital, we are going to continue to love you. You're fourteen and have your whole life ahead of you. Consider working with the staff; they're here to help you through your illness. We want you to feel better and make inroads and strides in the direction of picking up your life."

I hope her friends are permitted to visit; that may help as well. Hang in there—you have a long road ahead of you. Stay strong, and true, and don't forget about the meditations.

A GLOSSARY OF EATING DISORDERS

Anorexia Nervosa (AN)
One to two percent of American women suffer from anorexia nervosa.

It is an eating disorder characterized by an obsessive fear of gaining weight due to a distorted self-image, with rapid weight loss and failure to gain weight achieved through self-starvation. Anorexics are obsessed with counting calories and exercising frequently. Anorexia is one of the most common psychiatric diagnoses in young women, with a high mortality rate. Between 5 percent and 20 percent of anorexics die. The starvation leads to malnutrition, loss of periods, and eventually organ failure and death.

Bulimia Nervosa

Eighty percent of bulimia nervosa patients are female. One in every five college-age women is bulimic. Bulimia nervosa is an eating disorder characterized by a period of limiting food intake or fasting, followed by excessive eating, and then vomiting or purging to relieve feelings of guilt and low self-esteem. Purging may be achieved through self-induced vomiting, abuse of laxatives, or excessive exercise. This cycle can occur several times a week or in severe cases, several times a day. Symptoms may include chronic gastric reflux, dehydration, fluctuating weight, and inflammation of the esophagus, along with dental erosion due to contact between gastric acid and the teeth.

Binge Eating Disorder (BED)

Binge eating, or compulsive overeating, represents the greatest number of individuals with an eating disorder and is a leading contributor to obesity in the United States. It cuts across a wide range of ages and weights. You don't have to be obese to suffer from BED.

The eating has a frenzied and uncontrollable aspect to it. Among overweight and obese children and adolescents, the rate of BED ranges from 20 to 36 percent, and weight is gained at a younger age than those without the disorder. BED is estimated to affect fifteen million U.S. adults ages eighteen and over. Sixty percent of people who struggle with BED are female. Genetics; neurobiological and psychosocial influences, such as the increase in high fat/sugar foods; and a focus on body size and appearance all play a role in the high numbers of people with the disorder.

THIN = WIN

Dear Arden,

My daughter, Hope, is an amazing athlete who aspires to compete at the Olympics. She has been in training since she was seven. Now, at fifteen, she is under tremendous pressure. Her coach, Brian, suggested she step up her weight training and lose a few pounds. My daughter is a perfectionist. She is skipping meals and running to the point of exhaustion, and she has shin splints. I have told her that she is driving herself and her body to the outer limits. Her response? "Don't you want me to succeed and live my passion?" Her younger sister came to me the other day and said she saw Hope stick her finger down her throat and run to the bathroom. What is going on here, and how can I fix it?

Mom, it sounds like Hope is developing exercise bulimia along with purging. Unfortunately, any form of dieting is now going to cause an equal and opposite response. She is stressing beyond belief. Her coach is mostly responsible here, but so is our culture. There is a wave of exercise bulimia and eating disorders suffered by high-level athletes.

Where there is an overemphasis on hyperspeed or making weight, there can be a tendency on the part of these driven athletes to attain their goals in very unhealthy ways. As parents, we want our daughters to succeed, but we don't want our daughters to be driven to perfection and health-compromising behavior.

You need to speak to the coach about your daughter. Let her know that you are hurting for her and that Brian does not fully appreciate or realize his harmful impact on Hope. You must tell him what Hope is doing to herself. Once Brian sees what's going on, then you both need to help your daughter slow down. I know she is going to be furious, but she needs to heal and rest her body. A consultation with a counseling nutritionist, Mom, and Coach present will make a tremendous impact on your daughter.

She needs to be surrounded by love. Regaining her health right now is her—and your—priority. Her dreams, aspirations, and ambitions will come to pass once she regains her connection to her love, respect, and acceptance of her body.

> "Healing and recovery are about becoming whole, finding the parts of yourself you leave behind when you pursue food, weight, and body perfection at all costs and when food and eating disorder behaviors become your tools for negotiating life. Healing is about learning how to have feelings, to use these feelings as guides, and to find healthful ways of being present for what life lessons are coming your way. I teach them that the hard, scary, and uncomfortable is what creates growth and change. That staying safe and comfortable, while easier, keeps them stuck. My job is always to help them be in the moment and know that they can handle the feeling and make appropriate and good enough responses—not food responses but life responses."
>
> —Sondra Kronberg, MS, RD, CDN, CEDRD, and Director of the Eating Disorder Treatment Collaborative

IT'S A FAMILY AFFAIR

Dear Arden,
My sixteen-year-old daughter, Trisha, is chubby, about forty pounds overweight. We all are. After hearing so much about high blood

pressure, diabetes, cholesterol, and healthful eating, I wonder if I need to put my daughter on a diet. Her doctor suggested she should stop overeating French fries and sugary treats, her favorites. I have dieted and struggled with my weight my whole life, as did my mother. We love our food. To think of putting my daughter in the position I've been in my whole life frustrates and pains me. Is there another way?

This is a tough one, Mom. Your heart is in the right place. I am not a fan of any diet that becomes too restrictive and could create an equal and opposite reaction, a binge. Yo-yo dieting is definitely something we don't want your daughter to experience, right?

I would like your daughter perhaps to go to a counseling nutritionist who will help you all with food choices and lifestyle modifications. A counseling nutritionist can have meals with the family and make some wonderful interventions and help you all to understand what function and purpose food is serving for you. In addition, I know lots of people who have been on the Weight Watchers point system. This allows for a variety of choices, even of the previously mentioned "forbidden" foods. If there is an Overeaters Anonymous nearby, you and Trisha could check that out as well.

Perhaps the whole family can become more active walkers, hikers, or bikers. We don't want to make Trisha feel badly about herself, not at any cost. You know how you felt. The focus now needs to be more on one's health, not a diet. Be mindful and put a ban on diet and fat talk: yours, your mom's, and your friends'. Beauty is something that starts from within and manifests itself on the outside. Let your daughter know she is special and that this new active body and health project will be fun for all.

ANA AND MIA

Dear Arden,

My daughter, Tiffany, has been in treatment for anorexia and buli-mia for the past six months. She is five foot three and weighs ninety pounds. She was a compulsive overeater until last year. Her doctors felt that she had a mini-meltdown and was stressing out in her senior year, with applications, SATs, and ACTs. She is a perfectionist and an honor student.

I was listening at her door for signs of purging and I heard her chat-ting with another girl and it sounded like they were cheering each other on to lose more weight. They kept talking about these two girls, Ana and Mia. What's that about?

Ana refers to anorexia nervosa, and Mia stands for bulimia ner-vosa. Pro-"Ana" and pro-"Mia" sites first appeared about a decade ago. They discussed anorexia and bulimia as lifestyle choices, as opposed to life-threatening medical conditions. On such sites, an anorexic can talk about her weight and post pictures of herself as sources of "thinspiration" for other anorexics. It's perfection=starvation and emaciation. This personification of the disorders allows anorexics and bulimics to embrace their disorder as their "best friends." Recently, photos of model Isabelle Caro, whose struggle with anorexia and bulimia is documented in the 2008 memoir, *The Little Girl Who Did Not Want to Get Fat*, appeared on Ana and Mia sites after her death. Isabelle was involved in the Nolita campaign when the fashion industry was being challenged about hiring extremely underweight models on the catwalk. (You might remember Ana Carolina Reston, a twenty-one-year-old Brazilian model who died from anorexia in 2006.) Isabelle Caro's picture for the Nolita campaign was misused by Ana and Mia sites as a prototype of the ideal.

Yes, Mom, these are very dangerous sites that feed into your daughter's denial. It sounds like Tiffany has a very severe eating disorder. These sites validate your daughter's preoccupation with thinness and achieving "perfection" through starvation. This perfection comes at the cost of our daughters' bodies, minds, spirits, and beings. Please let your daughter's therapist and team know that she is involved in this world.

> "Most of my patients suffer from anorexia, bulimia nervosa, mixed eating disorders, and obesity. I believe that these patients all share a common disordered relationship with food and self. They almost all have altered body images and most struggle with self-acceptance. I spend a great deal of time getting to know and understand each patient. Compassion, acceptance, and setting limits and boundaries play an important role when trying to help my patients recover."
> —Dr. Maureen Cooney, DO, adolescent medicine and eating disorder specialist

IMPORTANT ADVICE FOR
THE PARENTS OF AN ANOREXIC

The Don'ts

- Don't force your daughter to eat or literally shove food down her mouth. She doesn't forget it and will make up for the "extra" calories by skipping a meal or two.

- Don't make her feel any worse than she already does. Try not to yell or have an outburst.
- Don't blame yourself. She will be disgusted and furious with you if she hears you blaming yourself.
- Don't come off sounding more expert than the experts.
- Don't tell her that she has to snap out of it.
- Don't punish her and take something special from her.
- Don't sit on your hands and hope it will go away. Get help for your daughter right away.
- Don't exercise excessively, well over three hours a day, to the point of injury, and obsessively focus on calorie reduction. You are a role model.

The Dos

- Do love her unconditionally, no matter what. Give her breathing space and encourage her self-expression.
- Do praise, affirm, and validate her whenever you can.
- Do be in her corner, offer hope, and encourage her to go to all of her helping professionals.
- Do be mindful about how you refer to people of different sizes and shapes. Your daughter is listening to you. She thinks you are talking about her, even if you aren't.
- Do exercise moderately for health and some stress relief.

Recovery is a slippery slope, and healing is a family affair. Everyone has to do their part to help themselves and to help each other. Your daughter's healing involves her emotionally and physically reconnecting to herself. Developing a healthy, nourishing relationship with food, while embracing, accepting, loving, and liking herself and her body and having a positive body image are all the keys, the ingredients, to wellness and recovery.

CHAPTER 12

Alcohol and Drugs

"The man who removes a mountain begins by carrying away small stones."

—Chinese proverb

It's the middle of the night when you hear your daughter returning home from a party. "Oh good," you think, "she's home," and roll over to go back to sleep. A few minutes later you are woken again, this time by a small and pitiful voice next to your bed. "Mommy," she says. "Mommy, I don't feel so good."

It's three in the morning. When you and your underage daughter get to the bathroom, her body begins to violently empty itself. In between her heaves, you ask what happened: *How much did you drink? What did you drink? Didn't you know when enough was enough?*

Your daughter looks pitiful, "I'm sorry, Mommy. I know you're mad at me. Are you going to punish me?"

Good question. Your daughter is a captive audience. Do you:

A) Yell and scream at her until you're hoarse;

B) Ground her and punish her until she's twenty-one;

C) Stay calm and resolve to talk to her in the morning; or

D) Ignore her and give her the silent treatment?

Well, if you had read my chapter on aerial parenting, you would know the answer is C. Personally, I think that feeling sick, with your head hanging over the toilet bowl, is punishment enough. You score extra points, Mom, if you table the discussion until tomorrow, when she is not looking so green. Your daughter, no doubt expecting the worst from you, will be relieved.

The next morning you tell her you're glad she got home safely, that you love her and you care about her. You tell her how concerned you are, that you hope she will take better care of herself. Most importantly, you tell her, "I'm glad you woke me up." See, that's the thing. If your daughter thinks of you as the punisher, she will never come to you for help.

As one sixteen-year-old patient told me, "She's not thinking. Kids get drunk. It's just for the moment. As a parent, I'd be upset. I would talk to her in the morning. I would ask her to tell me all about the party and get the details. Kids make mistakes. Maybe you did the same thing when you were a kid?"

It's difficult to telegraph to the teenage brain the consequences of acting out and experimenting impulsively at a time it is wired to do just that—act without thinking. Still, the evidence on even "harmless" and "fun" drug and alcohol usage is sobering. Parents need to stay alert and informed. Research indicates that alcohol consumption has the potential to trigger long-term biological changes that may have detrimental effects on the developing adolescent brain. A person who begins drinking early in life is more likely to become a heavy drinker during adolescence and to experience alcohol abuse or dependence on alcohol in adulthood. In 2004, over 142,000 teenagers between twelve and twenty years old visited emergency rooms with injuries related to drinking alcohol. Every day, approximately three teens die from drinking and driving accidents. If you talk to your daughter about not driving when she is drunk or getting in the car with a drunk driver, you could save her life.

Some Facts About Alcohol

- Alcohol is the most commonly used and abused drug among youth under the age of twenty-one in the United States, more common than tobacco and illicit drugs.
- Each year approximately five thousand people under the age of twenty-one die as a result of underage drinking.
- In 2005, 28 percent of fifteen- to twenty-year-old drivers who were killed in motor vehicle crashes had been drinking.
- It's estimated that 29.1 percent of high school students risk their lives by riding with a drunk driver every month.
- About 45 percent of people who die in car crashes involving a drunk driver under the age of twenty-one are people other than the driver.
- Teenage girls who binge drink are 63 percent more likely to become teenage mothers.

NOT SO FAST

Teenagers are curious. Their propensity for thrill-seeking and new adventures makes them willing subjects for experimenting with alcohol and drugs. If they suffer from depression or other mood disorders, they are at even greater risk of developing an addiction. Some teens pop pills to boost their energy levels so they can stay up all night to do homework and keep up with sports. Some girls with eating disorders take pills to lose weight. It's really getting out of hand. Consider these statistics:

- Nine million young people between the ages of twelve and twenty-five need treatment for substance abuse or addiction. Two million of them are ages twelve to seventeen.
- Ninety percent of the two million twelve- to seventeen-year-olds are not getting the help they need.
- Marijuana use is three times more likely to lead to dependence among adolescents than among adults.
- Treatment for marijuana is the number one reason teens get admitted to treatment programs—more than the admissions for all other illicit drugs combined.
- Every day, approximately 4,700 Americans under the age of eighteen try marijuana for the first time.
- According to the National Institute on Drug Abuse, 5.3 million Americans ages twelve and older abused cocaine in 2008.
- Nonmedical use of the opiates and prescription painkillers Vicodin and OxyContin increased during the last five years among tenth graders.
- According to the National Alliance on Mental Illness, 61 percent of individuals with bipolar illness also have a substance abuse disorder.

PHARM PARTIES

Dear Arden,
I heard my sixteen-year-old daughter, Stephanie, talking to her best friend about a "farm party" one evening. What is it?

Pharm parties are parties with pharmaceutical prescription pills. Teenagers and young adults raid medicine cabinets at home for Vicodin, OxyContin, Ritalin, Adderall, Dexedrine, Xanax, Klonopin, Prozac, Zoloft, Lexapro, and Paxil. At the party they mix up the pills, serve them in a bowl, and call it "trail mix." Then they grab a handful to swallow, crush, or snort.

Talk, talk, talk to Stephanie about how dangerous it is to take any prescription pill without medical supervision. Emphasize that mixing and ingesting pills in large quantities can be lethal. Ask her: has she ever popped a prescription pill? How about her friends?

A medicine cabinet is not a candy dispenser. You need to lock it up just as you would a liquor cabinet. Keep a number count of what you have used. Write the number of tablets left in the vial or bottle—just like you would draw a line across a liquor bottle with a Sharpie pen. Or keep your pills with you, for your teen's protection. When you're done with them, dispose of them properly and don't leave them lying around.

Tell Stephanie that her health and safety come first and you will be vigilant about her welfare. Let her know the seriousness of creating a drug dependence and addiction. Look at the warning signs for depression and anxiety. Often kids don't realize they are self-medicating for depression by abusing alcohol or drugs.

Fast Facts on Prescription Drug Abuse

- One in five teens report abusing a prescription pain medication, stimulant, or tranquilizer.
- Teens abuse more prescription drugs than cocaine, heroin, and methamphetamines combined.

- According to the Centers for Disease Control and Prevention, emergency room visits for nonmedical use of prescription and over-the-counter drugs doubled during a recent five-year period. (This puts the number of medical emergencies for abusing legal drugs on par with those for illegal drugs.)
- The most emergency visits were for reactions to oxycodone, hydrocodone, and methadone: 305,900 visits in 2008, up from 144,600 in 2004.
- The anti-anxiety drugs called benzodiazepines accounted for 271,700 visits in 2008, up from 143,500 in 2004.

CAUGHT SMOKING ON CAMERA

Dear Arden,

My thirteen-year-old daughter, Rachel, asked to borrow my camera last weekend. When she returned it, I noticed there were some images she had saved and forgot to delete. Arden, the pictures were of her and her friends smoking at a party! From the way she held the cigarette, I could tell she was very comfortable smoking and had been smoking for a while! When my husband and I confronted her about the pictures, she said that she and her friends were just posing. My husband says it is harmless and told me to let it go, but I feel sure that she has been smoking and sneaking around behind our backs for months now. She knows how I feel about cigarette smoking, and how her grandfather died from lung cancer. What can I do?

Think back to when you were a teenager and were caught with your hand in the cookie jar. An authority figure, perhaps your mom, asks, "What are you doing?" "Who, me?" you ask. "Nothing, I'm doing nothing. I'm innocent, I didn't do anything." Mom asks, "Why is there a pack of cigarettes in your bag?" "Oh," you reply, "I was holding it for my friend."

You get the picture, Mom.

Most kids, when confronted, go on autopilot with a knee-jerk reactive response, even when it would be so much easier if she just owned that she has tried smoking, or that she has been smoking for the past three months.

Approach Rachel with some cold, hard facts (see the following box). I have used this strategy with kids who were abusing steroids and those who were addicted to tanning beds. Their response, said with appreciation and relief: "I had no idea, Arden. Thanks!"

Ask Rachel to consider what you just shared with her and tell her that you would love to hear from her in a few days what she thinks and feels. We really want her to process everything that she's heard and read. I hope she does and thinks twice the next time she puts a cigarette to her lips.

And if she still insists that she's not smoking? Say, "Honey, this is a prevention talk, not a lecture." Finish up the talk by telling her that Grandpa died of lung cancer. Tell her about the health risks of being exposed to secondhand smoke. You say, "I don't want you to be in a position where you innocently experiment and find yourself hooked like Grandpa was. It's about safeguarding our health and well-being. We want to live for a long time and have productive lives, right? And not cut our lives short like Grandpa did."

Smoking Statistics

- Eighty percent of adult smokers started smoking before the age of eighteen.
- Twenty-five percent of young people have tried cigarettes by eighth grade.
- Fifty percent of young people have tried cigarettes by twelfth grade.
- More than 20 percent of twelfth graders smoked in the past month.
- Young adults, ages eighteen to twenty-five, had the highest rate of tobacco use (44.3 percent).
- Every day, close to three thousand young people under the age of eighteen become regular smokers.
- There is no safe level of exposure to second-hand smoke.
- Second-hand smoke is just as much of a risk outdoors as it is indoors.
- The younger you start smoking, the greater the likelihood you will become drug-dependent.

A HISTORY OF ALCOHOLISM AND DRUG ABUSE IN THE FAMILY

Dear Arden,
Both my husband and I grew up with one alcoholic parent, and there is a history of alcoholism and drug addiction in our families. How much can we tell our daughter, Melissa, age eleven, about her family history, and when is a good time to discuss it?

If you are beginning to open up an ongoing dialogue with Melissa, it's your current behavior that counts more than anything else. What is she seeing at home and with her extended family? I hope that if there is any drinking at all, it's minimal. The predisposing nature for both you and your husband puts your daughter at greater risk. If you do drink socially, keep a serious count, because she will learn her drinking habits by example. Sometimes it's our behavior, even more than our words, that counts. Ultimately our talk needs to meet up with our walk.

The earlier she experiments, the more likely she will become alcohol-dependent. Share with her that sometimes people cope with their anger, stress, and disappointment by overdrinking (binge-drinking). Some justify their excessive drinking by saying, "I only do it on the weekends."

If your parents or extended family are still drinking and are involved in your daughter's life, you can use that as a springboard for discussion. Get a sense of what she has observed, what she has overheard, and what she knows to help her put the puzzle together. If your parents are still drinking, I would **script** it and say: "I am unhappy that Grandma and Grandpa and other family members are hurting themselves and have not gotten help for themselves to deal with their drinking problems. I first became aware when I was your age, honey, around eleven years old. After I turned thirteen, I tried to convince them to stop, but they didn't listen. I was very frustrated and upset all those years and still am. Alcoholism and drug abuse are destructive to the person abusing those substances and emotionally painful and harmful to all the members of the family. The abuser drives good folks like me and your dad away."

Since Melissa is eleven, I would share some alarming statistics with her about underage drinking and becoming drug-dependent.

There are some parents who have spoken with their children as young as nine. I think that is okay as well. It's all about the exposure and not letting the drinking and drugging look like a normal part of family life. Don't sweep it under the rug and say that "all families do that." Always encourage her to share her confusions, concerns, and questions with you as she gets older, especially when she may start to think more about experimenting with substances.

SECRET STASH

Dear Arden,

I found marijuana and rolling papers in my fourteen-year-old daughter Erin's room. She said she was holding them for a friend whose parents were too nosy and strict, but then I found a jacket in her closet that reeked of pot-smoking.

Mom, as soon as you hear she is "holding them for a friend," nine times out of ten you can bet the "friend's" name is Erin. Where to go from here?

There is no doubt that there is a steady rise in the use of drugs at parties and social situations. Girls tend to view the use of marijuana as a positive in social situations—it makes them feel looser, more fun and cool, and less lonely. They don't necessarily see its potential to become addictive.

The younger she starts smoking, the more likely she will become seriously addicted. If she says, "Everybody does it," you answer, "Not everyone smokes. Some kids do." Over 40 percent of eighth graders and 73 percent of tenth graders consider marijuana to be easily accessible. That number jumps to 86 percent in twelfth grade. Marijuana is the most popular illegal drug in the country.

Erin needs to know that pot has more tar than cigarettes and can cause a nasty cough. If she is the kind of person who gets physically run-down easily, this drug will add to her fatigue.

Mom, you need to get personal and ask her directly: how long has her "friend" been smoking, how much, and how frequently? **Script** it: "If I tell you that you won't get into trouble with me, is the friend you?" You need to assess the severity of your daughter's habit. Then you need to realize that your daughter is more likely to smoke pot if either you or your husband do. Please do not be a hypocrite and hide behind the flawed "I can but you can't" line of reasoning. If you do, you won't have a leg to stand on. I hope you've had many talks with Erin about drug usage, experimentation, and abuse. If not, it's not too late to begin.

A DRUGGY PAST

Dear Arden,

My husband and I experimented a lot with alcohol and pot as teens and during college. We have three daughters, ages fifteen, fourteen, and eight. Is it okay for us to discuss the drugs we tried with them? If they ask us questions about the times we were hungover, stoned, or drunk, how honest can we be? If we are open with her about our own drinking and using experiences, will we be encouraging them to experiment and get drunk too?

Right now there is a hot debate about what to tell and how much, if any, to our tween and teen daughters when it comes to their parents' past risky behavior and habits, such as alcohol consumption and drug use and abuse. A few questions to consider: what is your current consumption? What do your children see? Are you both still smoking pot? How much, if any, are you still drinking?

I think we can have the greatest impact when our kids are young, before they begin experimenting with any substance. Approach the talk by focusing on "when and if you do" rather than telling them to just stay away from drugs and alcohol without explanation. You can talk about your past alcohol and drug use without extolling it. Research has shown that when parents provide information and better modeling early on, their children's risk of substance abuse decreases. The earlier this conversation begins, the better.

Let this coincide with what your child is learning in school. One program, the Drug and Alcohol Awareness Program (DARE), starts in elementary school. However, there are more spontaneous opportunities for discussion too. Let's say your precocious eight-year-old is watching a TV program with you and people are drinking. She may ask you about what they are doing. Give her a very simple explanation, and don't go into too much detail.

But what if her fifteen-year-old sister is drinking and your little girl hears arguing between her sister and you? Then what? You have to tell her that her sister is drinking and you are trying to help her see that she is harming herself.

I wouldn't get too detailed with your thirteen-and-under set, especially if you both were over the top. You don't have to tell her everything, but what you do say has to be honest.

If your fifteen-year-old comes home stoned, you can care-front her (a softened confrontation) instead of angrily confronting her. When she owns up to being high, say, "I was no angel." If she asks you, "What do you mean by that, Mom?" you can say, "I did do some drugs and drank as a teen. I was not thinking and not taking good care of myself. I was sneaking around, honey. I learned the hard way. I'm a very different person now, and I learned a lot from my mistakes."

While experimentation is understandable, addiction is another matter entirely. It could lead to even riskier behavior and more addictive drugs.

Mom, please be careful not to sound proud of your experimentation and glorify your drug use: "I was a cool hippie and man, those were the groovy days!" That's TMI, as the kids say.

For an older teenager, you could say (but only if it's true): "We made our mistakes and later realized we were polluting ourselves. Once we thought about having children, we decided to keep a drug-free home and lifestyle." Let her know you are not encouraging her.

She drives a car, right? Use that as a talking point. You want her to be safe, fully present, and very conscious and aware of herself and her physical safety. What's more, risky behaviors, date rapes, and other complicated situations are much more likely to happen when she is under the influence. Encourage your daughter to take precautions, be alert, and be aware.

ALCOHOLIC MOM

Dear Arden,

My name is Kate, and I am an alcoholic in recovery. I have maintained my sobriety through the help of Alcoholics Anonymous and my sponsor for the past eighteen months. I am still trying to pick up the pieces in my life. I have worked long and hard on myself. At one point, I was drinking up to a bottle and a half of wine a day. On the weekend, I could step it up and added about five to six drinks of hard liquor. I also owe my sobriety to my daughter Kelsey, seventeen, a graduating senior; my second husband, Bob; and my extended family that intervened over two years ago. I had no idea how much I was hurting all of them and myself. I guess I didn't care. Back then my addiction, my drug of choice, came first. I was told that I blacked out often and that I was a nasty drunk. I feel so guilty for putting my family, especially Kelsey and Tess, age twelve, through all of the chaos and turmoil.

My current predicament is with my ex-husband Peter, whom I divorced over six years ago. He is still an active alcoholic. Pete and I were drinking buddies in our abusive marriage. I have spoken to him about the kind of example he sets for the girls, and he could care less. He says, "Who are you to talk?" He's a big bully and becomes aggressive and intimidating when he wants to get his way. Last week, Tess told me that Pete was drinking and she was in the car with him. I am sick and tired of fighting him in court. Pete is so out of control. I don't know what to do.

It takes so much courage and fortitude to step forward, Kate, and admit that you are an alcoholic in recovery. Good for you that your commitment to AA, your sobriety, and your relationship with your daughters are taking first place.

Tess's safety is tantamount. How awful for her to be trapped in the car with her actively drinking alcoholic father. I have a feeling that this is nothing new for both of the girls. However, this time you see more clearly that you must be proactive and super protective of Tess. You have to imagine that your ex-husband's intimidating your daughters, running the show, and running you days are over. Kate, he tries to control you by pulling you down to his level.

You need help to rise above and continue to stand your ground, whether it's in a one-on-one with him or to see him in family court.

Script to your daughters: "Kelsey and Tess, I need to press forward. We can't let your dad continue to push us all around. I am going to court to fight for what's right. We will get more professional help to give us encouragement and support to do what's in your best interest. You girls come first. Tess, the days of worrying if Dad is or isn't sober are over. It's not fair for you to be put in that helpless position. If you don't feel safe, you don't have to get in the car with Dad. Call me and I will come and pick you up, or take a taxi."

Kate, a show of strength and standing tall on your part will be reassuring to your girls.

BACK FROM REHAB

Dear Arden,

My eighteen-year-old daughter, Dakota, is returning from rehab to live at home and go to college under our supervision. She was treated for mixed addiction to alcohol and painkillers. I am having a hard time trusting her and that she is where she says she is or doing what she is supposed to be doing. I am constantly afraid that she will have a relapse and I watch her like a hawk. It's really hard to trust her after knowing and remembering all the lies she's told her father and me. How do I know she's really cured this time?

This is a rough, tough time and an arduous journey for you and your daughter. Recovery is a very slippery slope, full of cravings, temptations, and near misses. It could take a good year and a half for Dakota to clean up her act and stay that way. For now, she is trying to replace unhealthy behaviors with healthy behaviors. It is a lifetime commitment to remain sober and alcohol-free. I would suggest you look into Alcoholics Anonymous. Attend Al-Anon meetings and get your daughter into Alcoholics Anonymous or Narcotics Anonymous. Having a sponsor will provide a safety net for Dakota, and it's a wonderful adjunct to her continued work with a counselor. I am presuming she has an outpatient therapist. If she doesn't, connect her to a therapist well-versed in addiction who is comfortable working with teens and young adults.

I would not expect a "cure." Recovery is a process that starts with discovering why Dakota did drugs to such an intense degree and frequency. She needs to learn how to identify and cope with her affective, feeling states, her body tension, and stresses in her life, rather than numb and run away from herself.

It's so understandable that you don't trust her. You don't have to for now. Over time it's all about the changes in her behavior, more accountability for her whereabouts, what she's doing and who she's with, her actions more than her words. She needs to re-earn your trust, and that will take as long as it takes. For now, being hypervigilant and watching out for your daughter like an eagle over its eaglets is protective and proactive and what any good mom would do. Dakota knows how you feel, and I bet at this point she doesn't even trust herself. Some rehabs last from ten days to two weeks to one to four months, not much time for an effective change, certainly not a cure, but it's a good beginning for her. Maintaining an open, authentic dialogue is the key to working on forgiveness. You both need to carry her baby picture and go through picture albums together of her childhood to remind yourselves of happier times. This will aid and abet healing for you both.

DRINKING DAD

Dear Arden,

My husband is a very social drinker, and has two or three cocktails during the week after work. I think he drinks more at business lunches too. I worry sometimes that his weekend drinking bouts set a bad example for our thirteen-year-old daughter, Cassidy. During the week, he is fine. He has never missed a day of work, but on the weekends, it is not uncommon for him to down one six-pack of beer after another, especially when he is watching sports. He tells me that I worry too much, and that our daughter is accountable to us for her behavior—and not the other way around. Cassidy asks me why her dad has to drink so much. What can I say to her without denigrating her father?

Uh-oh! I don't like the sound of this, Mom. Your daughter sees her dad's "bouts." What he's doing on the weekend is called binge-drinking. Dad may be a great guy, but he is rationalizing, in denial, and clueless about his impact on your daughter. Alcoholism is what it is, and for your husband it's having two or three cocktails perhaps after work during the week and a few six-packs on the weekend. He is offering you false reassurances and saying "you worry too much." Well, you know better, don't you?

His double-standard is very troubling to me. Get ahold of the Twelve Steps of Alcoholics Anonymous and read it out loud. He will look at you as if you have three heads and you are speaking another language. Let him know that you are tired of being an enabler and that you are going to Al-Anon for help.

Sorry, Mom, this is serious. Your husband is setting a very dangerous example for your daughter. These days it's so easy to have access to alcohol. Many kids are starting to drink as young as ten, eleven, or twelve. I hope that seeing her dad's weekend drinking is a turn-off for her

Here's a **script** for what you can say to her: "Cassidy, you are right. Dad is drinking too much, and I am concerned about him and the effect it's having on you. I have spoken with him, and he is acting like he has no problem, but he does, honey. I love your dad, but I don't like or agree with his drinking habits. I am going to a group called Al-Anon to get some help to figure out what my next step is. I think your going to an Alateen group could be helpful. There are other teens there who have parents who drink too much too. Dad does not want to get help for himself right now, but we need to help ourselves. Dad is clueless about how this is affecting you. Cass, tell me what have you seen that has upset you? It's okay to tell me if you have ever said anything to Dad about his drinking. Has Dad said anything to you? If so, what?"

Focus on verbally pulling Cassidy out of herself, and create a feeling of safety by telling her she can say anything to you now and that you won't repeat it to Dad. I don't want Dad being angry or defensive with her. These are positive and proactive first steps for you and Cassidy to get on the right track.

MIXING MEDS WITH DRUGS

Dear Arden,

Yesterday I overheard our sixteen-year-old daughter, Hannah, talking to one of her friends, who is on behavioral medication and abusing other drugs. I am concerned about any possible harmful side effects or interaction between the illegal, recreational drugs and his

prescriptions. Here's my dilemma: can we tell the friend's parents, or is it up to my daughter? Understandably, my daughter is afraid of any backlash it would cause for her.

You need to sit down with your daughter and share what you over-heard with her. Approach this with concern and without any judg-ment, with an emphasis on the health of her friend and his risky behavior. Reassure Hannah that she is not in any kind of trouble, and you are only there to help. Give her an opportunity to share her fear that he may get mad at her and she could lose a friend if you talk to his parents. She might say, "Lots of kids are on prescribed medication and smoke pot or pop pills."

Ask Hannah if she thinks her friend is harming or hurting him-self. If she says yes, you can empathize with her and say how dif-ficult this must be and how could she possibly know what to do? Find out if she has spoken with him already. This is the information you need to know, Mom, before you even involve the boy's parents. Let's say she spoke with him and got nowhere. Ask her, "Now is there anything we can do as a team of three to possibly help him?"

This is a very hard call. You don't know if this young man is going to feel angry and betrayed or relieved. Hannah needs to take a risk and speak with her friend and let him know that her mom overheard the conversation. She can then ask him what he wants her to do. She needs to let him know that her parents could talk to his parents or better yet, maybe they could speak to him directly. All of this depends on how comfortable and close he feels to you and your husband. We go one step at a time.

Unfortunately, combining drugs is not unique. His drug use could hamper the effectiveness of his behavioral medication. He may be abusing drugs for other reasons, like depression and anxiety, to numb any overpowering and negative feelings. You sound like a very concerned family. He is so fortunate to have people like you in his life.

WHEN ATHLETES AND DRINKING DON'T MIX

Megan, nineteen, was a scholarship athlete on her college soccer team. She contacted her mom to tell her that the coach would be calling her about a recent incident.

Britney, a freshman player, had fallen off the top of her bunk bed in the middle of the night and broken her arm. Megan and her teammates told the coach that she had just rolled the wrong way. The coach then relayed the news to the athletic committee. Then one of the girls on the team felt bad about lying to Coach and told him the truth.

Megan said, "Mom, this is what really happened. We were all drinking in the room and Britney was very drunk and fell off the bunk. None of us realized she'd have a hairline fracture and that Stacy would be a snitch. Now I am in real trouble. Coach is furious with me, because I'm the oldest and he feels that he lied to the committee. He is calling all the parents. Mom, I am so scared I am going to lose my scholarship and get kicked off the team! He's going to tell you everything, Mom."

Mom stayed calm. "Do you really think he is going to kick you off the team?"

"He threatened that he should, but I don't know. Maybe he won't let me play in a few games. Mom, I feel like such an idiot!"

Mom rolled her eyes, sighed again, and said, "Young lady,

you are so lucky that we have been in therapy with Arden. The old me would have killed you, grounded you, and yelled, but what's the point? Arden says teens learn from experiencing their lives, by making mistakes, and I have to expect that."

It's true. We know our children will make mistakes, but we hope that our teens won't make mistakes that can't be undone. That's where you come in, Mom—as her smart, calm, logical, compassionate, and resourceful secret weapon. Based on their work together in my practice, Megan and her mom were able to build a safe, secure, and open relationship where Megan could tell her mom the truth without fearing repercussions.

Mom said, "Well, let him call me, and I will call you back and let you know what he wants you to do."

The call came, and Coach was furious and beside himself. "Kids drink, even though it's against the school's and the athlete's code of conduct," he said. What really hurt him, though, was the lying and the position he was put in.

As he told Megan's mother, "I lied to the heads of the department. I could lose my job." Mom understood his predicament. She asked what would happen if the entire team went into the head of the department's office and apologized for lying and explained that it wasn't Coach's fault.

He said he'd think about that.

Days later I heard back from Mom and I was not surprised to hear that everything got straightened out. As she explained, "My daughter got an inkling of how much Coach had been relying on her to be the older, more responsible teammate, but she didn't fully appreciate the weight of it. This whole incident has scared her straight. She thanked me for being there for her and told me she felt incredibly relieved."

CASSIE: A CAUTIONARY TALE

I share the following true story as an eye-opener for parents and their teenage daughters.

Cassie was a smart young woman in a Midwestern college. She was a good student, with a close-knit group of friends. They all lived together in a sorority house. They all were casual drinkers but could step up their partying on the weekends. They were known on campus as the "pot heads." Everyone knew: if you needed pot, you went to the Delta house. The girls had quite the supply and reputation. In the past two years, business had been very good.

Cassie's parents, however, had no clue that their daughter was the campus drug dealer. They were so proud of their daughter, a full-time student on student loans who was working hard and hardly ever asked them for a penny. She would be the first college graduate in their family. When her parents visited Delta house, they would admire the wide-screen TV, the elaborate stereo system, and the fancy dinners that the girls prepared. They did not ever put together where all the money was coming from.

Well, little did anyone know that the house was under surveillance by school security. You guessed it, one day there was a big drug bust, and the only one home was Cassie. They uncovered one kilo of marijuana in the kitchen, and Cassie was held totally responsible. She denied it was hers, but it didn't make any difference.

The college administration contacted the sheriff's department, which led to the district attorney and a criminal case. It cost Cassie's parents thousands of dollars to hire a lawyer to defend her and reach a plea bargain for a first-time offender. Cassie risked graduation, a criminal record, a stint in jail, and embarrassment and humiliation to herself and her family. The case dragged on for almost a year. Cassie did get her degree and a two-year probationary period. She terribly regretted putting herself and her parents through such extensive agony.

The trust she had worked so hard to earn was destroyed, and it took years for her to rebuild her connection with her parents. Her parents felt totally hurt and had. They realized how gullible and naïve they had been and became wary of Cassie's ease in storytelling and lying. Cassie had to jump through many hoops for well over a year before her parents started to cautiously trust her again. Her parents nonetheless loved her unconditionally and stood by her side during the entire ordeal. They have all worked hard to rebuild their connection and have pressed forward with renewed faith and confidence in Cassie.

CHAPTER 13

Mental Health

"Every setback is a setup for a comeback."

—Joel Osteen

Being the mom of a tween or teen girl is challenging. Helping her to manage her stress levels and her ups and downs is no small feat. When they're young, our daughters learn coping skills and strategies from parents; as teenagers, they learn from peers. At times, your daughter's teenage brain can only take so much. She is susceptible to being stressed out and flooded by anxiety. She experiences mood swings and depression. How do you know what is typical teenage acting out—and what isn't?

Well, think about these kinds of things. Has there been a change in her behavior? Is she not like herself? How is she eating and sleeping? Does she appear lost, confused, anxious, or depressed? Are her outbursts and meltdowns, so typical of tweens and teens, now more frequent and severe in intensity? Do the writings and sketches in her journal disturb you, scare you? Does it feel like she is spiraling down into a dark abyss?

This is delicate work and no easy task. We keep a watchful eye on our children as we juggle our responsibilities, but sometimes paying attention is not enough. You get a gut instinct as a mother that something is terribly wrong. If you find yourself feeling helpless, hopeless, and overwhelmed, then it's time to seek professional help for yourself and your daughter.

Take a breath, Mom; what I'm going to say here is tough to swallow. According to the National Institute of Mental Health, mental disorders are the leading cause of disability in the United States and Canada for ages fifteen to forty-four. Studies have shown that one in eight teens may be suffering from depression, but less than a third of them receive any sort of treatment. Suicide is the second leading cause of death among college students.

Getting help for yourself and your daughter is the first step. Keeping a hopeful attitude is the next. Don't ever underestimate the healing power of your presence for your daughter. You can be the healing salve for her wounds by gently coaxing her to open up about what she is feeling and experiencing. Realize that there is so much you can do just by being fully emotionally present for her. Caring for your child can be very draining. It's important to keep in mind that it doesn't have to all fall on you. This is a time when you need the support of your family and friends, and all the patience, gentleness, and love they can provide. Going to a highly skilled psychotherapist can be a life-saver as well.

A recent survey done by the National Institute of Mental Health determined that:

- Eleven percent of teenagers ages thirteen to eighteen are severely impaired by a mood disorder such as depression or bipolar disorder.
- Ten percent are severely impaired by a behavior disorder such as ADD or a conduct disorder.

- Eight percent report being severely impaired by at least one type of anxiety disorder.
- Symptoms of anxiety disorders tend to emerge by age six, behavior disorders emerge by age eleven, mood disorders emerge by age thirteen, and substance use disorders by age fifteen.

LITTLE MISS PERFECT

Dear Arden,

My sixteen-year-old, Victoria, is a perfectionist. I frequently find her checking and rechecking her homework, school forms, and her purse. She spends hours lining up the shoes in her closet just so. When she has a paper due or has to study for a test, she gets all worked up until she is on the verge of tears. She tries so hard and is so conscientious, it breaks my heart. She's a good kid; I just wish she could take it easier. One of my friends suggested that she might be suffering from anxiety or OCD. How do I know if she is?

Underneath your daughter's drive for perfection is an inordinate amount of anxiety that she is struggling to manage and that gets played out through obsessive-compulsive rituals and symptoms. A little amount of anxiety or concern is okay—that's what motivates folks to improve themselves, work harder, and get the job done. Unfortunately, your daughter is being thrown off her track. A consultation with a clinical social worker or a psychologist will generate helpful suggestions and direction. Victoria needs counseling to develop alternative constructive behaviors that will help her deal with her high anxiety. Cognitive behavioral therapy, stress management, and guided visualization will help alleviate some of her body tension, lower the impossibly high bar of expectations she has set for herself, and reduce some of the pressure she puts on herself. It sounds like you also have a great friend who cares very much about you and your daughter.

Sit down with Victoria and calmly tell her you hate to see her so distressed. Gently suggest to her that with the help of some caring professionals, she can learn how to calm, soothe, and anchor herself and approach her challenges in a far less anxious manner with faith and confidence in herself. If you are met with fear and reluctance, ask her to go once for a consultation. Once she's there, hopefully she will find immediate relief from being heard and understood and pick up some helpful coping strategies and tactics as well.

JOURNAL OF DOOM

Dear Arden,

My sixteen-year-old daughter, Destiny, left her journal open on her bed. I peeked at what she had written. It was a very long and sad poem about dying and cutting and blood. I was shocked. She wondered what it would be like to die, and her descriptions were very graphic and bloody. She had doodled pictures of zombies with hollowed-out eyes. In some sections, it looked like she had spilled blood on the pages, not ink. Do you think she could hurt herself?

Her doodles, poems, and pictures are quite disturbing and concerning to me as well. If your daughter is thinking about cutting or hurting herself, we need to help her find some other means of healthy self-expression. These include:

1. Sculpting and ceramics class, working with a kiln and creating her own personal work of art.
2. Art and creative drawing classes; buy her art supplies and make her feel that you are a loving presence.
3. Sewing and knitting classes.
4. Walking outside and communing with nature, a change of scenery, a day trip, sitting near a lake, river, ocean, or other body of water.
5. Meditation and deep breathing.
6. Yoga/Pilates class, deep stretching.
7. Taking a warm bubble bath.
8. Listening to calming music.
9. Reconnecting with pals, going to concerts, movies, dinner, hanging out.
10. Having a facial/massage/manicure/pedicure.
11. Shopping.
12. Writing in a journal that contains her poems and doodles on one side and perhaps challenging with positive life-affirming thoughts on the other side (you need a therapist to guide and facilitate this process).
13. Cognitive reframing (this involves the rebuilding of your daughter's self- and body-esteem with the help of a therapist, with statements like "I believe that I have value and worth; my body is not a canvas to deface but my place of worship.").

If you put yourself into Destiny's skin, this is how you would feel. Imagine that you are experiencing excruciating, intolerable, emotional pain that doesn't diminish or go away. A flood gate of emotions—rage, loss, emptiness, abandonment, and numbness—engulfs you. You feel fragmented and dissociated from your usual self. You have no means of verbal expression for what you're experiencing, no outlet. Instead you turn to a sharp edge, scissors, a knife, a razor blade, a shard of glass, a pin, or your nails, and you dig in hard enough to draw your own blood.

There is a sense of relief, as emotional pain is fully realized in the physical. The physical pain is easier to handle. You have created a ritual and you have created a wound for the expression of your pain. In a strange way, the cutting is a relief from all this numbness—you can feel again. This cutting, this release from the pain, becomes addictive. Sometimes you feel ashamed of your secret; it would be humiliating for anyone to find out. You take special care to hide the scars.

The body weeps what the person is unable to articulate. If the body could speak, what would it say? If the cutting could scream, what would it say?

Hopefully you can get Destiny the help that she needs, and prevent her from tumbling down this path any further. If she is a cutter, then you will have to seek professional help, as her cutting could continue for years if left untreated and put her at greater risk for suicide and other self-punishing behaviors like eating disorders.

For signs of cutting, look at your daughter's wrists, arms, legs, thighs, and torso when she is wearing clothes that show her body parts. Look for scratches, unhealed open wounds, healed scars, stitches, and bandages. She may be cutting at night when she is alone and unable to manage upsetting thoughts and feelings.

Use this **script** for approaching her: "Honey, I noticed that you have an open gash. How did that happen?" She might say, "I accidently cut myself while shaving my legs. I was using scissors to cut paper. The knife slipped while I was cutting a sandwich." You reply, "This is happening more than ever. I am getting concerned about you. You didn't have those gashes or cuts yesterday. Are you hurting yourself at night? Maybe we need to get you some help to understand what you are doing to yourself?"

She will deny it and be furious, but that's okay; you are opening up a dialogue and from what you shared she really needs to speak to some professional. Sometimes, Mom does not have to do it all, especially when our daughters present us with such complicated symptoms.

WHAT LIES BENEATH THE URGE TO CUT

It is estimated that self-mutilation affects nearly 1 percent of people in the United States. Teenagers who cut themselves or practice other forms of self-mutilation and self-harm may turn to cutting because they feel invisible or unaccepted. They may suffer from an untreated clinical depression, physical and sexual abuse, incest, trauma, an eating disorder, panic attacks, or profound loss and delayed grief and bereavement. Loneliness, bullying at school, angst over sexuality, low self-esteem, an unwanted pregnancy, and previous suicidal attempts can all contribute to a teenager's desire to injure herself.

Cutters can cut, carve, and slash their wrists, thighs, legs, stomach, and face. They may reopen a wound or insert objects under the skin. Other forms of mutilation may include pulling out hair, burning oneself, and hitting oneself. Some cutters are furious with themselves, full of self-hate and self-loathing, and they want to punish themselves. Others may suffer from borderline personality disorder. These people have many cuts and bruises. They will go to great lengths—wearing long-sleeved shirts and wrist cuffs or bandannas—to hide their wounds and scars and keep their injuries a secret. Among those who are most likely to seek help for this self-injurious behavior are teenage girls from the middle class and upper-middle class.

Statistics on Self-Mutilation and Cutting

- In the United States, it's estimated that one in every two hundred girls between thirteen and nineteen years old cut themselves regularly.
- One in every five teenagers admit they have injured themselves on purpose.
- Self-abuse, including self-mutilation and eating disorders, affects nearly one percent of the population in the United States.
- Teenagers are particularly vulnerable to self-mutilation, with girls four times more likely than boys to self-harm. Over 10 percent of the teenage population is estimated to experiment with self-mutilation.
- The majority of people who self-injure are women between the ages of thirteen and thirty, with the onset of symptoms beginning when they are between ten and sixteen years old.

AN ALARMING UPDATE

Dear Arden,
The other day I noticed that my stepdaughter, Madison, age fourteen, updated her Facebook status and posted, "OMG I WANT TO RUN AWAY OR DIE!!" and this is not the first time. She often posts

things like "FML!" (fuck my life) or "Wish I could die to see if someone would actually care." She's always been a little dramatic and high-strung, but I suspect she may be depressed. My husband is not the custodial parent, and we only see her on the weekends; he lets his ex-wife be in charge and handle all of her doctor's appointments. I got some excellent recommendations for therapists, so how do I approach her mom about this? We aren't close and haven't talked much. We just see each other at drop-offs or school functions. I don't have any children of my own, or experience with them, although I have always wanted to be a mother.

Being a stepmom is a challenge, especially if you have not had children of your own. You astutely recognize that the biological mother and father are not picking up on their daughter's very strong and powerfully dramatic statements. Just a thought, but maybe she wouldn't have the need to be so dramatic if they were more attuned with her.

I would share what you read with your husband. Then he needs to decide, with your help, how he will approach his ex-wife. I don't know how friendly the ex and your husband are to each other, but they both need to get on their daughter's Facebook page and be impacted! Then they need to look at themselves and try to figure out what could have led up to Madison being so angry and upset. You are right: a therapist who specializes in working with families is the next step. Both her dad and mom need to be involved in the therapy and work together on their daughter's behalf.

Your stepdaughter's health and safety is of the utmost importance. Perhaps a neutral person who will listen and give a serious ear to Madison will help her begin to unravel all or some of her pain.

Expressions like "FML" have become part of the teenage vernacular, the equivalent of "I had a crappy day. Wait till you hear about this!" So how will you know if this is just adolescent moping on her part or something more serious? Check to see if other red flags and warning signs for depression are present: an inability to concentrate or focus well, plummeting grades in school, moodiness, temper tantrums, refusal to go to school, refusal to shower or get out of bed, poor grooming habits, erratic sleep patterns, crying, weepiness, chronic fatigue, threats to harm herself, and suicidal gestures. Also look at the context of Madison's posts and comments: saying "I give up" after a bad breakup may be alarming, but saying "I give up" because of the math homework is not. Statements that smack of suicidal gestures include: "I am going to kill myself. Life is not worth living."

When it comes to having a finger on the pulse of our vulnerable children that could be very traumatized by a divorce, impending divorce, or an incident at school, we as mothers and parents really need to be so *aware* of our children's mental, physical, and spiritual state.

DIAGNOSIS OF DEPRESSION

Dear Arden,

My daughter, Julia, seventeen, has been diagnosed as clinically depressed. I am meeting with her psychiatrist next week. What kind of questions do I need to ask the doctor? What do I have to consider before putting my daughter on medication? Are there any drawbacks?

Clinical depression, also known as major depressive disorder, is a mental disorder marked by an all-encompassing low mood and accompanied by low self-esteem and the loss of pleasure and interest in normally enjoyable activities. Major depression is very disabling. It can adversely affect a person's sleeping, eating, and general health, along with family relationships and performance at school and work. The most common time of onset is between the ages of twenty and thirty years, with another peak between thirty and forty years. Women experience depression at twice the rate that men do, and this statistic holds true for teenage girls and boys as well.

Julia has been diagnosed with *clinical* depression, which is different from *reactive* depression.

Reactive depression is situational and more connected to a recent loss or event, such as the death of a loved one, divorce, or a major transition, like moving. Patients with both clinical and reactive depression are often treated with a combination of antidepressant medication and psychotherapy or counseling. With any prescribed medications and drugs, you will need to be informed of the short-term side effects and the long-term side effects. Among the medications that could be prescribed for your daughter are antidepressants and SSRI's such as Prozac, Zoloft, and Lexapro; antidepressants like Wellbutrin or Zyban; and antianxiety medications such as Klonopin and Xanax. These have been useful in offering some symptomatic relief and facilitating a person's ability to concentrate and engage more in a therapeutic treatment process with her clinician.

Your daughter's unique brain and blood chemistry will dictate and gauge the dosage. We do not want her to be overmedicated or undermedicated. Based on Julia's receptivity, responsiveness, and personal feedback, it can take some time to achieve the right dosage. A good barometer is to ask the simple question about how she is feeling each time she is seen. Mom, you can ask Julia how she is doing and feeling, especially if she is on the younger side. You also can give the therapist feedback on how your daughter is doing and coping with her life (i.e., school, friends). If Julia is feeling better, less anxious, and able to get out of bed, that will give her therapist a sense of the effectiveness of both the therapy and medication.

Research bears out that the most effective treatment for a clinical depression is a combination of psychotherapies and medication. Medication alone is not as effective. Exercise and physical activities will help to release endorphins that will elevate your daughter's affective state and mood. The challenge of pushing oneself physically often creates movement and momentum in her life.

It's a long journey with no magic bullets or quick fixes. You will need to take developments one step at a time. In time, medication may be tapered off depending on how she is managing her life—school, family, peers, daily functioning, and stresses. The main focus is to help Julia feel better and rebuild her confidence and her capacity to make independent decisions for herself.

It's not uncommon for a clinically depressed person to resist getting help due to feelings of shame. The social stigma attached to mental illness can make a teenager feel like she is going crazy or that there is something wrong with her. Getting help is not a sign of weakness but an act of great courage. Please give Julia a hug. She will need the constancy, love, and emotional support of her parents, family, and friends.

Red Flags and Possible Signs of Depression

1. Thoughts of death, suicidal gestures, and suicide attempts.
2. Inability to focus and concentrate.
3. Suffering from anxiety, panic attacks, feeling like she is going crazy and losing her grip with any reality.
4. Withdrawal from people, including family and peers, and formerly enjoyable activities.
5. Development of dysfunctional eating habits: loss of appetite, weight loss, or binge-eating.
6. No motivation or ambition to exercise or move herself.
7. Fatigue, low energy level, deteriorating health.
8. Moodiness and irritability.
9. Low self-worth and body esteem.
10. Suffering from insomnia or sleeps too much to escape.
11. Refuses to go to school or leave home.

FED UP WITH HER DAD

Dear Arden,

My husband was diagnosed with manic depressive disorder several years ago. Along with having constantly racing thoughts, he would go on wild spending sprees, was unable to sleep at night, and talked in a grandiose manner. Sometimes he would take off from home and work for weeks at a time. For the past two years, he has been on medication and his condition has stabilized.

Now he's decided to stop taking his meds and is back to behaving erratically. Any coaxing on my part gets him riled up and in a rage.

He tells me I'm the crazy one, not him. My fifteen-year-old daughter, Wendy, is now demanding that I leave him. She no longer wants to live like this. She loves me but does not understand why I put up with his "abuse." I say he's sick and not abusing me. She says, "No excuse, Mom. Whether he is sick or not, this is no way to live."

I don't know what to do. I don't want to lose my daughter, or for her to feel that my husband comes first, which is how it's been since she was four years old. I am not looking for you to make a decision for me; I just need help in facing how detrimental this is to my daughter's health and well-being. She wants to go for help, for the family, but he refuses.

Wendy is very wise. She recognizes how urgently the family needs help. Yes, your husband has a mental disorder, but there is no excuse for him to be allowed to disrupt your lives again and again. Your daughter is right—this is no way to live.

If he refuses to go for help then I suggest you, Wendy, and the rest of the family go to a psychotherapist to figure out the next course of action. That will make your daughter feel seriously heard and understood. We do not want her to go underground and get more hopeless and depressed about his long-standing illness and the toll it has taken on the family.

Mom, it's time to put yourself and your family first. This actually may have some positive impact on your husband. Let your husband know what you and the family are doing. This may be a long and hard road, but at least Wendy will be getting the support she needs. She will have an opportunity to express her pain, upset, anger, and humiliation. I don't think your daughter really wants to leave home, but if that is what inspires you to take action and move forward, then believe it.

TOO CLOSE TO HOME

Dear Arden,

My sixteen-year-old daughter, Violet, lost a close friend to suicide recently. She knew he was struggling and felt depressed but she didn't think he'd really act on it. Well, he did. And now she feels tremendously guilty for going to a movie with her friends on the night he died and not picking up the phone when he called. She berates herself "for being alive" and asks, "Why didn't I know, Mom? How come I didn't see it? How could I have missed it?"

Each year over thirty-three thousand people in the United States die by suicide, leaving behind shattered family members and friends. Shock, guilt, anger, sadness, and depression are common reactions among those left behind, but each person grieves in his or her own way. Reassure your daughter that she was not responsible for his death and that the suicide was not her fault.

To help Violet through this terrible tragedy, Mom, continue to be empathetic. Put yourself in her shoes. Talk to her gently: "You feel that if you were with him, he would still be here?" She may nod and cry, "Why didn't he wait for me to get home? Didn't he realize how special he was, how much he mattered to us?"

Let your daughter talk and get any burdensome feelings off her chest. She might say, "Mom, if I was there, he wouldn't have done it," to which you can reply, "Sweetheart, you are expecting too much of yourself." Tragically, many show a happy, smiling face to the world while in excruciating pain. Let your daughter know that it will take some time to assimilate the trauma, grieve the loss of her friend, process her guilt, and heal.

Violet is in shock and disbelief and asking herself, "Why would he do such a thing?" I have worked with those who have attempted suicide. Usually they are in excruciating pain and not thinking past that. Some, in the midst of an attempt, realized the hurtful impact on their parents, siblings, and friends and stopped themselves.

The realization that life can hang on a thread is earth-shattering for an adult, let alone a teenager. Mom, you can gently and patiently share the losses you have experienced in your life with your daughter. Don't be surprised if she doesn't want to talk about it, or if she can't stop talking about it. Violet's grief and sadness will come in waves, sparked by memory and love. Hopefully, one day the emptiness she feels inside will be replaced by her happy memories of her friend's wonderful qualities. Birthdays and holidays may be especially hard. You will also need to stay alert to signs that she might be feeling severely depressed and suicidal herself.

A teenager in my practice describes being clinically depressed as "I'm in a hole, I can just see out of the hole with medication. I am hanging on the edge. Truly I don't care if I see anyone. Just go away and leave me alone and let me be." Another patient describes it as "a deep dark place, a big gravesite in the ground."

Suicide Statistics

- According to the Centers for Disease Control and Prevention (CDC), suicide is the third leading cause of death among fifteen- to twenty-four–year-olds, surpassed only by accidents and homicide.
- Girls ages ten to fourteen have the fastest growing suicide rate of any population group, increasing 75.9 percent between 2003 and 2004.

- Girls contemplate and attempt suicide twice as often as boys, usually by overdosing on drugs or cutting themselves.
- Nearly 60 percent of *all* suicides in the United States are committed with a gun. Make sure any gun in your home is unloaded, locked, and kept out of the reach of children and teens.
- According to a study conducted by Johns Hopkins Children's Center in Baltimore, children whose parents have committed suicide are three times more likely to commit suicide later in their lives.

CLINGY

Dear Arden,

My eighteen-year-old daughter, Claudia, has just moved back home after a semester away at college. She was an honors student on a full scholarship. We thought she was doing fine until we got a call from her a few weeks ago. On the phone, she sounded unsteady, disconnected, and unfocused. She begged us to pick her up, so her father and I drove six hours to get her. Growing up, she was my youngest and I babied her too much. She has always been dependent on me. Now she is home and complaining of feeling distressed and panicked. Our general practitioner put her on 20 mg of Lexapro and 250 mg of Wellbutrin.

Can you recommend what type of therapist would work well with her? I am willing to go with her for the first few sessions. I so much want her to get back on track so she can go back to school.

Over the years I have worked with a number of teenagers brought in by their overwhelmed and anxious moms. These girls were suffering from crippling anxiety and panic attacks as they struggled to make their way back to school.

Imagine you are taking a kindergartener to her first day at school. She is screaming, "Mommy, don't go! Don't leave me." Your daughter is carrying on hysterically, as if you have abandoned her for life. We can appreciate a small child suffering from separation anxiety but when it's your high-achieving teenager, it's much harder to understand.

Mom, it sounds like you see yourself as part of the problem with your daughter's struggle and "part of the solution." Your love and devotion to Claudia and helping to steer her in the right direction again are very evident. Taking a semester off to work on managing her high and intense levels of anxiety is the direction to go.

I suggest some cognitive work for her to see that Claudia is creating much of her anxiety. She needs to challenge the obsessive, anxious, negative thoughts running through her mind and replace them with calming self-talk so that she can begin to talk herself down.

This approach, along with additional self-soothing strategies like deep breathing, guided imagery, and visualization, will go a long way in rebuilding her self-confidence, self-worth, and competence as a person. She is moving from "I can't go" to "I think I can go" to "I can go" to "I must go." She has to know that she can do it.

Once Claudia is doing better, I would suggest that she take one class at her new school to help her adjust. Desensitization training could work too. Desensitization is a gradual exposure to what is frightening your daughter. For example, her therapist can go with her to the school a few days in advance, park where she will park, literally walk her through to her classes, to the cafeteria, etc. Imagining herself in class, picking out a desk, using her laptop (guided visualization) will familiarize her with her new routine. Most kids with panic attacks who suffer from separation anxiety do not like any changes in routine and cling to home.

What we are doing is rebuilding Claudia brick by brick, one baby step at a time. I have had much success with this approach, along with additional self-soothing strategies.

The other suggestion is to help her reconnect to an activity she loves that does not stress her out and brings her joy. If she enjoys swimming, for instance, she can join a fitness gym with a pool. Claudia needs opportunities to meet and make some new friends as well. Journal writing, listening to her favorite music, and connecting with her friends from college will all help her feel better.

PLEASE HELP ME HELP MY DAUGHTER

Dear Arden,

I am exhausted and spent with grief over my eighteen-year-old daughter, Anna. She was a beautiful child and still is a stunning young woman. Over the years, she's been diagnosed with everything from ADHD to clinical depression to bipolar disorder. Each time, the new doctor will make a diagnosis and prescribe new medications. Then they have to adjust the dosage because she can't sleep, or gets the shakes, or talks too fast, or sleeps too much. For a time she seems stable and calm, she can keep a job down, is sober, and shows up for classes. Then she goes numb, can't feel, and seems flat and depressed. She starts acting out, drinks to the point of blacking out, and engages in very risky behaviors, from sex to drugs. I've seen her weight balloon up on the meds, and I've seen her skinny when she steps off them. The last time I heard from her she sounded very agitated on the phone. I asked her to tell me where she was so I could bring her home and take care of her.

Sometimes I get so mad I want to shake her. Mostly, though, I just want to know she's all right. I wish she could find peace and feel good in her skin. I am desperate to help her, but I don't know how. Over the years she's lost many friends, and her relationships with her brother and sister are very strained. They can't stand the roller coaster.

I feel for the entire family. If the diagnosis is correct, having a bipolar daughter is such a draining, exhausting, and painful roller coaster ride. Please don't take this the wrong way, because I truly understand the devastating effect this illness can have on a family, but she sounds like Dr. Jekyll and Mr. Hyde. When she's good, she's great, but when she is off the deep end, she is so self-destructive that she blows up her relationships with the significant people in her life. What will happen is that her behavior will totally drive away her sister, brother, and the friends who love her and want to help her. There is only so much suffering that one can accept.

Here is where I get very firm. Anna needs to know that maintaining a connection with you and her siblings is contingent upon her taking her medication, probably lithium, and being in a supportive therapeutic program. At the very least, she needs to be having weekly sessions, or more, with an excellent psychotherapist. Anna is self-medicating with alcohol, sex, and food (binges and restricts). She is running scared and unable to be still enough to let herself be helped. Anna needs to own that she needs help. What is needed is a psychopharmacological evaluation and some supportive psychotherapy, perhaps of a cognitive nature to start. She could track her mood swings, learn to recognize some of the triggers, and begin to consider healthier alternative behavior. Be aware that Anna might not go for help. Don't expect the world of yourself.

I understand how much you want your daughter to let you help her find stability in herself and peace in her life, but please don't forget about you. No matter what happens, make sure that you find some inner solace. Please make an appointment with a psychotherapist. You will be heard, understood, and given helpful direction and support in dealing with a very difficult and heart-breaking situation.

CHAPTER 14

Special Needs

"The best and the most beautiful things in the world cannot be seen or touched. They must be felt with the heart."

—Helen Keller

Much has been written about how to handle and support children with special needs when they are young and recently diagnosed, but there is less information and advice out there for moms who are raising and caring for teenagers with special needs. Many parents have become the experts on their children's behavior, education, and needs, acting as both advocates and activists. A daughter who has been diagnosed with a physical disability, a learning disorder, autism, attention deficit disorder (ADD), attention deficit hyperactivity disorder (ADHD), or other issues will have special concerns and challenges to face throughout her lifetime.

Teens with special needs deal with a lot of the same issues that other teens do—they long for a boyfriend, seek acceptance from peers, and wish to be independent. As one strong-willed fourteen-year-old girl with ADHD told her mom, "I know what I need to do to be like everyone else, but that makes me very unhappy. I am only happy being myself!" Such unique-ness sets them apart—but also can make them susceptible to bullying and teasing. The National Center for Education Statistics reports that 25 percent of all students say they are bul-lied on a daily or weekly basis. For children with disabilities, that number jumps to 85 percent.

The way that moms handle and approach these situations requires special parental consideration. For example, what do you do when your daughter, who has Asperger's syndrome, starts talking about boys and sex? How do you handle it when your daughter with a learning disability is told by her class-mates that she is stupid?

The long-term care of a child with special needs can be very draining on a family, especially the mother. Along with under-standing the challenging and changing needs of your daughter and working to accept and cope with her special needs, you also need to take care of yourself, Mom, and we offer helpful strate-gies and tips for that.

ADHD

Dear Arden,

I have my hands full with my thirteen-year-old daughter, Kayla, who has ADHD. I adore her, but she is driving her friends away. She talks too much, she is very bossy, and she tries too hard. Then she gets hurt, angry, and withdraws. I try to support her to be her own person, but she is struggling socially. It's getting to the point where it's difficult for me to stay friends with the other moms. At school, Kayla has a hard time staying focused and on task. She can't prioritize or get organized. I feel locked in a power struggle with her most of the time. She can be very defiant and hard to help. Any suggestions?

Mom, it sounds like you are struggling to face many issues with your daughter, from social to academic. *How can I help my daughter fit in, make and keep friends, and still be true to herself? How can I begin to help Kayla see her part in the process of driving away her friends? How can I teach her study skills so she can be more organized at school and focus on her tasks?*

A mom whose daughter struggles with ADHD also faces a socially complicated set of circumstances. Your withdrawal from the other moms may not be the best alternative. Kayla sounds very anxious, which would explain the excessive talking, and I think you're feeling anxious too. I think a socialization group for Kayla would go a long way. Check into what's available at her school. There are private groups outside of the school as well. There, she could begin to see her impact on her peers and see that she does not have to try so hard. Her pushiness is about not feeling good enough about herself and wanting their attention.

It might be time for an educational evaluation too. Kayla could receive specific accommodations to meet her educational needs in school and outside tutoring to help with her organizational work/study skills. She might be an ideal candidate for 504 status, which would allow her to receive extra help in a resource room even if she does not qualify for special education services. Many students with ADHD or OCD receive additional support in school this way. (See "A Glossary of Special Education Terms.") Kayla sounds like a very sweet but frustrated and hurt thirteen-year-old. Once she is feeling better understood, she will probably settle down and not lash out at you. For now, it sounds like Kayla needs more acceptance and support, and Mom could use some more support too.

COPING WITH HER SPECIAL NEEDS—AND YOURS

Taking care of a daughter with special needs can be exhausting. One mom describes her daughter's autistic meltdowns as involuntary seizures: "It was hard when she was little. Now that she's older, it's even more challenging to soothe her." Every mom needs to recharge her batteries, relax, and regroup, but the mothers of children with special needs are especially prone to burnout. These strategies will help provide critical relief and TLC to worn-out moms:

1. Join a women's support group for moms. "Being in a support group is so empowering," says one mom. "There's so much give and take and relating to each other. We have helped each other countless times, and always say, 'You'll get through it.'"
2. Hire a college student to stay at home with your daughter so that you and your spouse can go out and take a break and enjoy each other's company. You can post ads for babysitters at the local teachers' college.
3. Hire a home tutor for your child to help with homework and ease her frustration over schoolwork. This will be one less thing for you to do.
4. Attend conferences to learn about the latest strategies, techniques, and research affecting your daughter's condition. Network and meet with other parents and experts.

5. Be an activist. Organize fund-raisers and events to raise public awareness. Stu, a father and activist, shares, "Knowledge is power. Some families believe that my child has a disease, that it's going to rub off on their child, or that a child with special needs is inferior just because they are different. By opening up the lines of communication, we're trying to raise tolerance."

6. Meet the parents of other kids with special needs to expand your daughter's social network and yours. There are also supportive groups and networks you can join online.

7. Take a yoga class, meditation class, or dance class. One mom swears by her Jazzercise.

8. Encourage your daughter to participate in activities. Help her find her passion. If she loves animals, encourage her to volunteer at an animal shelter or zoo.

9. Discover what kind of coping strategies help to calm your daughter, from rolling on a medicine ball, wrapping her in a blanket, or giving her a big bear hug.

10. Be creative, consistent, and loving.

DREAMY AND DISTRACTED

Dear Arden,

My eleven-year-old daughter, Ellie, has been acting very dreamy and distracted in class. She isn't disrespectful to the teacher and she doesn't draw any attention to herself, but it's hard for her to pay attention to the lesson plan. It takes her a long time to finish reading a chapter. The teacher says that Ellie looks out the window or scribbles in her notebook. The teacher recommended that Ellie be screened and evaluated for any learning issues like ADD or ADHD and dyslexia. She said that an IEP could benefit her greatly. My husband and I were too embarrassed to ask what an IEP is.

Every child develops at his or her own unique pace. When a child is tuning out, daydreaming, and having a hard time keeping up in class and obviously trying, then it's time to have an educational evaluation. The evaluation may include subject testing, reading comprehension, psychological testing, an IQ test like the Wechsler Intelligence Scale (WISC-R), and teacher feedback from all of her classes. Dyslexia needs to be ruled out as well. Based on the evaluation, certain recommendations will be set in place. She might benefit from having extended time to take her tests, or taking them in a quiet room with no noise or distractions. Ellie may also be eligible to go to a resource room to get extra help on specific subjects and do her assignments and homework with a teacher present. The teacher provides more organization, structure, and support to help Ellie stay on track. I knew kids who attended a resource room all through middle school and high school. They were able to attend a regular school and still receive the specialized services they needed and be part of the school social life.

Suffice it to say that Ellie may be struggling with learning deficits that are affecting her ability to concentrate and focus on the tasks at hand. She may have a mild learning disorder, a perceptual/ spatial problem, or a processing issue that could involve mild ADD or ADHD. She sounds more quiet, so my hunch is that there may be attention deficit disorder without the hyperactive component. She will need to be evaluated to see if she qualifies for special education services.

An IEP is an Individualized Education Plan that identifies how the school will provide specific support services to your daughter to meet her special educational needs. The IEP is tailored to the unique needs of a single student. It describes how she learns and outlines goals and objectives for her education and teachers. It specifies accommodations so the student can continue to enjoy mainstream classes and extracurricular activities in a regular public school.

A student's eligibility for an IEP is discussed and determined by the Committee on Special Education (CSE). The meeting is usually attended by the student's parents, the head of special education, a school psychologist, one of your child's teachers, a special education teacher, and a parent member. The group also can include the principal or any other service provider who works with the child, such as her speech language pathologist (SLP), occupational therapist (OT), physical therapist (PT), and therapist. I have attended many of these meetings to share what I see my patient struggling with, be it a learning issue or a behavioral issue.

Just be aware of the emotional impact an IEP may have on your daughter. Too often I have heard a child say, "I'm stupid or dumb; that's why I need help." It's important for parents to reassure their daughter that she has strengths in different areas, and just might need extra help and support in a particular subject, such as reading or math. Kids who are classified do feel different. She is in fifth grade now, and her feelings may be exacerbated in middle school. To be forewarned is to be forearmed. We need to bolster Ellie and provide other affirming and positive experiences and activities to help her feel more confident and good in her skin.

A GLOSSARY OF SPECIAL
EDUCATION TERMS

IEP (Individualized Education Plan)

This is the educational plan for a student. It's basically a contract that states what special education services your child needs and justifies why she needs them. An IEP is for students who qualify for special education in a public school. The IEP runs for one year and is changed annually at the child's annual review meeting.

BIP (Behavior Intervention Plan)

The BIP is a concrete plan of action for managing a student's behavior that may include positive reinforcement to promote good behavior. Also known as a Behavioral Management Plan or Behavioral Support Plan, the BIP is written with clear goals and expectations to change a behavior or prevent a student from acting out due to frustration or fatigue. The parents and student are involved in this plan.

504 Plan

A 504 plan provides accommodations for students who do not qualify for special education services but would benefit from classroom accommodations or testing accommodations and modifications. Often a diagnosis of ADHD/ADD, OCD, or anxiety disorder from a neurologist will qualify a student for a 504, if the disability negatively impacts the student's academic progress. Accommodations for 504s may include but are not limited to testing modifications such as preferential seating in class, modified homework assignments, and having test directions read out loud or explained.

Resource Room

A resource room is a designated room in a public school where students with learning disabilities and educational accommodations receive one-on-one instruction or instruction in small groups by special education teachers and aides. Depending on the specifications of their IEPs or 504s, students can receive assistance in specific subjects, homework, and study skills.

TIPS FROM A SPECIAL EDUCATION TEACHER

Amy works with students who are classified with learning disabilities or behavioral conduct disorders such Asperger's syndrome, autism, dyslexia, obsessive-compulsive disorder, ADD, and ADHD in middle school. Here's the advice she had for the parents of children with special needs:

1. Educate yourself about what services and support your child is entitled to receive.
2. Once there is an IEP in place, follow through and make sure that your child is receiving the services and is retested and reevaluated periodically. You will know the IEP is effective if she is making headway or showing improvement.
3. Meet regularly with the people who are providing services to your child and get feedback from them. This could be your child's aide, a teacher, or a speech therapist.
4. The squeaky wheel is the one that gets oiled. People who speak up and "yell" the loudest (in a respectful way, of course) are the ones who are heard first.

5. If your child is classified and not thriving in the school system, then it is the school district's responsibility to find an alternative placement or school for your child.

6. Some students do very well and do benefit from a mix of special education classes and mainstreamed classes.

7. Not every child belongs in a public school setting or thrives in mainstream classes, even with additional support. Every child has special individual needs that must be addressed.

8. Kids in special education classes are more frequently bullied, picked on, and teased. Some of these kids have a hard time standing their ground and can be ostracized unmercifully.

9. The focus for parents of kids who feel and are different is to aim for acceptance and respect for self and from peers.

10. Make sure that school officials are doing everything they can to ensure that your child is learning and thriving in a safe environment.

11. Be your child's advocate.

12. If you feel unheard and dismissed, connect with an education lawyer who specializes in special education issues. The attorney will make sure that your daughter is fairly represented and that she receives the services and treatment that she is entitled to under the law.

LEFT OUT

Dear Arden,
My eleven-year-old daughter, Tyra, gets teased at school for being slower than her classmates. They make fun of the way she talks and

reads and trip her for being less coordinated. Yesterday, she came home crying because nobody picked her to play on their team in P.E. When she was younger, she got invited to the same parties as everyone else, but not anymore.

Oh, I can't stand this mean-girl behavior. I understand how painful it is for her. It's so much different when they are younger, isn't it? Tyra needs just one friend to pal around with. That will make a huge difference for her. And there you are, standing by and wondering what to do. It sounds like she used to play with some of these girls and they have turned on her. We need to find places where your daughter feels more comfortable and secure. What are the areas and activities in which she excels? What makes her feel good about herself and confident about her capabilities? Plenty of times these nasty girls pick on and tease the girl they see as vulnerable, different, and lacking in the capacity to stand up for herself. Remember, friends can be made outside of school as well. Does Tyra belong to the Girl Scouts? Is she involved in any outside activities?

I know that none of these suggestions address the immediate issue of these mean girls trying to push your daughter around. Exclusion is a very hurtful way to push someone out of a group and make them feel less than, so I am brainstorming ways we can build up Tyra from the inside. Activities like dance, karate, kickboxing, and yoga can help center your daughter and improve her gross motor coordination. Yoga especially can be very calming. Being able to release stress and let off steam will do wonders for your daughter. We need to bolster her morale.

Unfortunately, if this distressing and hurtful behavior continues, you need to bring it to the attention of her guidance counselor, teachers, and principal. Sometimes when the girls are young, guidance counselors can intervene and talk to the group without suspending anyone. The emphasis, of course, will be on respecting differences and developing kindness and consideration for the feelings of others. Plenty of schools host antibullying assemblies and diversity days, but it just can't be said (or done) enough: you treat your peers the way you want to be treated.

HANDLING "THE TALK" WITH SPECIAL CARE

Dear Arden,
My thirteen-year-old daughter Marissa, who has Asperger's Syndrome, is starting to talk about boys and sex. How do I approach this with her?

You need to speak in very concrete terms and not expect your daughter to follow or understand the hypothetical or the abstract. Try this **script**: "Marissa, guys may tell you how cute you are and put their arms around you and try to kiss you."

Marissa may say, "What's wrong with that?"

You say, "It's not that it's wrong, but if he is looking to go further, know that you have the right to say, 'That's enough, no thank you.' If he presses further and you start to feel uncomfortable and he is not listening, he's being too pushy and aggressive. You need to ask someone to help make him stop. Marissa, try not to be all alone or walk off with a boy at a party. Because you are mildly Asperger's, he could possibly take advantage."

Mom, naming and identifying that your daughter has Asperger's validates and affirms why she is feeling different, processes differently, and struggles to read social cues the way most kids do. It's important that you create a knowledge base and a foundation for the rest of her life.

Your daughter is not crazy; she does not have to feel ashamed, though she may at times, but this is her special uniqueness and limitation that she needs help with. This is something that she will have to manage. You let her know what she is dealing with—and that her mind, her brain, needs extra explanations patiently provided by her parents who are there to help her.

You can see how going step-by-step leaves room for her questions, but you really need to fill in any gaping holes and what-ifs. As it is, most thirteen-year-olds have a hard time thinking past the present. Your daughter is emotionally younger than her years, and it's okay to tell her so. She can mistakenly read that a boy likes her or loves her when he does not, if she likes the boy a lot. It's so much more delicate and complicated for her. We don't want her to feel badly about herself. We are bolstering her self-worth and self-esteem, but at the same time, we are building social-relatedness skills too. Always reassure her that you appreciate her trying to listen to you and that you are trying to teach her in small steps. She is feeling what any teen feels; she just needs extra help in expressing herself. Your kindness and an extra dose of patience will go a long way. You are teaching your daughter, by the way you relate to her, how to manage moments of impulsivity, have tolerance for frustration, and connect with potential friends.

Some of these youngsters have a hard time making and keeping friends. You and other caretakers can help her develop the capacity to put herself in her peers' shoes through fun role-playing and acting exercises. I have found this to be a successful strategy for Asperger's tweens and teens.

TOO SMART?

Dear Arden,

My twelve-year-old daughter is super bright. In fact, she did so well last year that she skipped a grade. We went to our first parent-teacher conference, and the teacher explained that while Maddie's academic performance was excellent, she was having some social difficulties and issues with her peers. The teacher referred us for counseling. I don't understand why my daughter has to go to therapy just because the other kids aren't as advanced and feel dumb around her.

I am sure that you and your husband are so very proud of Maddie's intellectual achievements. She sounds like a very bright girl who may be having a hard time adjusting socially to kids who are nine to twelve months older. I know it sounds like a minor detail, but there is some validity to this. I am thinking of a few tweens I know who skipped a grade or had a very late birthday and were having a hard time connecting to their peers. A few of the kids avoided making contact with their classmates because the content of some of the conversations were a bit over their head. You need to ask Maddie how she is feeling, not how she's doing. She may be keeping up and excelling academically, but socially she may be really sweating it out and unable to share this with you and ask for your help. She does not want to disappoint her parents.

Who knows? Maybe you are right that the other kids may feel intimidated around her, that she is too smart, and they may be envious or jealous. I don't know, but I have a feeling Maddie can tell you.

The teacher's suggestion to speak to a therapist—someone outside of school, who could lend some objectivity—is a wise recommendation. Please try not to take this personally, Mom. Go for a consultation and see for yourself. Everybody knows how smart your darling daughter is; I am just concerned that her emotional development may not be on par with her intellectual achievements. Because she is so young, now is the time to help her, rather than wait until she is older when the discrepancy is too wide. Let's look at this as a step that will be in Maddie's best interest.

A TALE OF THREE SISTERS

Dear Arden,

I have three daughters. Fifteen-year-old Sunny is the oldest and autistic. My middle daughter, April, fourteen, is sweet and gets along with everybody. It's my youngest daughter, June, twelve, who's been giving me grief. I've been noticing changes in her diet, sleeping patterns, and habits. She recently got her period—could that be it?— but she complains that Sunny gets all of the attention and she looks at Sunny sometimes with daggers in her eyes.

June is not herself. She is mad when Sunny is home and acts curt and short-tempered and withholding around her. I thought I was imagining this, but my girlfriend noticed it too and asked me, "What's up with June?" I am not sure how to approach June. I feel anything I say to her will be taken the wrong way.

It's hard to know if June has been harboring anger, hostility, and resentment toward Sunny, but it does sound as if June has been having a bit of a bodily and mental adjustment to having her period. Are there times of the month where she calms down? Has she been hard on Sunny in the past? Has that recently escalated?

Have you given her ample opportunities to express herself directly about what it's like to have a sister with special needs like Sunny?

Your daughter, now in middle school, could be feeling more self-conscious and want to fit in; she may be having some very uncomfortable feelings coming up. Perhaps there are times that June understandingly wishes she didn't have an autistic sister, especially when she is stressed out and doesn't have the patience for her.

Sunny is an easy target for jealousy and envy. A little tape may be running through June's head asking, "Why are you here, Sunny? You get more attention than me...Sunny, Sunny, Sunny!"

It sounds like she is so frustrated she is fairly screaming with anger, so start a dialogue with her. I feel she needs to unload and unburden herself. I would **script** a conversation for you like this: "June, dear, you seem so out of sorts, honey. Can Mom help? What's troubling you? Whatever you share with me, June, it's okay. You seem angry."

For all we know, Sunny may be getting some of the displaced frustration, anger, envy, and jealousy that June feels about an incident in her new school. It's tough to read, but don't leave June's side until you get some feedback from her. You both will feel better. As for Sunny, she must be wondering, "What did I do?" With lots of love and patience, explain to Sunny that it's probably nothing. Here's a **script** for what you can say: "Sunny, your sister June is not herself. I am so sorry she is hurting your feelings. You have done nothing wrong; you are just being yourself. June thinks I give you too much attention. She is a little right. I have to figure out how to balance my interest and attention I give to you three girls. June needs to talk to me, and I will help her figure out what's bothering her. Let's give each other a hug and say 'I love you.' That always makes you feel better, right?"

CHAPTER 15

How to Choose a Therapist

*"Too often we underestimate the power of a touch,
a smile, a kind word, a listening ear, an honest
compliment, or the smallest act of caring, all of
which have the potential to turn a life around."*

—Leo F. Buscaglia

It can be hard enough for your daughter to ask for help when she needs it, but sometimes it can be even harder for a mom. Moms can feel like failures—overwhelmed, exhausted, and defeated. If you've approached life and parenting expecting to make mistakes, then it follows you can expect to need help too, from time to time. You can set a good example for your daughter by knowing when to reach for it.

That's because you want your daughter to know that, if she is feeling overwhelmed and scared and exhausted, it's okay to ask for help, and it's okay to come to you.

It actually takes courage to admit that you need help. The worst thing you can do is pretend you don't.

HOW TO CHOOSE A THERAPIST

The thought of choosing a therapist—let alone going to a therapist—can be foreign territory for a mother. For a mom, asking for directions from a well-intentioned stranger can be like visiting another planet. Until now, Mom has been able to figure out how to deal with her daughter and family with little or no outside help. She can't imagine sharing the intimate details of her life or the history of her relationship with her daughter and her family. She already feels inadequate and like a failure. The last thing in the world she thought could happen was landing on a therapist's couch for a consultation. How awkward and uncomfortable that it has come to this.

It's important to get a good recommendation from a trusted friend who has experienced success with her therapist and received excellent advice on how to deal more effectively with her teen daughter. If you don't have such a friend, a recommendation can come from your family physician, your pediatrician, a clinical social worker, a psychologist, or a psychiatrist. It can come from a teacher or a guidance counselor at your daughter's school, or any person who has known you and your daughter for a long time and can be trusted to have your daughter's best interests at heart.

Now, Mom, I am going to ask a lot of you. I feel it's my sacred task to steer you in the right direction. No matter what, please trust your gut, that small voice within you. It's the common sense you instinctively hear and turn to during times of trouble. It's like your own personal GPS system that leads you to your path and directs you so you can find your way home. Keep in mind that the hardest time to make a clear-headed choice is when you are feeling vulnerable and stressed out. Unfortunately, that is how one feels in a crisis, and that feeling will coincide with the first time you meet your potential family therapist for a consultation.

When it comes to working with the mom of a tween or teen daughter, your potential therapist needs to know how to make you feel unbelievably comfortable and be capable of listening and understanding you while giving you helpful feedback. She or he needs to be a down-to-earth, authentic person who can show tremendous compassion and gives you reassurances that she is in your corner.

Consider a therapist who puts a positive spin on recent developments and offers hope that this new collaboration between therapist, Mom, and daughter will help to build, maintain, and strengthen your relationship with your daughter. Remember, she is there to guide you and help the two of you get through some really tough times.

She offers you assurances and reassurances that she has helped many teens and moms for many years and has had great success. Here is where Mom can ask specifically for concrete examples and the therapist can share a small vignette to help assuage Mom's anxiety. This is a good time to ask about licensing, insurance, fees, and where she has been trained as well.

During the first session, Mom needs to observe a therapist who takes her seriously but who has good timing and insightfully uses humor to lighten some of the darkest moments. A therapist who is well-related, connected, caring, authentic, human, and approachable can serve as a wonderful role model for both Mom and daughter. Your daughter can spot a phony a mile away, so ask her after the session, if she is part of it, how she felt being with this new therapist. Her feedback is invaluable, and then you respectfully have her in the loop. A good therapist will ask you both at the end of the session how it went for you. Please try to be as open and honest as possible.

If you choose this particular therapist, notice if she goes the extra mile sometimes and is available during crises for telephone calls, additional sessions, and extra last-minute rescheduling because of a shift in your daughter's schedule. She needs to be flexible and demonstrate good limits and boundaries.

The sessions become a mini-testing ground for both you and your daughter. You need a therapist who is grounded and capable of keeping the two of you grounded as well. Sometimes your therapist will seem like a referee and coach. She will teach both of you how to negotiate an argument, disagree respectfully, and help you manage your anger more constructively.

The best therapists who work with tweens and adolescents tend to have a more creative and stimulating approach. Look for a therapist who is comfortable giving feedback, scripting and coaching Mom in what she can say to her daughter, and who will suggest readings and articles on the subject areas to be discussed. This psycho-educational interactive approach can be very effective with teenagers.

As mothers, we need to put so much energy, effort, and work into becoming effective, communicative, warm, and loving parents. Our children need our unconditional love and emotional support, with age-appropriate expectations, firm limits, and boundaries put into effect.

Conclusion

*"Keep your eyes on the stars and your feet on the
ground."*

—Teddy Roosevelt

We are not here forever; we are passing through. The universe
is so vast and awesome. With that in mind, I make sure to
appreciate every day and be grateful that I and my precious
family are alive. I do my best to encourage and teach through
example acts of kindness, thinking outside of myself by being
considerate of others, giving back, and being mindful of how
important it is for our daughters and family to see that we are
great self-caretakers. It's quite the challenge to create balance
in one's life.

After all, parenting and motherhood are probably the most
amazing and hardest chosen professions in the world.

Remember, you can make today the day to start afresh. You
can make a difference in one moment just by challenging and
changing your perspective and attitude. Parenting, like life, has
a very long learning curve and is an experience packed with
great lessons. Like your children, expect to make mistakes.
That's okay; just learn from them, move on, and press forward.

I'm seeing the biggest picture. It goes so fast. It was just yesterday that Samara started college. This May, she is graduating, and will be moving into Manhattan, auditioning for roles, and hunting for jobs. I try so hard to make the most of it and enjoy the ride.

I hope that I have been able to help you have a deeper appreciation of all the effort that goes into creating a strong, healthy, hopeful, and happy relationship with your precious daughter and children that will last a lifetime. I am grateful to have had this opportunity to make a difference in your lives.

Resources

For more information on bullying, eating disorders, gay and lesbian youth, mental health, sexual health, special needs, and substance abuse, please consult these websites.

BULLYING

PACER's National Center for Bullying Prevention and Teens Against Bullying
www.pacerteensagainstbullying.org

Fight Crime: Invest in Kids
www.fightcrime.org

Striving to Reduce Youth Violence Everywhere
www.safeyouth.org

Olweus Bullying Prevention Program
www.olweus.org

Stop Bullying Now
www.stopbullyingnow.hrsa.gov/adults

EATING DISORDERS

National Eating Disorder Association
www.nationaleatingdisorders.org

Binge Eating Disorder Association
www.bedaonline.com

The Renfrew Center Foundation
www.renfrew.org

Something Fishy (for support in positive behavior and prevention)
www.something-fishy.org

Eating Disorder Referral and Information Center
www.EDReferral.com

Academy for Eating Disorders
www.aedweb.org

Eating Disorder and Awareness Prevention
www.edap.org

GAY, LESBIAN, BISEXUAL, AND TRANSGENDER YOUTH

Gay, Lesbian and Straight Education Network (GLSEN)
www.glsen.org

GLBT National Help Center
www.glnh.org

Parents, Families, and Friends of Lesbians and Gays
www.pflag.org

RAPE AND ABUSE

Rape, Abuse & Incest National Network
www.rainn.org

National Teen Dating Abuse Helpline
www.loveisrespect.org

MENTAL HEALTH AND
SELF-INJURIOUS BEHAVIORS

The National Institute of Mental Health
www.nimh.nih.gov

The National Alliance on Mental Illness
www.nami.org

S.A.F.E. Alternatives (Self Abuse Finally Ends)
www.selfinjury.com

Secret Shame: Self-Injury Information and Support
www.selfharm.net

SEXUAL HEALTH

Centers for Disease Control and Prevention
www.cdc.gov

The Guttmacher Institute
www.guttmacher.org

SUBSTANCE ABUSE

Substance Abuse and Mental Health Services Administration
www.samhsa.gov

National Institute on Drug Abuse
www.nida.nih.gov/nidahome.html

NIDA for Teens
teens.drugabuse.gov

Alcoholics Anonymous
www.aa.org

Al-Anon and Alateen
www.al-anon.alateen.org

The National Youth Anti-Drug Media Campaign
www.theantidrug.com

Partnership for a Drug-Free America
www.drugfree.org

Check Yourself
www.checkyourself.org

SPECIAL NEEDS

National Association of Parents with Children in Special Education
www.napcse.org

Parents Advocacy Coalition for Educational Rights (PACER)
www.pacer.org

Office of Special Education and Rehabilitation Services (OSERS)
www2.ed.gov/about/offices/list/osers/osep/index.html

About the Author

Photos by Dennis Kwan

ARDEN GREENSPAN-GOLDBERG is a nationally known family and marriage psychotherapist, specializing in parenting, pretween, tween, teen, and young adult issues.

She has her BA in psychology, a master's in social work from Hunter College School of Social Work, City University of New York, and two certificates in psychotherapy and psychoanalysis from the National Institute for the Psychotherapies in New York, where she completed five years of post-master's training. She was the president of the local chapter of the New York State Society for Clinical Social Work Psychotherapists, a fellow of the National Association for Social Workers, a board-certified diplomate in clinical social work, and a member of the American Federation of Television and Radio Artists.

She currently maintains private practices in New City, New York, and New York City. She taught courses at St. Thomas Aquinas College in New York dealing with women's issues and eating disorders. She runs eating disorder groups for people struggling with anorexia, bulimia, binge-eating disorder, and obesity. A sought-after speaker for colleges, high schools, middle schools, elementary schools, and for-profit and non-profit organizations, she has written a monthly advice column for the *Journal News* (Gannett Newspaper) and ran a monthly discussion group with local teens called "Teen Talk," covering all teen-related issues.

She has been a featured expert on numerous national news and talk shows over the past fifteen years, including MSNBC, CNN, *The View*, *Maury Povich*, *Sally Jesse*, and *John Walsh*. She has appeared on local radio and TV in New York and Chicago, including *Fox Morning News*. She has been featured in national and local publications such as *Ladies' Home Journal*, *Family Circle*, and syndicated newspapers around the country.

Recently she has been seen on Meredith's productions of Parents.tv and Better.tv, aired across numerous national markets on Comcast Digital Cable as well as many local TV stations.

Many of her segments can be seen on YouTube and on her website, www.askarden.com.